T0294810

Growing Business in Delaware

Growing Business in Delaware

The Politics of Job Creation in a Small State

William W. Boyer and Edward C. Ratledge

UNIVERSITY OF DELAWARE PRESS
Newark

Published by University of Delaware Press
Copublished by The Rowman & Littlefield Publishing Group, Inc.
4501 Forbes Boulevard, Suite 200, Lanham, Maryland 20706
www.rowman.com

Unit A, Whitacre Mews, 26-34 Stannary Street, London SE11 4AB

British Library Cataloguing in Publication Information Available

Library of Congress Cataloging-in-Publication Data

Names: Boyer, William W., author. | Ratledge, Edward C., author.
Title: Growing business in Delaware : the politics of job creation in a small state / William W. Boyer
and Edward C. Ratledge.
Description: Lanham, Md. : University of Delaware Press, [2015] | Includes bibliographical refer-
ences and index.
Identifiers: LCCN 2015036278| ISBN 9781611495942 (cloth : alk. paper) | ISBN 9781611495959
(electronic)
Subjects: LCSH: Industrial policy--Delaware. | Job creation--Delaware. | Labor policy--Delaware. |
Delaware--Economic policy.
Classification: LCC HD3616.U48 D325 2015 | DDC 331.12/04209751--dc23 LC record available at
http://lccn.loc.gov/2015036278

Printed in the United States of America

Contents

List of Abreviations   vii

Acknowledgments   ix

Preface   xi

Map of Delaware   xiii

Introduction   1

1   AstraZeneca   21

2   Delaware's Port   41

3   Wilmington's Riverfront   63

4   Fisker Automotive   79

5   Bloom Energy   99

6   Delaware City Refinery   117

7   A Potpourri of Grants   139

8   Growing Business by Other Means   157

9   Politics of Economic Development   179

10   Lessons Learned   199

Selected References   209

Index   213

About the Authors   225

List of Abreviations

AAA — American Automobile Association

AP — Advanced Placement

BGC — Brandywine Gateway Corporation

BP — British Petroleum

CADSR — Center for Applied Demography & Survey Research

CEO — Chief Executive Officer

CMB — Center for Molecular Biotechnology

COO — Chief Operations Officer

CZA — Coastal Zone Act

DCR — Delaware City Refinery

DEDA — Delaware Economic Development Authority

DEFAC — Delaware Economic and Financial Advisory Council

AFC — Affiliated Finance Companies

AZ — AstraZeneca

BofA — Bank of America

BPG — Buccini-Pollin Group

CDF — Council on Development Finance

CHP — Combined Heat and Power

CNBC — Consumer News and Business Channels

CRG — Citizens for Responsible Growth

DCM — DuPont Capital Management Corporation

DCRAC Delaware Community Reinvestment Action Council

DEDO — Delaware Economic Development Office

DelDOT — Delaware Department of Transportation

DET — Division of Employment & Training

DNREC — Department of Natural Resources and Environmental Control

DOE — Department of Energy

DSPC — Diamond State Port Corporation

EPA — Environmental Protection Agency

EO — Executive Order

FCDA — Financial Center Development Act

FDA — Federal Food and Drug Administration

FDIC — Federal Deposit Insurance Corporation

FY — Fiscal Year

GM — General Motors

HSBC — Hong Kong and Shanghai Banking Corporation

HUD — Department of Housing and Urban Affairs

ING — International Netherlands Group

IT — Information Technology

JPM — JPMorgan Chase & Company

JPMC — JPMorgan Chase

LNG — Liquefied Natural Gas

M&A — Mergers and Acquisitions

MBNA— Maryland Bank National Association

NCRC — National Community Reinvestment Coalition

NJPP — New Jersey Policy Perspective

NRAPP — Newark Residents Against the Power Plant

PAC — Political Action Committee

PSC — Public Service Commission

R&D — Research and Development

RDC — Riverfront Development Corporation

REPSA — Renewable Energy Portfolio Standards Act

RPS — Renewable Portfolio Standards

SEC — Securities Exchange Commission

SOC — Save Our County

STAR — Science, Technology and Advanced Research campus at UD

STEM — Science, Technology, Engineering, and Mathematics

TDC — The Data Centers

TIS — Traffic Impact Study

UD — University of Delaware

UDAG — Urban Development Action Grant

Acknowledgments

We are especially indebted to David S. Swayze, Esq., former legal counsel, chief of staff, and executive assistant to the governor of Delaware, and former solicitor of Wilmington, for reading and critiquing in detail the entire draft manuscript of this book, and for offering many helpful suggestions. Likewise, we are equally indebted to Professor James L. Butkiewicz, Chairman of the Department of Economics of the Alfred Lerner College of Business and Economics, University of Delaware, for his critique of the complete draft of this book and for his helpful suggestions. And we wish to acknowledge with gratitude Julia Oestreich of the University of Delaware Press for her excellent editing of our manuscript.

We wish also to acknowledge Hon. Edward J. Freel, former Delaware secretary of state, and Judy McKinney-Cherry, former director of the Delaware Economic Development Office, who read and critiqued portions of our manuscript and offered helpful suggestions.

We have benefited, too, from those who have assisted us in one way or another in the preparation of this book. They are, alphabetically, Rebecca Bedford, Nancy Boyer, Daniel Brown, Simon Condliffe, Amirah Ellis-Gilliam, Roberta Gibson, Joan Jacoby, John Laznik, the late Gerard Mangone, Don Mell, David Racca, and Tibor Toth.

In addition, we wish to acknowledge the support and assistance of the staffs and resources of the University of Delaware's School of Public Policy and Administration, the University of Delaware Morris Library, the University of Delaware Press, and the Rowman & Littlefield Publishing Group, Inc.

Regardless of the assistance we have received, we alone are responsible for the content of this book.

WWB
ECR

Preface

This is the fourth book in our series about public affairs and public policies in the small state of Delaware. The first book—*Governing Delaware: Policy Problems in the First State* (2000)—was written by one of us as the sole author, but the other of us was one of the few colleagues who read and critiqued the entire draft manuscript. That proved to be the catalyst of our collaboration as coauthors of the remaining books in our series. Our second book is *Delaware Politics and Government* (2009), and our third is *Pivotal Policies in Delaware: From Desegregation to Deregulation* (2014). In progress is the fifth book in our series, to be entitled *Public Education in Delaware: Politics of Public School Reform*.

In this, the fourth book in our series—*Growing Business in Delaware: The Politics of Job Creation in a Small State*—we examine Delaware's economic development strategies to maintain a business-friendly environment, especially by subsidizing efforts to attract, keep, and grow businesses and employment. The book addresses the nation's financial crisis that ushered Delaware into the Great Recession beginning in 2008, which was still especially severe in the state into 2014. Among the larger Delaware employers that disappeared after the onset of the recession were Chrysler, General Motors, and Avon. Meanwhile, the state's largest employer, MBNA, was sold to Bank of America, causing the loss of many jobs. We analyze this small state's strategy to deal with this overwhelming crisis, especially during the administrations of Governors Ruth Ann Minner and Jack Markell. Accordingly, the book's analysis is timely with respect to public policy choices involving education, jobs versus the environment, leadership, competition with other states, and a host of other problem areas.

Our introduction provides the book's context by considering the relevant historical background of state-sponsored incentives regarding private investment, and how Delaware attempted to grow its economy in partnership with private enterprise. Hence, the importance of Delaware's unique landmark comprehensive incorporation law of 1899 is stressed, inasmuch as it was responsible for the incorporation of about one million firms in the state by 2013, unmatched by far by any other state in the nation, or by any other polity in the world for that matter. But the background to a transition from a somewhat passive strategy to a proactive management approach toward business in Delaware had its beginning with the Farmers Bank Crisis during the administration of Governor Sherman W. Tribbitt (1973–1977) and the ensuing financial mess inherited by Governor Pete du Pont (1977–1985). From this time onward, this introductory chapter and the book as a whole is liberally laced with "behind-the-scenes" activities describing how this small state experienced successes and failures in its manifold attempts to keep, grow, and attract businesses and jobs.

As noted in the preface of the first book in our series, *Governing Delaware*, Delaware's small size helps explain the dearth of policy-related research in the state, compared to larger, more populous states with multiple and highly differentiated media and institutions specializing in policy analysis that serve to enrich policy studies. Researchers in Delaware must rely on sparse resources. Moreover, as our study indicates, transparency is lacking concerning the financial information of firms subsidized by the state government to create jobs, and is unavailable even in the state archives. Such business information is considered confidential and not to be shared with the public. Fortunately, Delaware's lone investigatory newspaper, the Wilmington *News Journal*, serves as a valuable resource, both historically and currently. The newspaper fills information gaps by providing frequent balanced articles on policy issues, businesses, government, and political activities. More important, these articles comprise information routinely used by Delaware citizens and policy makers alike. In addition to *News Journal* articles, readers may find many other primary and secondary sources cited in the notes and bibliography.

Finally, as we made clear in the prefaces of our other books in this series, we have refrained from interviews in order to mitigate research bias. We considered that complete fairness would require interviews of notables on all sides of each issue. Inevitably we would miss interviewing some important persons, or those who would be unavailable. We relied on pertinent printed sources only, citing them frequently, extensively, and unambiguously, so that our readers will know our sources, and unlike interviews, be able to find them if needed.

Map of Delaware

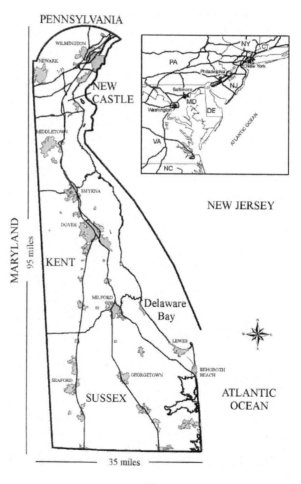

Introduction

This book is about Delaware's economic development. It emphasizes history and strategies providing direct grants and loans to businesses, which accelerated and reached their zenith through the first decade of the twenty-first century. But first it is important in this introduction to provide context by considering the relevant historical background.

BACKGROUND

One of the original thirteen states, Delaware was predominantly rural from its inception through the nineteenth century. Its economy was agriculturally based like that of most other states until the 1890s, when manufacturing surpassed farming in importance. Besides the establishment of E. I. duPont's company in 1802, which became Delaware's leading firm until recently, the state's economic activity became increasingly fueled by railroads, shipbuilding, and other water-powered factories.

Delaware was one of only a few states, however, without a general incorporation law. In a state whose government was structured to establish weak gubernatorial authority, the General Assembly essentially ran the state government by licensing corporations on a piecemeal, ad hoc, case-by-case basis, with little or no oversight or constraint. The incorporation process was thus open to lobbyists, bribery, vote-buying, and other corrupting influences. Indeed, the General Assembly in the 1890s was spending most of its time granting corporate franchises. One delegate of the Constitutional Convention of 1897 estimated that two-thirds of the legislature's time was consumed by granting corporate charters and divorces.

By the time the constitutional delegates began their consideration of proposed Article IX to the 1897 Constitution, the Delaware legislature was . . . granting . . . in 1897 . . . a total of 115 special acts of incorporation, . . . and the average wait for a corporate charter was approximately two years. In addition, the special act procedure had . . . been taken over by . . . "wild-cat" lobbyists who would secure for their clients the . . . vote of the legislature for a fee.[1]

Meanwhile, New Jersey's experience greatly influenced Delaware. At the turn of the century, New Jersey's economy was dominated by the incorporation of the nation's largest industrial enterprises, including Standard Oil, General Motors, and even DuPont. It was later reported that by 1917, roughly one-third of American industrial enterprises with assets exceeding $20 million, and 42 percent of the country's largest firms, held New Jersey charters.[2]

New Jersey's success in raising revenue, by attracting the legal domicile of firms, influenced several states to follow its example—notably Delaware. William Saulsbury, while a delegate of Delaware's 1897 Constitutional Convention, said: "I want our State to reach the highest possible point of development. I do not want to give unjust powers to corporations. . . . But if corporations can be induced to come to our State to take out their charters and pay their money into our State Treasury and relieve our people from taxation, instead of going to New Jersey to get their charters—I would like them to come here."[3]

INCORPORATION IN DELAWARE

Article IX of the Constitution of 1897 ordained that incorporation could only be enacted "under general law," not by "special act," and that no general incorporation law could be enacted without the approval of two-thirds of the members of each house of the General Assembly. With remarkable foresight, this high vote requirement was inserted in the Constitution to assure stability in Delaware corporate law.

Pursuant to Article IX, Delaware's legislature in 1899 enacted a comprehensive incorporation law that copied New Jersey's liberal corporation statute of 1896 almost verbatim. Not until New Jersey passed seven strict antitrust laws under Governor Woodrow Wilson, however, did Delaware replace New Jersey as the so-called "Mother of Trusts."[4]

This momentous change in Delaware corporate law led both DuPont and General Motors to reincorporate in Delaware in 1916. But DuPont's reincorporation in Delaware did not thereby add jobs to the state's economy, because DuPont was already located in the state. Nor did General Motors' reincorporation necessarily add jobs, because its manufacturing activities were located elsewhere at the time. And so it was with many other firms that were to incorporate in Delaware, because Delaware's 1899 law, that passed both houses of its legislature unanimously, permitted companies incorporated in Delaware to do business anywhere in the United States. They were not required to do any actual business in Delaware.

So why incorporate in Delaware? One answer is that Delaware legislation relating to corporations (Title 8, *Delaware Code*) became very detailed through the twentieth century in providing explicit benefits for the majority stockholders and management of companies doing business in other states to incorporate in Delaware. For example, they could avoid paying income taxes imposed by those other states on profits from "passive" or "intangible investments"—such as stocks, bonds, patents, etc. By merely moving their intangibles to a Delaware incorporated subsidiary, a corporation—wherever chartered—could avoid state taxes on intangible earnings all together. Using Delaware as a tax haven was only one reason to incorporate in Delaware. According to one observer: "There is no one . . . reason that gives Delaware its edge over other states in the corporate charter market. It is the combination of its flexible corporate code, the responsiveness of its legislature, the wealth of legal precedent, its efficient and knowledgeable court system, and its business-like Secretary of State's Office that allows Delaware to remain the leader in the corporate charter market."[5]

By the end of 2013, there were over one million business entities incorporated in Delaware, including 64 percent of the Fortune 500 companies. Although the actual annual fee for an incorporated business entity in Delaware had remained as low as $75, the aggregate yield to the state was significant. Revenue from incorporations (including escheat) in fiscal year 2013 accounted for more than a third of the state's budget. Responding to the "Why Delaware?" question, Delaware's Secretary of State Jeffrey Bullock stated:

> Businesses choose Delaware not for one single reason, but because we provide a complete package of incorporation services. Our Court of Chancery is a unique centuries-old business court that has written most of the modern U.S. corporation case law. It interprets Delaware's General Corporation Law, which is the most advanced and flexible business formation statute in the nation, as a result of our state government's emphasis on being business friendly and accessible.[6]

In 1992, Attorney Norman Veasey became chief justice of Delaware's Supreme Court. In law review articles, Veasey claimed that Delaware's court system was largely responsible for "a very significant contribution" to Delaware's economy and that its "glittering" reputation in business law "is driven by the national respect for our Court of Chancery and Supreme Court, as well as the historic and . . . modern statutes and outstanding service to Delaware corporations."[7] Veasey was referring to the scale and productivity of Delaware's entire legal industry—the employment generated, wages paid, and services consumed—that contributed significantly to Delaware's economy. It was no accident that the U. S. Chamber of Commerce annually ranked Delaware the best in the nation "for excellence in civil litigation."[8]

Regardless of the hundreds of thousands of businesses incorporated in Delaware, primarily to access its courts and services, very few of them actually conduct any business in the so-called "Corporation Capital of the World." Accordingly, state officials have sought other means to attract entities to conduct business that create jobs in the state and keep them there. Indeed, the challenge of creating and keeping jobs has topped the agenda of every governor in modern Delaware, as well as those in many other states.

THE ESSENCE OF DELAWARE'S ECONOMIC STRATEGY

Delaware's economic development strategy has consisted not only of maintaining a business-friendly environment for industries *incorporating* in the state. Not all companies doing significant business in Delaware are even incorporated in the state. For example, McDonald's had thirty-eight locations and 550 employees in Delaware in 2012 but was not incorporated in the state. Perhaps more important are efforts to attract, keep, and grow businesses and hire employees that pay corporate and personal income taxes, respectively. These two strategies—incorporating and subsidizing businesses—have formed the core of ongoing government economic development in the first state. The expectation is that loans and grants to businesses will increase employment and generate tax revenue.

A *subsidy*, according to the dictionary, is "monetary assistance granted by a government in support of an enterprise regarded as being in the public interest."[9] For our purposes in this book, *monetary assistance* may be direct or indirect, and in the form of tax relief, loans, or outright grants; *government* may be national, state, local, or intergovernmental; an *enterprise* or business may be public or private, existing or proposed; and *public interest* may be rationalized or understood as economic development and/or job creation.

Beginning with Governor Sherman Tribbitt's administration (from 1973 to 1977) and through the first term of Governor Pete du Pont's administration (from 1977 to 1981), a series of adverse business-related events convinced state leaders to replace *reactive* crisis management with a *proactive* management approach to economic development. The state government could initiate and/or respond to new opportunities for economic development by making such a management approach a major policy initiative. Obviously, not all economic crises in the future could be avoided.

How did these developments move the state toward adopting a proactive management approach to economic development? To answer this question, we must first consider the Farmers Bank Crisis during the administration of Governor Sherman Tribbitt. That crisis was a catalytic event in the sense that it precipitated an elongated process toward framing the proactive management of economic development in the First State.

THE FARMERS BANK CRISIS

The administration of Democrat Governor Tribbitt was plagued with misfortune, so much so that former Senator Roger Martin in his 1998 book about Tribbitt concluded that "it will be a long time before another chief executive will endure such trying times as Sherman Tribbitt." His "greatest calamity," according to Martin, was the near-failure of the Farmers Bank. [10]

The Farmers Bank of the State of Delaware, regardless of its name, was not an agency of the state government. It was a private bank founded on February 4, 1807, and headquartered in Dover, but also having branches in Sussex and New Castle Counties. Although a private bank, the state government's relationship with the bank became significantly intertwined. Originally, the state owned only a minority of the bank's stock, but over time the state became the owner of a majority of the bank's shares. Moreover, the state's dormant funds were required by law of the General Assembly to be deposited in the bank without interest. Though some of its directors were elected from the General Assembly, the bank itself was run by a board of directors and a president who were private citizens and not state employees. The bank's officials had the authority to make loans, and were answerable to its stockholders, but not necessarily to the state—the majority stockholder.

In January 1976, the bank was on the verge of being bankrupt, a major crisis for Delaware. The bank's capital had gone "negative." It was simply in the "red" without enough money to pay its creditors. The directors had used its capital, including state deposits that were not collateralized, to make $22.5 million in bad loans. Nancy Cook, chair at the time of the General Assembly's Joint Finance Committee, characterized the crisis as "the most serious problem we have ever had."[11] Attorney Frank Biondi explained:

> There was a crew running the bank who were . . . trying to convert it from the local community bank to a bank that was financing economic development in other states. It was trying to become a big credit card operator. The executives . . . were trying to change the character of the bank. They tried to grow too fast and got themselves into speculative and unprofitable lines of business. They wound up with a lot of bad real estate loans out of state . . . a lot of uncollectible loans, credit card loans. . . . It was too aggressive with respect to growth and . . . not adequately capitalized for what they were trying to do. [12]

Democrat Governor Sherman Tribbitt feared all the state's deposits in the Farmers Bank would be lost, a crisis that would put the state government back decades. Accordingly, the plight of the bank was given top priority on his agenda. Many depositors, especially in southern Delaware, mistakenly thought the bank was a state government agency. They irately blamed Tribbitt for the crisis.

Fortunately, the federal government intervened through its Federal Deposit Insurance Corporation (FDIC). Governor Tribbitt then brought in bank experts as consultants and appointed a committee to oversee negotiations with the FDIC. Finally, a deal was struck when—on May 20, 1976—Tribbitt signed a "bailout" with the FDIC. Roger Martin described the agreement as follows:

> It was a complicated agreement that began to restore capital in the bank through preferred stock purchases, bond sales, belt tightening and the state's leaving deposits in the bank without accruing interest. The idea was to build the bank's position in order to attract a buyer. . . . The massive state account . . . kept in Farmers, by law, was disbursed. Accounts were let out to other banks on competitive bids. The Farmers Bank of the State of Delaware, in operation since 1807, would never be the same.[13]

Finally, after Tribbitt's tenure as governor, and a second bailout with the FDIC, the Farmers Bank was bought on December 30, 1981, by Girard Trust of Philadelphia for $38.6 million.

GOVERNOR DU PONT'S PROBLEMS

Former Republican state legislator Congressman Pierre ("Pete") du Pont won election for governor in November 1976 with 57 percent of the electorate. He had defeated incumbent Democrat Governor Sherman Tribbitt's bid for re-election.

After taking office in January 1977, Governor du Pont not only inherited a financial mess from the Tribbitt administration, but he also faced a hostile Democratic majority in the General Assembly. For example, the Democrats first rejected du Pont's proposed budget, then sent him their own budget bill, which he vetoed, and finally they overrode his veto of their budget bill—the first such override in the state's history. And du Pont otherwise was failing to make headway in achieving his policy objectives.

Governor du Pont, from the summer of 1977 to the beginning of 1978, wisely worked to change confrontation into bipartisan conciliation, cooperation, and consensus. But this was a work in progress. In April 1978, President Al Giacco of Hercules Corporation, the state's second largest employer, launched threatening salvos at the state government. That was when Democratic leaders decided to join with Governor du Pont's administration to respond to Al Giacco's onslaught against the state government.

Alexander Giacco became president of Hercules the same year that Pete du Pont became governor of Delaware. In April 1978, Giacco launched an attack during a speech to the Wilmington Rotary Club—a blistering broadside excoriating the state government as anti-business, epitomized by the state's 19.8 percent income tax on annual personal taxable income over $100,000, the highest among the states.

Giacco, in his 2008 autobiography, recounted his confrontation with Tribbitt's predecessor, Governor Russell Peterson, after a luncheon meeting, appearing to blame Peterson for raising the tax rate to 19.8 percent:

> The state was drawing almost half of its revenue from the personal income tax, so when faced with deficits, the governor and the legislature had to raise the tax rate to 19.8 percent. . . . After lunch, Governor Peterson took off on a friendly tack, describing himself as a businessman. . . . For someone like me, who had just paid his taxes, it was almost enough to make me lose my lunch. . . . I could not resist making the comment, "Governor, I wish you would stop calling yourself a businessman; you're giving us a bad name." . . . [W]hen I told him that the cost of services as measured by the high tax rates had skyrocketed, his answer was, "Yes, that is so, but I only raised the taxes at the upper levels." . . . This incident left me feeling as though I swallowed a fish bone, and it was caught in my throat. Needless to say, he was not reelected.[14]

Actually, the top tax rate enacted during Peterson's administration was 18 percent. The rate was increased to 19.8 percent during the administration of Governor Sherman Tribbitt, Peterson's successor. Curiously, Tribbitt's name is not even mentioned in Giacco's autobiography.

One may note that a factor considered in locating a business is the taxes to be paid by the company. Moreover, CEOs are also interested in their personal tax rates, a factor that does not necessarily affect the company. Many CEOs, such as Giacco, may be concerned about both their company and their own tax bills. In any event, Giacco coupled his 1978 salvo with a threat to move Hercules out of Delaware to Texas. Irv Shapiro, then CEO of the DuPont Company, gave credence to Giacco's threat by announcing that he also could not in "good conscience" encourage CEOs elsewhere to move to Delaware given its 19.8 percent tax rate. Although there was some "bluff" in Giacco's threat to move Hercules from Delaware, state leaders took his threat seriously. After all, Giacco was CEO, president, and chairman of Hercules—all wrapped in one. Governor du Pont's budget director Nathan Hayward said Giacco's threat "put the fear of God into everyone," even though "some people said it's political blackmail."[15]

Governor du Pont's response to the criticisms from Giacco and Shapiro took time. By enlisting the support of Democratic leaders in the General Assembly, the top tax rate of 19.8 percent was reduced in May 1979 to 13.5 percent—the first of two income tax cuts during du Pont's administration that were to set a precedent for a succession of such cuts through the end of the twentieth century.[16]

The governor then established an internal task force to explore the means by which Hercules could be induced to remain in downtown Wilmington. Hayward recalled: "Once we got that (tax cut) bill passed . . . we then set about working on the project to try to save Hercules' location downtown. That was the first sort of major economic development initiative that we had in Pete's administration. . . . Frank Biondi helped us put together a strategy to deal with financing to buy some land for Hercules and to give them a place to build their new corporate headquarters."[17] According to Glenn Kenton, Governor du Pont's secretary of state, the task force even helped locate a site for a new building for Hercules and arranged for its "architectural renderings." Giacco "had no clue about . . . this huge presentation," said Kenton, "and I think he was quite taken." Kenton noted that the effort to keep Hercules in Wilmington started because of Giacco's remarks about Delaware's high taxes, but the early planning was in process without any involvement by Hercules officials, "So we were really working on economic development a lot starting in 1978–79."[18]

Regardless of the state's efforts on behalf of Hercules, Al Giacco made little mention of them in his autobiography. Nor did he reveal details of the "deal" that allegedly induced Hercules to stay, except to acknowledge that the Wilmington city government was able to obtain federal urban renewal funds to purchase the site for and to construct the new Hercules building, although the funding was not adequate ("the city and state's efforts didn't fully remedy our cost differential"). Giacco also acknowledged that the city provided two parking garages for the building. But his autobiography did not mention that the state acquired adjacent property to develop a park, nor that the city waived Hercules' payment of property taxes for eleven years. Nor did his autobiography reveal what targets Hercules agreed to on its part in return, namely to create 1,775 new permanent jobs, about nine hundred of which would be filled by lower income workers including seventy minority workers. Those targets were never met, although Giacco in the end acquired what he wanted. Instead, he claimed in his autobiography, "Hercules indeed was a catalyst for revitalizing Wilmington."[19]

Construction of the Hercules building was completed in 1983. The authors of a study, published six years later, commented: "An uncharitable interpretation of the situation is that Hercules was never interested in . . . and only talked about relocation as a means of getting as much of its center city development as possible."[20]

Throughout the 1970s, the Chrysler Corporation was struggling financially, mostly because of soaring interest rates. To survive, Chrysler's CEO Lee Iacocca sought loans at below-market rates from states where it had auto assembly lines, including Delaware in which Chrysler operated a large auto assembly plant in Newark. He asked Delaware's state government for a loan of $50 million. Although that subsidy was more than the du Pont administration could approve, Pete du Pont's legal counsel David Swayze recalled: "One of us—I believe it was Nathan [Hayward]—said that if we cannot contribute what Chrysler is asking, we at least can be the first among the Chrysler production states to provide financial relief."[21] The state gave Chrysler the $5 million loan, becoming the very first state to offer a loan to Chrysler. Iacocca was able to parlay that loan into loan offers by other states, but Delaware's loan was the one that started Chrysler on its way to recovery. Iacocca had personally promised Governor du Pont that Delaware's loan would be the first to be repaid, and that he would deliver the check himself. He did just that on the floor of the Chrysler assembly plant in Newark.

DELAWARE ECONOMIC DEVELOPMENT OFFICE

Taken together, the du Pont administration had initiated three groundbreaking economic development successes: keeping Hercules in downtown Wilmington; being the first state to help Chrysler to stay alive; and, of course, overseeing the Farmers Bank sale to Philadelphia's Girard Company.

Governor du Pont and the General Assembly then saw fit to create the so-called Cash Management Policy Board to oversee operating cash balances. But, more important, the economic development initiatives led to the establishment in 1981 of the Delaware Development Office—later renamed the Delaware Economic Development Office (DEDO)—thus institutionalizing in Delaware at the time a nationally unique proactive state management agency for economic development.

Nathan Hayward, the first director of DEDO, later recalled in a 2006 oral history how DEDO evolved:

> Well, there were offices of tourism, there were various other kinds of offices, but from a standpoint of having a statewide development initiative, what we had in mind was certainly on the cutting edge in 1980. And a group of us had been meeting from time to time—business developers and some legislators and what have you. Frank Biondi was in the middle of it all and I sat down with Frank and I said okay, we need an authorizing statute to do this and we worked together on what the office should be able to do and wrote a bill to create one which was introduced in the General Assembly in January of 1981. . . . It was structured to be a professional office where its employees were outside the merit system and where people would be hired and fired based on their productivity and where you could pay competitive wages. It was a hell of a novel idea . . . and it passed . . . with strong support of the business community.[22]

Oral history writer Larry Nagengast, in his 2006 Delaware Heritage Press book, added this comment about DEDO:

> Not only was the Economic Development Office instrumental in identifying businesses that would relocate to Delaware, but it also served as a broker to ensure that the needs of these businesses were met. . . . By cutting taxes, reforming state finances and creating the Economic Development Office, the du Pont administration and the General Assembly transformed Delaware from a state with a fading economy and an anti-business image into a well-managed operation that was responsive to corporate leaders and to the entire work-force.[23]

The new office was not created too soon, because it was established just before the landmark Financial Center Development Act (FCDA) was enacted in February 1981. FCDA deregulated credit card banking and ushered into the state an unparalleled economic bonanza of sorts. DEDO's director, Nathan Hayward, had a hand in paving the way for FCDA. This is not to say that Hayward was responsible for FCDA, but he was a major player at the time. He had joined Governor du Pont, Frank Biondi, Glenn Kenton, and other notables to negotiate many times with Chase Bank and Morgan Bank officials, both in New York and Wilmington, about moving their credit card operations to Delaware. And it was Hayward who suggested that the new law be named the Financial Center Development Act (FCDA). The mission of DEDO has been to attract and keep businesses in Delaware in order to create jobs for Delawareans, or as stated by DEDO itself: "to be responsible for attracting new investors and businesses to the State, promoting the expansion of existing industry . . . and creating new and improved employment opportunity for all citizens of the State."[24]

The importance of DEDO is not just to attract new businesses to the state, and thus create jobs, but also to support them to be successful in Delaware so that they will remain. Accordingly, FCDA was amended to remove an impediment for credit card banks by adjusting the bank franchise tax that was levied at the same rate as the corporate income tax at 8.7 percent. The tax rate was reduced on a sliding scale from 8.7 percent for banks with incomes not in excess of $20 million to as low as 1.7 percent on incomes in excess of $650 million. This tax replaced the corporate income and corporate franchise taxes for banks.

The banking industry overall grew from a pre-FCDA level of about 4,600 employees to 43,000, a total of about one-tenth of all Delaware employees, by the year 2000. Moreover, the state government's collection of about $2.5 million in 1980 from the bank franchise tax increased to more than $175 million by 2007, which was over 5 percent of all state government revenue.

Large government surpluses replaced shortfalls. So successful was the financial sector of the state's economy that it threatened to dwarf the manufacturing sector. DEDO's role thereby was substantially reduced during the state's economic heydays. But the advent of the Great Recession beginning in 2008, together with federal intervention, most notably via passage of the Credit Card Act of 2009, deflated Delaware's credit card boom and otherwise portended hard economic times for Delaware. DEDO's proactive activities became even more important than ever before. Spurred by negative business developments and job losses, reliance on subsidizing businesses to create jobs became the state government's highest priority.

THE STRATEGIC FUND

To buttress DEDO, the Strategic Fund was created in 1994. The legislation creating the fund, as amended, stated its "findings and purpose" as follows:

> The General Assembly finds that Delaware's development finance programs are necessary to compete for new and existing businesses. Furthermore, the General Assembly finds the number and limited previous funding of the Delaware Economic Development Office do not maximize efficiency of administration by the State or the business community. It is the intent of the General Assembly to solve this problem by consolidating the existing development finance programs of the Delaware Economic Development Office into a Delaware Strategic Fund. . . . The Fund shall initially consist of $2,250,000 as authorized . . . to the Office on behalf of the Delaware Economic Development Authority. . . . Moneys appropriated to the Fund . . . may be used for the following purposes: (1) Retention and expansion of existing firms; (2) Recruitment of new firms; (3) Formation of new businesses.[25]

According to the same legislation, the Strategic Fund may be used for these activities listed below:

> (1) Working capital; (2) Renovation, construction or any other type of improvements to roads, utilities and related infrastructure and public facilities; (3) Assistance for equipment, machinery, land and building acquisition and development; (4) Assistance with relocation expenses; (5) Loans or loan guarantees; (6) Assistance for the development of startup strategies such as seed capital and incubator programs; (7) Assistance for the development of re-use strategies and implementation plans for sites located in the State and targeted for development by the Office; (8) Assistance for the development and implementation of modernization strategies for existing manufacturing firms to strengthen their competitive position in regional, national and international markets; and (9) To develop and implement strategies to maintain or enhance important economic sectors in the State.[26]

The legislation also explicitly lists the criteria, upon which the "amount and type of assistance" provided by DEDO to a firm through the fund, is to be determined:

> (1) Consistency with state economic strategies; (2) Number of jobs created or retained; (3) Competitiveness of Delaware versus other locations under consideration measured by tax comparison and relative site location factors; (4) Quality of jobs using measures such as the average wage and benefits of the jobs to be created or retained as compared to labor force characteristics of the county and community in which the project will be located; (5) Comparative overall impact of the project at the state, county and local levels as measured by job creation and retention, private investment leverage and revenue generation; (6) Feasibility of the project as determined by the applicant's business plan, business history and collateral or other financial resources available to adequately secure assistance; and (7) Any environmental consideration related to siting decisions, manufacturing processes or byproducts.[27]

The General Assembly's bond bill, of June 30, 1995, allocated $10 million for the Strategic Fund as part of the total of $17,425,000 appropriated for DEDO.[28] Thereafter, the Strategic Fund became the principal funding mechanism for DEDO's subsidies to businesses.

DELAWARE ECONOMIC DEVELOPMENT AUTHORITY

The legislation creating the Strategic Fund also established the Delaware Economic Development Authority (DEDA). The authority is a government corporation that "shall draft rules and regulations pertaining to the Fund eligibility, and establish criteria to administer the Fund."[29] For example, DEDA requires applicants for a Strategic Fund loan and/or grant to complete its application form that provides "a detailed description of the project to support the Authority to determine that the project maintains or provides gainful employment for the people of Delaware, maintain or increase the tax base of Delaware's economy and maintain diversity, or expand business and industry in Delaware."[30]

The actual financing of organizations approved for assistance is a rather complicated process in which DEDA has a central role. Organizations that are exempt from federal income taxation are financially assisted by DEDA issuing tax-exempt bonds and lending the proceeds of such bonds to them. The interest rates of tax-exempt bonds are lower than those of taxable bonds, for the reason that the interest paid to bond holders is exempt from both federal and Delaware income taxes. So DEDA can pass the lower interest rate to the assisted organizations. After DEDA approves a bond issue, the assisted organization is responsible for arranging for the sale of the bond and for paying the interest and principal. According to DEDA, tax-exempt financing may be cost effective for projects involving the issuance of more than $1.25 million. But the availability of tax-exempt status, for the issuance of bonds to finance a given project, is governed by the Internal Revenue Code and detailed IRS regulations that restrict the amount of tax-exempt bonds a state may issue.[31]

DEDA, in conjunction with DEDO, has several other flexible ways it can add to incentives for a firm to do business and create jobs in Delaware. For example, DEDA may waive service fees that typically amount to over 2 percent of the bond issue—a move that may loom as very important for a company that needs cash. Although the full faith and credit of the state are not invested in the bond issuance process, the fact that Delaware's state government enjoys a top bond rating is certainly a benefit.

COUNCIL ON DEVELOPMENT FINANCE

Still another state entity involved in this seemingly complicated subsidy process is the Council on Development Finance (CDF). Once an application for financial assistance is completed and submitted by a firm, DEDA—via DEDO's staff—evaluates it in terms of criteria as specified in relevant law and regulations. If DEDA approves the application after review, CDF holds a public hearing on the proposed project.

According to its governing legislation, CDF is established to serve in an "advisory capacity" to the director of DEDO. CDF's membership is required by law to be bipartisan in its make-up and to serve without compensation. Moreover, CDF may hold its hearings, in part, in "executive sessions closed to the public for the purpose of discussing certain confidential commercial and financial information submitted by the applicants for assistance.[32]

According to the minutes of one of its 2012 hearings, for example, among the items under "New Business" considered were the following: the Henry Francis du Pont Winterthur Museum's application for $5 million to fund costs associated with the capital budget; the Delaware City Refinery's request for $10 million for converting combustion turbines to natural gas; the E. I. DuPont de Nemours company's request for $920,000 to help develop a new product; and the Hughes Delaware Maid Scrapple's application for $10,000 to help rebuild its business.[33]

CDF's role is an advisory one only. Once it holds a public hearing, CDF makes its recommendation to the chairperson of DEDA, who must approve an application for financing before financing can take place—for example, before DEDA can issue a bond.

THE GOVERNOR'S ROLE

Although this process appears complex, circumstances permit the state to complete the process in a much shorter time compared with other states with which Delaware competes. Because Delaware is so small, DEDA can act quickly and may issue a bond within thirty-two days, if necessary, from the time an application is submitted. It is true that each of the various state administrative entities involved in the subsidy process—principally DEDO, DEDA, and CDF—has important decision-making authority. Red tape and jurisdictional conflicts are avoided, however, by the fact that the director of DEDO is also the chairperson of both DEDA and CDF. In effect, therefore, both DEDA and CDF function as arms of the director. Moreover, DEDO is part of the executive office of the governor. The director is appointed by, and serves at the pleasure of, the governor, who thereby is vested with ultimate authority in the subsidy process. This authority is shared, of course, as the General Assembly appropriates money in its annual bond bill for the Strategic Fund, and the DEDO director's appointment is subject to Senate confirmation.

The nation's financial crisis, which began in 2008, was still not resolved through 2013. The crisis appeared especially severe in Delaware. Symptomatic was Delaware's hotel occupancy rate, which was hit hard during the recession; the rate was reported to have been only 53.8 percent statewide in 2011, compared with 60.1 percent nationally. The occupancy rate was even worse in Kent County at 47 percent.[34] Although Delaware's unemployment rate of 7.6 percent in November 2011 continued to be lower than that of the nation as a whole, the state lost an additional 2,700 jobs that month. The Wilmington *News Journal* reported:

> In Delaware, from February 2008 to December 2008, as the recession gained steam, economists originally estimated that employers here cut 5,800 jobs. After benchmarking those numbers against actual payroll data that employers submit for unemployment insurance claims, economists counted 13,700 Delaware job reductions over that critical eleven-month span. . . . From November 2010 to November 2011 . . . the U.S. Department of Labor survey of businesses recorded 3,900 job losses across Delaware.[35]

Among the larger Delaware employers that either closed or were merged with other firms with the onset of the recession were Hercules, Chrysler, General Motors, Avon, and Merck, while some remaining firms—such as AstraZeneca and DuPont—cut a significant number of jobs. In August 2011, the Wilmington *News Journal* reported: "Delaware Department of Labor economist George Sharpley said the state's construction industry was one of the hardest hit by the recession, losing more than 7,200 jobs from 2007 to

2010. But the building sector was already sliding before the recession began, losing an estimated 3,000 jobs in the lead-up to the housing crash."[36]

Politically, attracting and keeping jobs ranked at the top of both the governor's and General Assembly's agendas during the Great Recession. In general, as the state's economy declined during hard times, the Strategic Fund—hence DEDO subsidies—tended to increase. When Democrat Jack Markell was campaigning for governor in 2008, many Delawareans assumed that Alan Levin, CEO of Happy Harry's, the nation's tenth largest drugstore chain, would become Markell's Republican opponent. However, Levin withdrew his name from contention, and Markell, a former businessman himself, was elected governor. Soon after he took office in 2009, one of Markell's first appointments was of Levin to become director of DEDO. With the recession at its worst, Governor Markell made it known that attracting businesses and new jobs to Delaware was going to be his top priority, and that Alan Levin and DEDO would have his strongest support.

In 2010, the Delaware Economic and Financial Advisory Council (DEFAC) projected that over $100 million would be added to the state's revenue. Governor Jack Markell at the time optimistically proposed a plan to move the newly found revenue into the Strategic Fund to preserve jobs and induce new businesses to come to Delaware. Noting that the fund was very active during the economic downturn, Markell said that it "is the tool that helped us bring companies like Fisker Automotive, PBF Energy and so many other employers to Delaware."[37] In June 2011, DEFAC had projected revenues to increase up to a $365 million surplus. However, in September 2011, DEFAC's projected revenue was down $108.9 million, prompting one Finance Department analyst to say: "We're skating on thin ice."[38]

DEFAC projections notwithstanding, Governor Markell adopted an aggressive strategy to establish the so-called "Delaware New Jobs Infrastructure Fund," which was created in June 2011 by the General Assembly's fiscal year (FY) 2012 Bond Bill to provide "economic assistance for renovation, construction or any other type of improvements to roads, utilities and related infrastructure in order to attract new businesses to Delaware, or for the expansion of existing Delaware businesses, when such an economic development opportunity would create a significant number of direct, permanent, quality, full-time jobs." The Bond Bill appropriated $40 million to the Infrastructure Fund for FY 2012, supplemented with $15 million bonding authority set aside for the fund.[39]

Governor Markell's FY 2012 budget proposed $55 million for the Infrastructure Fund, surpassing even the $31.9 million he proposed for the Strategic Fund.[40] Markell's motivation to create the special Infrastructure Fund to attract business may have been precipitated to support in part Amazon's construction of a large distribution center in Middletown with a $4 million grant from the fund, to be used to build extensions of roads to the site. The fact that Amazon expected to produce 850 new jobs at the $90 million center was certainly a factor. Moreover, the company had already been awarded a grant from the Strategic Fund.[41]

The question remained whether a project that expected to create few full-time jobs would also qualify for an Infrastructure Fund award. That question was raised after Dover's City Council approved a request from Calpine, a Houston-based power plant company, for $6 million in city bonds for roads and other infrastructure to support building a Calpine generation plant on city-owned land. Calpine was considering in February 2012 applying for another $6 million from the state's New Jobs Infrastructure Fund. But one state senator from Dover, Brian Bushweller, questioned whether its application would fit the Infrastructure Fund. Although the plant would create up to 250 construction jobs, only about fifteen permanent jobs would be filled, noted Bushweller. DEDO director Levin was more sanguine, however, saying: "Assuming that it gets built, the city will have the ability to bring in more business."[42]

Governor Markell did not stop with creation of the New Jobs Infrastructure Fund. He was successful in having still another fund established to cover opportunities that might arise and not be funded by the Strategic Fund or the Infrastructure Fund. The new fund was established by the General Assembly's Bond Bill of June 2011, named the "Building Delaware's Future Fund," that authorized an appropriation of $115 million for FY 2012. The Future Fund included the $40 million Infrastructure Fund, plus its $20 million set-aside bonding authority.[43]

In addition, the Future Fund also included tax-related components, namely: (a) it made permanent certain elements of the state's so-called "Blue Collar Jobs Tax Credits," used to recruit and expand businesses for twenty-five years; (b) it increased the basic ten-year corporate and personal income tax credit amount from $400 to $500 for each qualifying job, and from $400 to $500 for every $100,000 of qualifying investment; and (c) it extended 50 percent higher income tax credits and a lower gross receipts tax rate to "green" businesses that manufacture clean-energy systems, such as wind, solar, and fuel cells.[44]

In other words, besides including the Infrastructure Fund money authorizations, the Future Fund merely tweaked existing legislation by increasing certain tax credits to qualified businesses. It is important to note that some of the taxpayers' money spent by the state to attract and/or enhance businesses to create jobs can sometimes be recovered, or clawed back, by the state, but a tax credit is tantamount to money permanently lost. One should also note that claw-backs usually come from loans or grants, and that businesses generally prefer having cash rather than receiving tax credits.

Delaware was not the only state using tax credits to grow or attract business. Indeed, most states were engaged in such activities. New York's state government was sponsoring primetime nightly TV commercials in 2013 promising ten years of tax exemption for start-up companies attracted to the state. In April 2012, the *New York Times* reported that New Jersey Governor Chris Christie after taking office in 2010 had approved a whopping $1.57 billion in state tax credits for dozens of his state's largest companies that threatened to move to other states. Opponents claimed the Christie administration was mortgaging the state's future by forgiving so much tax revenue for the next ten to fifteen years.[45]

CONCLUSION

Activist Governor Jack Markell came close to rationalizing the state's revitalized and renewed subsidies with these remarks:

> We want to support existing employers' efforts to expand here in Delaware. We want to keep attracting more businesses to make our state their home, and we want to be ready to act quickly when the next great opportunity comes. These tools build on the success of previous efforts and months of conversations with businesses about how we could be a better partner in building their work force.[46]

Delaware had come a long way since the 1899 enactment of its landmark incorporation law. Many thousands of firms had chosen to incorporate in the first state. But very few made Delaware their home. The early years of the twenty-first century—during the administrations of Governors Minner and Markell—were different. Delaware had developed a multidimensional management approach to grow and/or attract businesses and jobs in the first state.

The following chapters examine the successes and failures of Delaware's economic development strategies—strategies that may be characterized as comprising a spectrum from "grow-your-own" to "beggar-thy-neighbor" as well as hybrids in between. Delaware is a small state that may not realize the measure of success in handing out grants compared with the success of other states that have far more resources. Delaware possesses certain advantages, however, in terms of flexibility in governance, including the relative ease of adjusting regulations, tax laws, and other legal barriers that pose more difficult hurdles for more populous states with larger bureaucracies.

NOTES

1. A. Gilchrist Sparks III and Donna L. Culver, "Corporations, Article IX," in *The Delaware Constitution of 1897: The First One Hundred Years*, ed. Harvey B. Rubenstein, et al. (Wilmington: Delaware State Bar Association, 1997), 161.
2. Christopher Grandy, "The Economics of Multiple Governments: New Jersey Corporate Chartermongering, 1875–1929," *Business and Economic History*, Second Series 18 (1989): 19.

3. Quoted by Carol E. Hoffecker, *Democracy in Delaware: The Story of the First State's General Assembly* (Wilmington: Cedar Tree Books, 2004), 133.

4. Grandy, "Economics," 19.

5. Demetrios G. Kaouris, "Is Delaware Still a Haven for Incorporation?" *Delaware Journal of Corporate Law* 20, no. 3 (1995): 1011.

6. Jeffrey W. Bullock, Secretary of State, *Delaware Division of Corporations 2010 Annual Report* (Dover: Delaware Department of State, April 5, 2011), 1. See also, Lewis S. Black, Jr., *Why Corporations Choose Delaware* (Dover: Delaware Department of State, 2007).

7. See E. Norman Veasey, "It Is Time to Give Credit," *Delaware Lawyer* 12, no. 4 (1994): 6; and Veasey, "I Have the Best Job in America," *Delaware Lawyer* 13, no. 4 (1995): 21, 23.

8. See, for example, Editorial, "Distinguished Record," Wilmington *News Journal*, April 7, 2004, A12.

9. *American Heritage College Dictionary*, 3rd edition, s.v. "subsidy."

10. Roger A. Martin, *Sherman W. Tribbitt, Governor of Delaware, 1973–1977* (Wilmington: Delaware Heritage Commission, Oral History Series, 1998), Introduction.

11. Cook quoted in ibid., 203.

12. Biondi quoted in ibid., 203–4.

13. Ibid., 201–2.

14. Al Giacco, *Maverick Management: Strategies for Success* (Newark: University of Delaware Press, 2003), 214–15.

15. Larry Nagengast, *Pierre S. du Pont IV: Governor of Delaware, 1977–1985* (Dover: Delaware Heritage Press, 2006), 92.

16. See, for example, Celia Cohen, "Tax Cut a Proven Road to Del. Re-election," Wilmington *News Journal*, May 19, 1996, B3.

17. Hayward quoted by Nagengast, *Pierre S. du Pont IV*, 98.

18. Kenton quoted in ibid., 99.

19. Giacco, *Maverick Management*, 28–29.

20. Timothy Barnekov, Robin Boyle, and Daniel Rich, *Privatism and Urban Policy in Britain and the United States* (New York: Oxford University Press, 1989), 86.

21. Swayze quoted by Nagengast, *Pierre S. du Pont IV*, 101.

22. Hayward quoted in ibid., 102–3.

23. Ibid., 103.

24. See, for example, this mission statement of the Delaware Economic Development Office (DEDO), in its Membership Directory, www.delawarebio.org/delaware-economic-development-office (accessed July 14, 2015).

25. *Delaware Code*, Title 29, Chapter 50, State Economic Development, Subchapter I-B, Delaware Strategic Fund, Sections 5027, 5208(a).

26. Ibid., Section 5208(b).

27. Ibid., Section 5208(d).

28. See "A Bond and Capital Improvements Act . . . for the Fiscal Year Ending June 30, 1996," Chapter 210, Vol. 70, Formerly Senate Bill No. 260, June 30, 1995: Section 44: 536, and Section 1 Addendum: Fiscal Year 1996 Capital Improvements Project Schedule.

29. *Delaware Code*, Section 5029, supra, note 23. For DEDA's rules and regulations, see *Delaware Regulations, Administrative Code*, Title 1, 402: "Procedures Governing the Delaware Strategic Fund."

30. See DEDA, Application for Financial Assistance: General Information, at inde.delaware.gov/dedo_pdf/BusinessServices_pdf/BusinessFinancing/DelawareEconomic-DevelopmentAuthority.pdf.

31. See DEDO, *Tax-Exempt Bond Financing* (accessed February 3, 2012) at dedo.delaware.gov/BusinessServices/BusinessFinancing/BusinessFinancingTaxExe. See also DEDO, *Tax-Exempt Bond Financing Application*, on the same site.

32. See, for example, CDF, "Notice of Public Hearing . . . ," Monday, December 12, 2012.

33. See CDF Public Hearing Minutes, January 23, 2012, inde.delaware.gov/dedo_pdf/NewsEvents_pdf/minutes/2012/January23_2012_CDF_Meeting.pdf.

34. Maureen Milford, "Troubled Hotel Firm Has $1M in Debts," Wilmington *News Journal*, February 27, 2012, B1–B2.

35. Jonathan Starkey, "Jobs Data Full of Ups and Downs," Wilmington *News Journal*, December 7, 2011, A1, A2.

36. Wade Malcolm and Doug Denison, "With Work Scarce, Construction Firms Clamor for Public Projects," Wilmington *News Journal*, August 15, 2011, A1, A2.

37. Mark Eichmann, "Governor Wants Delaware Surplus to Repay Strategic Business Fund," *WHYY News and Information*, May 20, 2010.

38. Editorial, "Revenue Forecast Shows How Tight Budget Will Be," Wilmington *News Journal*, September 20, 2011.

39. See Section 39 (b) (1), Senate Bill 130, Fiscal Year 2012 Bond and Capital Improvements Act; and DEDO, Guidelines Governing the Practice and Procedure for Administering the Delaware New Jobs Infrastructure Fund, accessible at www.budget.delaware.gov/fy2012/capital/cap_bond_bill_sb130.pdf, and at blogs.delawareonline.com/delawareinc/files/2011/10/DRAFT-Infrastructure-Investment-Committee-Guidelines.pdf.

40. Office of the Governor, *Fiscal Year 2012 Operating and Capital Budget Summary* (Dover: State of Delaware, 2012).

41. See Council on Development Finance, December 12, 2011, Public Hearings, 5, accessible at inde.delaware.gov/dedo_pdf/NewsEvents_pdf/minutes/2011/December12_2011_CDF_Meeting.pdf.

42. Doug Denison, "Energy Firm Looks to Dover," Wilmington *News Journal*, February 20, 2012, A1, A2.

43. See Senate Bill No. 130, Section 39: "A Bond and Capital Improvement Act," June 28, 2011.

44. See *Delaware Code*, Chapter 20: Subchapter IX: New Economy Jobs Program Credits; Subchapter V: Clean Energy Technology Device Manufacturers' Credits; and Subchapters II–III, V: Tax Credit for Creation of Employment and Qualified Investments in Business Facilities (otherwise known as the "Blue Collar Jobs Act").

45. Charles V. Bagli, "Pursuing Jobs for New Jersey, Governor Leans on Tax Breaks," *New York Times*, April 15, 2012, A1, A18.

46. Quoted by Alan Levin, director, DEDO, January 2012, governor.delaware.gov/news/2011/1103march/20110314-bluecollarcredit.shtml (accessed February 27, 2012).

Chapter One

AstraZeneca

Delaware's 1981 enactment of the Financial Center Development Act (FCDA), which provided beneficial statutory changes and special tax considerations for credit card banks, proved to be a major job growth investment for Delaware that lasted for almost three decades.[1] The next major job growth strategy by the state, which it pursued toward the end of the 1990s, though on a lesser scale, involved the AstraZeneca pharmaceutical company. Events leading up to that effort, as well as its aftermath, comprise a dramatic and ongoing story that may be long remembered by many Delawareans. Reliance on many issues of the Wilmington *News Journal*, extending from 1999 through 2013, enables us to piece together highlights of this story.[2]

PROSPECTIVE MERGER OF ASTRA AND ZENECA

In late 1998 and early 1999, it became widely known that two large European pharmaceutical companies—London-based Zeneca and Stockholm-based Astra—were considering merging later in 1999. This prospect created quite a stir in both Delaware and Pennsylvania, because Zeneca's American headquarters was already located in an area of northern Delaware commonly known as Fairfax, and Astra's U.S. headquarters was located seven miles north of Fairfax in nearby Wayne of southern Pennsylvania. Astra had been considering moving its operations to East Goshen, Pennsylvania, even closer to Delaware's northern border.

Observers assumed that the merged company, to be known as AstraZeneca, would choose to locate its combined headquarters either at its Zeneca site in Delaware, which housed 2,400 pharmaceutical jobs, or at its Astra site in Pennsylvania, which employed 1,600. In other words, at least four thousand high-paying jobs (average salaries of about $50,000) and millions in tax revenue were at stake.

Long before the merger, Delaware officials became engaged in a bidding war with Pennsylvania officials to locate the merged North American headquarters at Zeneca's location. Officials of both states, looking toward a $37 billion merger of these two drug-making heavyweights, began courting the new company even though it did not yet exist.[3]

For a number of reasons, it seemed clear that Delaware had the edge. Delaware officials were cautiously optimistic, if only for the fact that a majority of the employees were already housed at the Zeneca site. Moreover, Zeneca already owned the eighty-eight acres on which it was located, while Astra was leasing its buildings and was considering a move elsewhere in Pennsylvania. In fact, Astra reportedly had bid $18.2 million to acquire 312 acres in East Goshen where it could build a new headquarters.

Still other factors appeared to favor a Delaware location. Through then-Governor Tom Carper and the Delaware Economic Development Office (DEDO), Delaware offered a package that included open land across the street from Zeneca's headquarters on its eighty-eight-acre site. Delaware bought that land in February 1999 to sweeten the deal, offering a reported $12.6 million for a 156-acre site. It was anticipated as part of the proposed deal that AstraZeneca would expand to a portion of that property, with the remainder left as open space. Officials also stressed that Delaware was well on its way to becoming a biotechnology center. They pointed to these facts: AstraZeneca's Fairfax location would be quite close to DuPont's Experimental Station; DuPont had recently formed DuPont Pharmaceuticals by buying half of Merck & Company in a joint venture; and Delaware's state government had earmarked $10 million to help build a local biotechnology institute.

Meanwhile, Pennsylvania officials did not reveal details of their package of incentives. With regard to taxes, both states emphasized their strengths while pointing to the other's weaknesses. Delaware highlighted its favorable corporate taxes and the absence of a sales tax. Although Pennsylvania imposed a 6 percent sales tax, it stressed that its personal income tax rate was lower than Delaware's rate.[4] However, Pennsylvania had substantially higher property taxes and taxed personal income based on gross income rather than taxable income.

THE MERGER OCCURS

The $35 billion merger deal occurred as scheduled in early April 1999, creating the world's third largest drug maker. Its North American senior management team was faced with two major issues: how to merge Zeneca and Astra operations in the United States and whether to locate its North

American headquarters in Delaware or Pennsylvania. Within days of the actual merger, both Governor Tom Carper of Delaware and Governor Tom Ridge of Pennsylvania and their staffs met independently with the new company's senior management team to offer their respective final pitches.

Delaware offered a package of incentives that included $18.7 million in cash grants and land, about $70 million in roadwork, $30 million in tax credits, plus training, infrastructure, and many other perks—labeled the most expensive package Delaware had ever offered to keep a company in the state. Carper spokeswoman Sheri Woodruff said: "We are just trying to be real attentive to their needs and to answer any questions."[5]

However, it was finally revealed that Pennsylvania officials offered roughly $20 million in grants, road work, and tax breaks, but not enough to offset Delaware's total tax structure. Nor could Pennsylvania match Delaware's biotechnology advances including the new Delaware Biotechnology Institute and DuPont Company's kindred interests and commitments. Indeed, the Carper administration projected the state's future economy precisely on the kind of biotechnology business that the behemoth AstraZeneca represented. Still, the decision of where to locate the new company's headquarters was clothed in secrecy, and officials of both states had no prior inkling which state would be selected.[6]

On April 30, 1999, just a few weeks after Astra and Zeneca merged, the Wilmington *News Journal* broke the news that AstraZeneca chose Delaware's Zeneca site as its new North American headquarters. It was quite a bonanza that one of the world's largest drugmakers, with annual sales of $15 billion, chose little Delaware over populous Pennsylvania for its North American headquarters.

It was revealed that key reasons the company settled on Delaware were the company's study pinpointing where its employees lived (most already lived in Delaware) and Delaware's lower business taxes, including its lower corporate tax rate and lack of a sales tax. Moreover, Delaware's cash and land package of $18.7 million was the largest the state had ever offered to a company. That package included $10.7 million for purchase of new land for the company, plus $8 million in cash to move the company, in addition to the tax breaks and other perks. Governor Tom Ridge of Pennsylvania was so disappointed with the decision that, reportedly, he asked AstraZeneca's North American CEO whether there was any chance that the company would reconsider if Pennsylvania could improve its offer. Pennsylvania had relied upon its lower income tax rate and its allegedly superior public schools to no avail.[7]

When Governor Carper heard the good news, he canceled a meeting in the White House with President Bill Clinton and hurried back to Delaware. Standing on the future site of AstraZeneca's North American headquarters, Carper lifted a glass of champagne with a toast to AstraZeneca's decision:

"This is the whole nine yards. This is the big enchilada. This is one of those deals where we never stopped working, where we didn't take anything for granted." Having AstraZeneca and DuPont in Delaware would "bring international attention for Delaware as a cradle for biotechnology." Saying that he hoped Delaware was on its way to developing a regional biotechnology corridor that would encourage other biotechnology firms to consider locating in the area, Carper added: "It's great to have one anchor for a corridor. But it's even greater to have two." DEDO Director Darrell J. Minott chimed in that DuPont officials were among those who helped Delaware attract Astra-Zeneca to Delaware. "We needed to have a mecca," Minott commented, "Today, the best and the brightest don't want to come to a one-company town."[8]

Mention also could have been made that two smaller Delaware companies were already involved in biotechnology—Hercules in Wilmington and Strategic Diagnostics in Newark. Moreover, the University of Delaware was a partner in the recently created Biotechnology Institute and had already been hiring new faculty to expand research in that field and teaching students destined for related high-tech positions. Its director, David Weir, exulted: "Life sciences has been referred to as the industrial revolution of the twenty-first century, so this [AstraZeneca's decision] is of particular significance. We've got a critical mass now and this will be a huge magnet. These kinds of companies feed on one another."[9]

DEDO Director Minott was particularly upbeat about Delaware's future economy when he commented:

> We have a strong base of the kinds of companies we want and the kinds of jobs that will lead us into the twenty-first century in a strong position and we're building on that. We're going to be a presence, globally and nationally. Technology will play a tremendous role. That's where all the businesses are placing their bets. Delaware has positioned itself to be last into a recession. All of the surrounding states will be the first into a recession before Delaware, and Delaware will be the first one out, and the reason is diversification. You can't rely on one industry. Every sector goes through its bad times.[10]

It was evident that Delaware state officials were taking aim on what they saw as the next growth area, namely high technology, or more specifically biotechnology. Such an effort was particularly timely given the fact that the DuPont Company had publicly committed to becoming more of a life sciences company instead of a pure chemical maker.

CONFRONTING TRAFFIC CONGESTION

The expected influx of thousands more employees working in the expanding AstraZeneca site in Fairfax, together with the planned expansion of the nearby DuPont Experimental Station, portended even greater congestion of the already traffic-choked network of roadways in the area. Road improvements had already been approved previously and were not directly related to AstraZeneca's expansion. However, since the company planned to move roughly two thousand more jobs to its headquarters area during the next three years, roadwork construction, including rerouting, became critical not only to AstraZeneca but also to residents of contiguous upscale neighborhoods. Spokesperson for the Delaware Department of Transportation (DelDOT) Michele Ackles said: "These are ongoing traffic improvements to this area. Future road improvements are still being designed and there will be a lot of opportunity for the key players to comment as to how we make it all work."[11]

One factor that induced AstraZeneca to choose Delaware for its headquarters was the commitment that DelDOT had already budgeted $70 million for road improvements in the vicinity. Now that the company had made its decision, DelDOT planned to go even deeper in debt to fund its assorted highway projects, including boosting its planned expenditure to $76 million in upgrades to accommodate AstraZeneca.[12]

The issue of traffic congestion in the area involved major actors within all levels of Delaware government. New Castle County's Executive Thomas Gordon and four county council members agreed to lift traffic and deed restrictions linked to AstraZeneca's new site. Such promises were made with the signatures of the county's elected officials in an April 1999 letter drafted without any required public hearings. Civic leaders expressed concern about how much power they had in the planning process. "How can they say yes . . . when there was no public input to this at all?" one civic leader asked. Greg Lavelle, then chairperson of the local council of civic organizations, questioned whether the county was appeasing major employers.[13] The Wilmington *News Journal* weighed in to allay a threatened donnybrook of sorts, by editorializing: "To win residents' approval, the state promised to involve them in the planning. This has been done. The reconfigured road and intersections may be the most democratically designed anywhere." However, a subsequent editorial acknowledged: "The arrival of AstraZeneca . . . and the almost certain expansion of the DuPont Co.'s Experimental Station threatened to make a marginally acceptable traffic situation a disaster."[14]

A full year after AstraZeneca chose Delaware for its North American headquarters, Governor Carper intervened, together with New Castle County Executive Tom Gordon, to postpone the decision of how to handle area traffic, by asking for more traffic analysis by DelDOT. Meanwhile, the state's General Assembly approved a nonbinding resolution supporting New

Castle County Council's proposal to waive traffic regulations and deed restrictions for AstraZeneca to proceed with its expansion in the area. Finally,
in July 2000, over one-and-a-half years since AstraZeneca's decision to
move to Delaware, the New Castle County Council voted unanimously to
approve the company's development plans, and to change deed restrictions
on the company's construction site.[15]

Whereas construction of AstraZeneca's new buildings was scheduled to
begin as early as the Fall of 2000, the Brandywine Civic Council's executive
committee adopted a resolution in April 2001 to support a clover-leaf traffic
interchange nearby. But the DelDOT plan for improvements called for the
construction of two underpasses and a bypass as part of an escalated $127
million package to accommodate increased traffic in the area, as AstraZeneca
expanded, bringing an estimated 3,350 new jobs to the area within the next
decade. Despite the case made by nearby residents for an interchange, Del-
DOT's Secretary Nathan Hayward rejected the interchange, by saying: "Each
of these decisions represent a series of compromises. . . . We promised the
residents of this state that we were going to stay within the budget, and meet
deadline with this project and that's what we intend to do." What Hayward
did not say was that the cost of DelDOT's projected construction improvements had increased from its original estimate of $70 million to $127 million—a whopping increase of 81.4 percent within a span of two years.[16]

With the advent of AstraZeneca in the new millennium, together with
DuPont joining the bandwagon of life sciences, plus the soaring rise of credit
card banking, Delaware economically was becoming a high performer in the
region. Its business climate remained healthy. Its unemployment remained
the lowest in a decade. Job creation remained very impressive. Median
household income and per capita personal income were well above the national average. And the prospect for further economic growth was never
higher.[17]

While AstraZeneca was zipping ahead constructing buildings with
800,000 square feet as part of its first phase of establishing its North
American headquarters at a cost of $200 million to $300 million, the company made it known that it also wanted to expand its pharmaceutical manufacturing plant near Newark, in its first-ever public acknowledgment of the
Newark plant's existence. A total of 615 people—not an insignificant number—were already employed at the Newark site. Roughly three-quarters of
the new space would be devoted primarily to production, with the remaining
quarter used for warehousing, cafeteria, and meeting rooms. AstraZeneca's
plan would add 214,034 square feet to its existing buildings on its 144-acre
site, and would take place over five to ten years, resulting in the consequen-
tial addition of 150 new jobs. All of this was independent of AstraZeneca's
expansion of its headquarters at its Fairfax site.[18]

But not all of the news about AstraZeneca in Delaware was to be good news.

STRUGGLES WITH ASTRAZENECA BEGIN

In September 2000, it was reported that England-based AstraZeneca and Switzerland-based Novartis were in the process of forming a new crop protection business named Syngenta, and would be deciding within the following month whether the U.S. headquarters would be located in Delaware or in North Carolina where Novartis already employed six hundred employees at its pesticides unit. About three hundred employees of Zeneca's farm unit would be joining Syngenta. It was also revealed that Delaware state officials offered an incentive package of grants and tax breaks of about $5 million from the state's Strategic Fund to attract Syngenta's headquarters, whereas North Carolina offered about $2.2 million. Neither company's executives would speculate as to how many jobs were at stake, but it became clear that the choice of headquarters would be crucial, as the parent company of Syngenta, to be based in Switzerland, would be the largest crop protection business in the world with about 23,000 employees worldwide and combined sales of $18 billion.

Delaware, however, lost this one. AstraZeneca decided that Syngenta's U.S. headquarters would be located in Greensboro, North Carolina, partly because of the existing Novartis campus there. A DEDO officer lamented: "Delaware really faced an uphill battle. We were at a distinct disadvantage." The decision resulted in some job losses in Delaware, the exact number undisclosed. Zeneca's farm unit, however, numbered about three hundred workers, and most of them would likely relocate to North Carolina near Syngenta's headquarters.[19]

A few years would pass before other ominous signs regarding AstraZeneca in Delaware would surface.

In 2002, AstraZeneca's profits soared. The company earned $2.84 billion that year on sales of $17.8 billion. But in June 2003, AstraZeneca pleaded guilty in the US District Court in Wilmington to a felony conspiracy charge requiring it to pay $355 million in a criminal fine, civil penalties, and restitution for helping urologists to defraud federal agencies. The company gave urologists free samples of its expensive prostate cancer drug Zoladex—AstraZeneca's biggest-selling cancer drug worldwide—so that the doctors could bill Medicare, Medicaid, and other U.S. government insurance programs, while pocketing the difference. The samples were marked "not for sale," and reselling them was illegal. Doctors were found to sometimes bill Medicare $300 for a one-month dose.

The government's case originally applied to Zeneca, the predecessor to AstraZeneca. According to the government's criminal complaint, "The core objective of this conspiracy for Zeneca was to obtain money from increased sales of Zoladex, while the core objective for the physicians was to obtain money from reimbursement for samples of Zoladex." Edward T. Bradley, a federal government agent, said: "They would defraud any program that had money to drain as long as it increased their profits."[20]

The heyday of the drug industry was in the 1990s, at the end of which Astra and Zeneca chose to merge and make its headquarters in Delaware. While AstraZeneca prospered, the industry as a whole declined over ten percent in growth by 2005. Market conditions caused AstraZeneca to eliminate five hundred sales representatives, including contract workers.

AstraZeneca stock fell 23 percent between September 2004 and January 2005, although the cuts did not affect the 4,800 AstraZeneca employees in Fairfax. The decline was attributed to the federal Food and Drug Administration (FDA) regulators' rejection of AstraZeneca's stroke medication Exanta, costing the company estimated losses of $1 billion to $3 billion a year. Moreover, in December 2004, a study of AstraZeneca's lung cancer drug Iressa showed that the drug did not increase survival rates, while sales of its anti-cholesterol drug Crestor had been below expectations. Nevertheless, AstraZeneca's overall profits jumped sixteen percent over the same quarter in the previous year, in part because of increased sales of its blood pressure drug Toprol-XL and its schizophrenia drug Seroquel, developed in Fairfax, which became a market leader in the United States.[21]

AstraZeneca executives acknowledged at a 2005 cancer conference that AZ had relatively few drugs nearing the market.[22] To cut costs, AZ reportedly was engaged in outsourcing by contracting with outside companies for its information technology services, human resources, copying, food services, and some research. AZ announced in 2007 it was also exploring outsourcing the manufacturing of active pharmaceutical ingredients for some of its newer drugs. It followed up in 2008 by contracting with Chinese and Indian companies to produce its drug compounds, as well as outsourcing services to a Swedish information technology company.[23]

Meanwhile, there were even rumors circulating in 2006 of a takeover of AstraZeneca. Noting that AZ was the smallest of the four large European drugmakers, a London financial analyst said: "If you take a long-term view, I see AstraZeneca as a target. . . . All the others are too big to be taken over."[24]

As the second decade of the twenty-first century began, AstraZeneca announced that it would not seek FDA approval of its experimental antidepressant drug TC-5214 after it failed testing against a placebo in multiple trials. Benjamin Strutt, AstraZeneca's global communications director in England, commented: "It's always disappointing, but it's worth pointing out that this is the nature of innovation in modern medicine, and you cannot possibly know the outcome when you start out."[25]

THE R&D PIPELINE DRIES UP

AstraZeneca's greatest setback was the shock, as it entered the second decade, of facing the loss of patent protection of the firm's three best-selling drugs in its product pipeline. Its antipsychotic Seroquel, that accounted for $5.8 billion in sales in 2011, was scheduled to lose its patent in 2012, as had its blood pressure medicine Antacand in 2011. Nexium, its heartburn pill, with $4.4 billion in sales in 2011, was scheduled to lose patent protection in 2014. Similarly, Crestor, AstraZeneca's cholesterol fighter, with $6.6 billion in sales in 2011, was scheduled to lose its patent protection in 2016.

When patents of a pharmaceutical company expire, the onset of generic competition—an anticipated "parade of horribles" for AstraZeneca—threatens the loss of billions of dollars for the company. Analysts refer to the loss of patent protection as a "cliff," as illustrated by AstraZeneca's breast cancer drug Arimdex. After generic versions of Arimdex entered the market in June 2010, AstraZeneca's worldwide sales of that drug dropped 62 percent to $181 million, and down 95 percent in the United States to $10 million. To make matters possibly worse for drug companies, the U.S. Supreme Court ruled in mid-2013 that the Federal Trade Commission could sue pharmaceutical companies for potential antitrust violations. That decision was described in the *New York Times* as follows: "Drug developers may now find it harder to ward off generics, which typically cost about 15 percent of the brand-name's price and cause the original to quickly lose up to 90 percent of its market share."[26]

The trouble with bringing new drugs to market was the fact that AstraZeneca's pipeline was struggling mightily. In addition to the problem of losing multiple patents, four potential "blockbuster" drugs during 2006–2008 were withdrawn during trials and never made it to market. In April 2012, a senior analyst was quoted as saying: "AstraZeneca is currently at the beginning of its patent cliff and we expect sales and earnings to decline as a result, and we do not believe the newly launched and pipeline products will be able to make up for the decline in revenue."[27]

While the R&D pipeline was faltering, among its options were: (1) acquire or make deals with other companies that were successfully marketing their own drugs; (2) litigate competition from generic drugmakers; and (3) eliminate jobs. The beleaguered company settled on a combination of these options.

OPTION 1: ACQUIRING OTHER COMPANIES

An option for AstraZeneca was to acquire, or make cooperative deals with, other successful drug companies. But such deals were not as easy to complete as they sounded. AstraZeneca did pay about $15 billion in 2007 to acquire Maryland-based MedImmune in 2007, a deal some industry analysts called too expensive and risky. AstraZeneca's stock fell five percent following that announcement. MedImmune's top-selling product was Synagis, a treatment for a common respiratory virus that garnered about $1.1 billion of that company's total of $1.2 billion in sales in 2008. Yet, in 2013, AstraZeneca was betting its future on MedImmune, whose scientists were upbeat about its biologics, as AstraZeneca's new CEO had been since October 2012.[28]

After acquiring MedImmune, AstraZeneca's next largest purchase was the $1.26 billion acquisition of San Diego–based Ardea Biosciences, announced on April 23, 2012. Ardea's focus was on developing small molecule prescription drugs. At the time of the announcement, AstraZeneca's CEO David Brennan said he was not looking for any "transformational" deals, and that other potential acquisitions would be smaller than the MedImmune purchase. Accordingly, AstraZeneca had embarked on a strategy of acquiring smaller companies engaged in the final developmental phases of new drugs, with AstraZeneca hoping to replenish its depleted pipeline. Martin MacKay, head of AstraZeneca's R&D, was quoted as saying that "we've got to do these kind of deals, and these will be pure relationships, licensing agreements, bolt-on acquisitions, and I expect to be talking more of these such deals as the year progresses."[29]

AstraZeneca was surely not out of the woods. It was struggling more than most big pharmaceutical companies. Its strategy of acquiring smaller companies appeared insufficient to assure a major turnaround. Symptomatic was the abrupt announcement by fifty-eight-year-old CEO David Brennan—just three days after the Ardea announcement—that he would resign from Astra-Zeneca on June 1, 2012. He was under some pressure from shareholders, as the first-quarter report for 2012 showed that AstraZeneca's revenue fell 11 percent and earnings per share plunged 38 percent. One industry analyst, Navid Malik, said that AstraZeneca needed bigger deals rather than smaller ones: "If you can't grow your way out of your problems, you buy your way out of them. Several single-digit billion-dollar deals don't solve short to medium-term issues." He added: "When a business needs radical surgery to solve its issues, I think you've got to think about the $10 billion–plus level. At that valuation point, you're buying a business with meaningful revenue and hopefully a meaningful pipeline." Another analyst, Naresh Chouhan, agreed: "The two options are to do a big deal or dramatically cut R&D," he said. "If the company is to exist in five to ten years time, they need to do a big deal." Still other industry analysts, however, doubted acquisitions were the answer. For example, Mike Mitchell said: "The much maligned activity in M&A [Mergers and Acquisitions] will have limited impact, in our opinion, in terms of significantly bolstering the near-term pipeline for the business." But departing CEO David Brennan remained optimistic, saying: "I'm confident that AstraZeneca has the capability, the courage and the determination to be successful in the future."[30]

OPTION 2: LITIGATING AGAINST GENERIC COMPETITION

British-based AstraZeneca's two leading drugs for 2011 were Crestor and Seroquel. Its second-best-selling drug, antidepressant Seroquel—developed at Fairfax, and produced and packaged at its Newark plant—accounted for 17 percent of AstraZeneca sales that year.

The U.S. patent for Seroquel expired on March 26, 2011. In order to block approvals by the FDA of generic forms of Seroquel, AstraZeneca brought suit against the FDA in the U.S. District Court of Washington, DC. It claimed that FDA did not require the eleven generic competitors to have the same detailed patient information on their labels that was required for Seroquel, including side-effect results from clinical trials. Thus, AstraZeneca tried to extend its exclusivity. It alleged that should the court refuse to reverse the FDA's approval of generics without parallel labeling and consumer warnings, the company could lose $2 billion in revenues. Meanwhile, the FDA announced its temporary delay of final approvals of tentatively approved generics until all patent exclusivity issues were resolved. In the end, AstraZeneca lost its suit. A result was that its first-quarter earnings report for 2012 revealed that sales of Seroquel already had precipitously fallen 25 percent to $754 million.[31]

AstraZeneca's top-selling drug, cholesterol fighter Crestor, generated almost 20 percent of AstraZeneca's earnings in 2011. Its main patent covering the major compound of Crestor was scheduled to expire in 2016. However, two minor patents for Crestor, due to expire in 2018 and 2021, covered methods of using the active ingredient rosuvastatin calcium for certain types of patients. A Delaware judge had dismissed AstraZeneca's lawsuits against generic drugmakers that sought approval to sell copycat medicines only for treatments not covered by those minor patents. AstraZeneca thereupon appealed that decision to the U.S. Circuit Court of Appeals in Washington, DC. The Circuit Court ruled against AstraZeneca, on the ground that it did not have the right to block competition, until as late as 2021, of generic drugmakers for using medicines not covered by AstraZeneca patents.[32]

Thus, litigating against generic competition proved to be an unsuccessful option for AstraZeneca.

OPTION 3: ELIMINATING JOBS

In October 2004, AstraZeneca's chief executive officer announced that the company would "consider more creative ways of reaching physicians, ways that are more cost-effective and more time-effective." What he meant became clear on January 7, 2005, when it was reported that the company had eliminated five hundred contract representatives from its sales force. Although none of AstraZeneca's approximate 4,800 Delaware employees were affected, the cut—in the wake of a series of setbacks for some of its major drugs—appeared to be the company's first such move since the 1999 merger. AstraZeneca's sales force of six thousand people had grown by more than a third since the merger, said AstraZeneca's spokeswoman.[33]

More ominous was the company's announcement two years later, in February 2007, that it planned to eliminate three thousand manufacturing and distribution jobs over the next three years, a total representing about 4.6 percent of its worldwide workforce of about sixty-five thousand employees. AstraZeneca was facing the fact that its patent for its high blood pressure drug, Toprol-XL, was due to expire in September 2007. Although company officials declined to say at which of its facilities the cuts would come, there was speculation that the company's Newark plant of 650 workers could be impacted, because that plant packaged Toprol-XL, among many other drugs. But AstraZeneca was not the only pharmaceutical company during the decade to eliminate jobs. In 2002, Bristol-Myers Squibb, Inc., eliminated more than five hundred jobs, and departed from Delaware, an early warning of sorts of possible industry problems ahead. On January 22, 2007, Pfizer, Inc., announced it would eliminate ten thousand positions from its total workforce and close manufacturing plants as well as R&D facilities. Moreover, Merck & Company had already announced in 2006 it would eliminate seven thousand jobs and would also close plants.[34]

The DuPont Company had entered into a joint venture with Merck & Company to form DuPont Merck in 1991. After eight years had passed, the two decided in 1998 to split, with DuPont paying Merck $2.6 billion for the drug company's half of DuPont Merck Pharmaceutical Company. One may recall that DuPont Pharmaceuticals was widely touted as one of the reasons that the newly merged AstraZeneca drug company was attracted in late 1999 to establish its North American headquarters at Delaware's Fairfax site near DuPont's revamped Experiment Station. Indeed, AstraZeneca's decision was said to be attributed in part to DuPont's active influence. Thus, Governor Carper and other Delaware notables had claimed that DuPont and AstraZeneca together would bring international attention to Delaware as the "cradle of biotechnology" and establish a "corridor for life sciences." DuPont Pharmaceuticals, however, was sold in 2001 for $7.8 billion, a far cry from DuPont's posture in 1999. Enthusiasm that two kindred drug companies were better than one in Delaware had proved unsustainable. With accelerating layoffs by AstraZeneca and the selling of DuPont Pharmaceuticals, the heyday of the drug business in Delaware had ended.[35]

As AstraZeneca came closer to the end of its blood pressure drug patent in September 2007, it announced another cut of 7,600 jobs worldwide, more than double the three thousand positions it had announced less than six months previously. This cut included positions in information systems, sales and marketing, and even research and development. Although once again the company refused to reveal where the cuts would occur, it was nevertheless certain that AstraZeneca's Fairfax site would be included this time.

At the time that AstraZeneca chose to locate its headquarters in Delaware, the state had stipulated as part of its incentive package that AstraZeneca sign a five-year agreement that its Delaware workforce would total at least four thousand. Noting that the agreement expired in 2004 and that AstraZeneca's workforce was then about five thousand, DEDO Director Judy McKinney–Cherry said, "Not only did they fulfill the agreement, they went way beyond it. Their value to the community has far exceeded their investment." David Brennan, AstraZeneca's CEO, commented: "We believe we can operate our business more efficiently"—a familiar refrain. McKinney-Cherry agreed that job cuts are the kind of move global companies need to stay competitive. "I'd rather see them take these steps than dissolve into something worse," she said.[36]

AstraZeneca's patent cliff with the onset in 2008 of the Great Recession and the growing popularity of generic drugs combined to make even deeper cuts in its global workforce. Thus, AstraZeneca announced dropping six thousand positions over the next four years, and once again refused to specify which cuts it made in Delaware. CEO Brennan said: "It's definitely not a reaction to the recession. It's just a good look at our business and where we can move some things around."[37]

Meanwhile, Delaware was experiencing job losses almost across the board, and those surely included AstraZeneca's Delaware workforce. Indeed, the company publicly announced plans to cut 550 Delaware jobs in 2010 and four hundred more jobs in 2011.[38] In 2011, it announced plans to lay off about 1,150 of its US employees, or about one-fourth of its U.S. sales force. Although only fewer than ten employees in Delaware were expected to be affected by that cut, it was conjectured that AstraZeneca's total Delaware workforce had fallen from a high of about five thousand to about three thousand, though the company would not divulge the actual numbers. Globally, AstraZeneca announced in 2012 that it planned to cut even 7,300 more jobs by 2014, but without projecting the size of still new cuts in Delaware.[39]

Of all factors influencing AstraZeneca to make such massive cuts in its global workforce, the most important factor remaining constant since the merger was the patent cliff it was facing. "AstraZeneca faces one of the most challenging patent cliffs within the pharmaceutical industry," said industry analyst Damien Conover in 2011.[40] Logic might seem to have indicated that increasing—not decreasing—reliance on R&D could replenish the company's pipeline with new drugs to replace those lost to the ending of patents. Nevertheless, such reasoning appeared to be absent. The company announced in March 2010 that it planned to eliminate 550 research and development jobs at its Fairfax site. Governor Markell traveled to London in an effort to minimize the impact of the cutbacks. Fairfax spokesman Tony Jewell reassured him that Wilmington remained an important part of AstraZeneca's global and U.S. R&D presence as well as its U.S. business. But senior company executives were not made available for comment. AstraZeneca's future appeared to continue to darken when it became known in March 2013 that another 2,300 AstraZeneca workers worldwide would be laid off, thus lifting the total reduction of AstraZeneca's workforce to 5,050 within fifteen months, including—most ominously for Delaware—1,200 positions at its offices in Fairfax.[41]

The enormity for Delaware of AstraZeneca's decision to cut 550 R&D jobs at Fairfax had not been immediately apparent. The Wilmington *News Journal* later revealed: "In March 2010, the company started to lay off *all* its 550 research scientists working in Delaware [emphasis added]. AstraZeneca plans to tear down the buildings that housed that research."[42]

To some observers, the demise of the company's very presence in Delaware appeared to be under way. AstraZeneca announced in April 2011 that it planned to demolish three buildings comprising 450,000 square feet of laboratory space at its decade-old Fairfax campus that housed all the company's Delaware-based research efforts. Reporter Jonathan Starkey commented: "The end of AstraZeneca's research presence in Delaware and the partial demolition of a campus the state battled hard to secure in 1999 is a psychological blow to the state's economic fortunes." Mike Bowman, president of the Delaware Technology Park, called AstraZeneca's decision a "shocking ending" of its research presence in Delaware. State officials had pleaded in vain with the company to lease its laboratories for use by life science companies experiencing a shortage of lab space. DEDO Director Alan Levin asserted that, given the short supply of lab space for Delaware's biotech industry, the "ideal outcome" would have been a deal to lease the buildings for start-up companies. But AstraZeneca refused, stating through its spokesman that "it would not be cost-effective for us to lease or repurpose the buildings for a variety of reasons." Those reasons were unstated, and Levin lamented, "We never got to that discussion."[43]

Following the quick departure of AstraZeneca's CEO David Brennan, amid the series of pipeline setbacks, interim CEO Simon Lowth seemed to sum up AstraZeneca's troubles in July 2012: "In addition to the challenges from our specific portfolio due to generics, we continue to face the same difficult market conditions that the whole industry faces as the global economy struggles to return to sustainable growth."[44] On February 1, 2013, AstraZeneca's new CEO, Pascal Soriot, delivered the company's 2012 earnings report, reflecting a 37 percent drop in net profit.[45] The company also announced its decision to redesign its Wilmington site by selling two more buildings it had constructed in 2002.[46]

But all was not lost. AstraZeneca's purchase of Medimmune was finally paying off, as witness this item in the Wilmington *News Journal* in October 2013: "AstraZeneca acquired Medimmune for $15 billion in 2007. Since the acquisition, the biotech has come to represent nearly 50 percent of AstraZeneca's overall research and development pipeline, with key targets in oncology, cardiovascular and metabolic disease and respiratory inflammation and autoimmunity."[47] Moreover, after AstraZeneca fought off a proposed acquisition by Pfizer in May 2014, it reported a second-quarter increase in revenue in August 2014, regardless of a decrease in operating profit. The company also announced the acquisition of rights to develop and market other drugs. AstraZeneca further claimed there were over one hundred products in its development pipeline, with fourteen in late-stage development. Perhaps to stave off subsequent Pfizer proposals to acquire the company or other such proposals, CEO Soriot boasted: "The quality of transformation we are seeing across all core areas of our business further underpins our confidence in AstraZeneca's longer term prospects."[48]

Optimism about AZ's future in Delaware, however, appeared weak at the end of 2014 in light of its sagging earnings. Net profits for that year stood at $1.23 billion, roughly a 24 percent decline from its 2013 net profit of $2.56 billion. The pharmaceutical industry's accelerated merger experience, moreover, influenced analysts to label AstraZeneca as a likely acquisition target.[49]

CONCLUSION

The AstraZeneca experience in Delaware left some very interesting and difficult questions to answer. Delaware's state government made a sizable investment (over $200 million in all) in AstraZeneca, hopefully to gain a merged company employing thousands of people who would expand the state's economy and also pay taxes. The question remained how long the payback period should be to recover the state's hefty investment, given the vagaries of competition, the unpredictability of product development, and the strategic planning/executive decision making of companies. A reasonable estimate for state income taxes paid by the 2,500 new employees would be $9 million a year. There would usually be secondary economic impacts but this was considerably lessened since the employees who were previously living in Pennsylvania chose to commute to work. Based on this one case, then, it appears that fifteen to twenty years might be a plausible estimate for a relatively mature firm to recover the state's investment.

While the AstraZeneca case was in a sense serendipitous, the merger had created the opportunity to attract the headquarters. Yet, AstraZeneca ceased to be a growing firm after it reached the level established by the merger. Indeed, AstraZeneca's North American headquarters ultimately declined in employment, following the experience of DuPont Merck and DuPont Pharmaceuticals.

Certainly, Delaware's mantra was not unique—namely to "create or retain jobs." This was surely evident even though the majority of Astra employees remained after the merger at their homes in Pennsylvania and commuted across the border to the nearby Fairfax site in Delaware. This was probably the best example of Delaware's "beggar-thy-neighbor" strategy.

Another lesson learned from the AstraZeneca experience in Delaware is how exceedingly important it is to exercise "due diligence" in the decision-making process by talking with financial and industry analysts to better assess the longer-term viability of involved firms and their industry. Such assessments should render better upfront understanding of the payback period needed to recover "investment" of taxpayer dollars.

NOTES

1. See chapter 8 on "Credit Card Banking" in William Boyer and Edward Ratledge, *Pivotal Policies in Delaware: From Desegregation to Deregulation* (Newark: University of Delaware Press, 2014).

2. Note that the Delaware Public Archives has no Delaware Economic Development Office (DEDO) holdings related to AstraZeneca.

3. See Trif Alatzas and Nancy Charron, "Delaware Courts AstraZeneca," Wilmington *News Journal*, January 9, 1999, A1; Trif Alatzas, "Del., Pa. Compete for AstraZeneca Site," ibid., January 12, 1999, A1; and "State Closes Land Deal," ibid., February 2, 1999, B5.

4. See articles by Trif Alatzas in the Wilmington *News Journal*: "Delaware and Pennsylvania See the New Company as a Boon, But Residents Have Varying Opinions," February 2, 1999, A1; and "Del. and Pa. Hope to Sway AstraZeneca," April 4, 1999, A1.

5. Trif Alatzas, "Governors Meet with AstraZeneca," Wilmington *News Journal*, April 15, 1999, B7.

6. See these articles by Alatzas in the Wilmington *News Journal*: "Merger Heralded on Wall St.," April 8, 1999, B7; "Governors Meet with AstraZeneca," April 15, 1999, B7; and Alatzas and Michelle Darnell, "Nerves Give Way to Elation," April 30, 1999, A6. Note that some details of Delaware's offer to attract AstraZeneca were not made known until much later; see Seth Agulnick, "Bridging the Old and the New," Wilmington *News Journal*, August 25, 2001, F1.

7. Alatzas, "AstraZeneca Picks Delaware," Wilmington *News Journal*, April 30, 1999, A1.

8. Michelle Darnell, "State Savors Sweet AstraZeneca Success," Wilmington *News Journal*, May 1, 1999, A1.

9. Ibid.

10. Quote by Jonathan D. Epstein, "State is Counting on a Biotech Future," Wilmington *News Journal*, November 3, 1999, E10.

11. Quote by Trif Alatzas, "AstraZeneca Is Open for Business," Wilmington *News Journal*, June 2, 1999, B7.

12. Robert Long, "DelDOT Plans More Borrowing," Wilmington *News Journal*, May 4, 1999, B1.

13. Dennis Thompson, "AstraZeneca's Private Deal Worries Civic Leaders," Wilmington *News Journal*, May 9, 1999, A1.

14. See editorials: "Concord Pike," Wilmington *News Journal*, December 21, 1999, A20; and "Concord Pike," ibid., May 7, 2000, A6.

15. See Dawn Ang, "Carper to Decide on Blue Ball This Week," Wilmington *News Journal*, January 25, 2000, B3; Dawn Ang and Charlotte Hale, "Road Work Set for Expansion of AstraZeneca," ibid., May 12, 2000, B1; "Around Our Towns," ibid., June 22, 2000, B3; and Charlotte Hale, "AstraZeneca Expansion Plans Clear Final Hurdles," ibid., July 12, 2000, B2.

16. See Stephanie L. Arnold, "DelDOT Ready to Start on Blue Ball Plan," Wilmington *News Journal*, June 15, 2001, B5.

17. See Trif Alatzas, "State Business Climate Healthy," Wilmington *News Journal*, June 27, 1999, L41; and Seth Agulnick, "AstraZeneca Project Zips Along," ibid., September 27, 2000, B7.

18. See Charlotte Hale, "AstraZeneca Asks Plant Expansion," Wilmington *News Journal*, August 8, 2001, B1; and Seth Agulnick, "Bridging the Old and New," ibid., August 25, 2001, F1.

19. See Seth Agulnick, "State Battles to Get New Company," Wilmington *News Journal*, September 14, 2000, A1; and Seth Agulnick and E. Janene Nolan, "Del. to Lose Jobs to N.C.," ibid., October 18, 2000, B7.

20. Fred Biddle, "AstraZeneca Guilty of Felony," Wilmington *News Journal*, June 21, 2003, A1.

21. Richard Sine, "AstraZeneca Profits Jump 16%; Company Makes $1.26 Billion in Quarter, Despite FDA's Rejection of Exanta," Wilmington *News Journal*, October 22, 2004, B7.

22. Richard Sine, "AZ's Drugs Get Scant Attention; Competitor Stars at Cancer Meeting," Wilmington *News Journal*, May 18, 2005, B7.

23. See Luladey B. Tadesse, "Outsourcing: A Necessary Business Tactic or Betrayal? Del. Experiences a Higher Rate than the National Average," Wilmington *News Journal*, October 9, 2005, A1; Gary Haber, "AstraZeneca: No Wholesale Outsourcing," ibid., September 18, 2007, B6; and Andrew Eder, "AstraZeneca Announces Outsourcing in Two Departments," ibid., June 13, 2008, B6.

24. See Gary Haber, "AstraZeneca Focus of Takeover Talk; GlaxoSmithKline, Novartis Likely Looking to Bolster Portfolios, Analysts Say," Wilmington *News Journal*, March 9, 2006, B7; and Haber, "AstraZeneca Buyout: A Fish Story? Deal Fraught with Difficulties for Any Likely Bidder," ibid., March 26, 2006, C1.

25. See, for example, Cori Anne Natoli, "AZ Not Seeking Approval for Drug," Wilmington *News Journal*, March 11, 2011, A7.

26. See Edward Wyatt, "Justices Rule for the F.T.C. in a Generic Drug Case," *New York Times*, June 18, 2013, B1, B7; Jonathan Starkey, "AstraZeneca Blames Generic Drugs for Stagnant Profits," Wilmington *News Journal*, July 29, 2011; and Jonathan Starkey, "Another Tough Week for AZ," ibid., December 23, 2011, A7, A8.

27. Cori Anne Natoli, "AstraZeneca Sees Stock Fall on Double-dose of Bad News," Wilmington *News Journal*, April 27, 2012, A1, A2. For AZ's continuing patent expirations that caused its 2013 profit to drop 26 percent, see Cori Anne Natoli, "Patent Expirations Cause AZ Profit Dip," Wilmington *News Journal*, February 7, 2014, A9, A10.

28. See Aaron Smith, "AstraZeneca's Big, Risky $15 Billion Bet," *CNN Money* (New York: Cable News Network, April 23, 2007); Cori Anne Natoli, "Feeling Upbeat, MedImmunes is AstraZeneca's Bet on Future," Wilmington *News Journal*, March 24, 2013, E1, E5; and Cori Anne Natoli, "AZ Cancer Drugs Move to Clinical Trials," ibid., May 17, 2013, A8.

29. See Lou Gutheil, "AstraZeneca Announces Ardea Acquisition," ADVEN StockWiki, April 23, 2012, wiki.advfn.com/en/Astrazeneca_Announces_Ardea_Acquisition (accessed June 1, 2012); and Cori Anne Natoli, "AstraZeneca to Pay $1.3B for Ardea Biosciences," Wilmington *News Journal*, April 24, 2012, A1, A2. Note also that early in 2014, AstraZeneca acquired Bristol-Myers Squibb's interests in a diabetes drug franchise. See, for example, these Wilmington *News Journal* articles by Cori Anne Natoli: "AZ Bets Big on Diabetes," December

20, 2013, A14, A15; "Diabetes Drug Approved," January 10, 2014, A8; and "AstraZeneca Completed Diabetes Deal," February 4, 2014, A6, A7.

30. Quotes from Rachel Cooper, "AstraZeneca Is in Need of Radical Surgery after Chief Brennan Retires," *The Telegraph*, April 26, 2012. See also, Andrew Pollock, "AstraZeneca C.E.O. to Step Down," *New York Times* (Business Day, Global Edition), April 26, 2012.

31. See articles by Cori Anne Natoli: "Seroquel XR Patent Ruled Invalid," Wilmington *News Journal*, March 23, 2012, A13; "As AZ Patent Expires, Generic Seroquel Looms," ibid., March 27, 2012, A8; "Floodgates Open for Seroquel Clones," ibid., March 28, 2012, A9; and "Generics' Labels Back in Court," ibid., March 30, 2012, A8.

32. "AstraZeneca Loses Crestor 2018, 2021 Patent Appeal," Wilmington *News Journal*, February 11, 2012, A6, citing *Bloomberg News*.

33. Richard Sine, "Following Drug Setbacks, AstraZeneca Cuts Sales Force; Number of Contract Workers Eliminated Put at 500," Wilmington *News Journal*, January 7, 2005, A1.

34. Gary Haber, "AstraZeneca to Eliminate 3,000 Jobs by 2010," Wilmington *News Journal*, February 2, 2007, B6.

35. See, for example, Claudia H. Deutsch, "DuPont to Buy Merck's Share of Venture," *New York Times*, May 20, 1998; and Harold Brubaker, "DuPont: Seeking a Strategy, DuPont's Strategy Unclear as Firm Sheds Units after Casting Off Oil, Seed and Drug Units, the 200-Year-Old Firm Fights Image as Rudderless," *Philadelphia Inquirer*, July 7, 2002.

36. Gary Haber, "AstraZeneca to Cut 7,600 Global Jobs," Wilmington *News Journal*, July 27, 2007, A1.

37. See Andrew Eder, "AstraZeneca Turns Profit, Plans to Cut 6,000 Jobs," Wilmington *News Journal*, January 30, 2009, A7; and "AstraZeneca Buyout Trimming Sales Force," ibid., October 20, 2009.

38. See Eric Ruth, "AstraZeneca Overhaul Leaves 550 Jobless Here," Wilmington *News Journal*, March 3, 2010, A1; and Jonathan Starkey, "AstraZeneca to Cut 400 Jobs," ibid., February 7, 2011, A1, A2.

39. See Jonathan Starkey, "AstraZeneca Plans to Lay Off 1,150 People in US Sales Force," Wilmington *News Journal*, November 8, 2011, A9, A12; and Aaron Nathans, "AstraZeneca to Eliminate 7,300 Jobs by 2014," ibid., February 3, 2012, A1, A11.

40. Quote by Jonathan Starkey, note 35, supra, at A2.

41. See Eric Ruth, "AstraZeneca Overhaul Leaves 550 Jobless," Wilmington *News Journal*, March 3, 2010; Cori Anne Natoli, "1,200 AstraZeneca Jobs Leaving Del.," ibid., March 19, 2013, A1, A6; and Cori Anne Natoli, "AstraZeneca: Another 2,300 Cuts Globally," ibid., March 23, 2013, A1, A7.

42. Aaron Nathans, "AstraZeneca to Cut 7,300 More Jobs," Wilmington *News Journal*, February 2, 2012.

43. Jonathan Starkey, "AZ to Demolish 3 Buildings," Wilmington *News Journal*, April 23, 2011. See also Aaron Nathans and Eric Ruth, "AstraZeneca Cuts Jobs Despite Help from State," ibid., March 3, 2010; Jonathan Starkey, "Lack of Lab Space Dogs Delaware Biotech," ibid., October 17, 2011; Editorial, "Demolishing Three Labs Is a Missed Opportunity," ibid., April 28, 2011; Letter to the Editor by Edmund Dohnert, Wilmington, "AstraZeneca Plan Shows State Needs Diversity," ibid., April 28, 2011; and Letter to the Editor by Al Denio, Newark, "AstraZeneca Wasting Our Tax Dollars on Labs," ibid., October 26, 2011.

44. Quote by Cori Anne Natoli, "Generics Whittle AZ Earnings," Wilmington *News Journal*, July 27, 2012, A14, A15.

45. See Cori Anne Natoli, "Patent Cliff Scuttles AZ," Wilmington *News Journal*, February 1, 2013, A12, A13; Allison Connolly, "Can a Merger Rescue AstraZeneca?" ibid., February 17, 2013, E1, E3; and Cori Anne Natoli, "Soriot to Push AZ Plan," ibid., March 21, 2013.

46. Cori Anne Natoli, "AZ Buildings for Sale," Wilmington *News Journal*, October 2, 2013, A8. JPMorgan Chase was reported in 2014 to have reached a deal to purchase for $44 million AstraZeneca's fifty-eight-acre south campus of its Fairfax site. See Cori Anne Natoli, "JP Morgan Eyes Fairfax Site, Deal with AstraZeneca Unconfirmed; State Incentives Likely," Wilmington *News Journal*, February 28, 2014, A1, A2.

47. Cori Anne Natoli, "AZ Targets Cancer Technology," Wilmington *News Journal*, October 17, 2013, A10.

48. Jen Rini, "AZ Second-Quarter Earnings See Increase," Wilmington *News Journal*, August 1, 2014, A8.

49. Jeff Murdock, "Takeover Threats Loom for AZ, DuPont," Wilmington *News Journal*, February 22, 2015, E1, E5.

Chapter Two

Delaware's Port

Wilmington is the largest city in Delaware. The city is located at the confluence of the Brandywine River and the Christina River, which flows into the Delaware River. The Port of Wilmington, a small and specialized port, at one time was wholly owned by the city. Since the city of Wilmington's finances are constrained by its inability to annex land, raise its wage tax, and extend taxation to tax-exempt properties (almost half of the city's land), property supporting the port and its more than two thousand employees was an economic strain.[1] The Port of Wilmington was purchased by Delaware's state government in June 1995. This chapter examines the past and ongoing efforts to make Delaware's port a viable contributor to the state's economic development. These efforts have been fraught with multiple political, policy, and regional conflicts that in sum are unique in the economic history of the first state.

FROM SILTED HARBOR TO MODERN PORT

After the Revolutionary War, the United States was formed with Delaware becoming a state. Meanwhile, Wilmington became a major milling center, with flour exported from its harbor. In the 1800s, Wilmington transformed from a milling center to become an industrial city where ships, railroad cars, carriages, and iron works were built. The Civil War created wartime demands that spurred greater harbor activity in Wilmington. According to a brief history published by the University of Delaware Graduate College of Marine Studies:

> By the beginning of the twentieth century, the harbor of Wilmington included piers along the Christina River, and in 1901 a harbor project to provide a

channel 21 feet deep and 250 feet wide, from the Delaware River to the mouth
of the Brandywine River, was completed. But the channel silted rapidly and
could not sustain shipping needed for the development of Wilmington's industries, yielding business to the larger port of Philadelphia on the Delaware
River.[2]

Wilmington citizens voted in 1913 to build their own deep-water port to
support the city's industries. As World War I exploded in 1914 and engulfed
European nations, demands for shipments of munitions, industrial products,
and food from the East Coast surpassed the export capacity of New York and
Philadelphia to meet growing war needs.

The United States declared war on Germany on April 6, 1917. Given the
fact that in Delaware, as Paul Dolan observed, the legislature had "supreme
power in respect of municipal government,"[3] the General Assembly on April
12, 1917, created the so-called Wilmington Port Terminal and initiated the
Board of Harbor Commissioners, appointed by the city's mayor, to have full
powers over the terminal: "The purpose of the act was to provide for planning for waterfront improvement through an increase in harbor and shipping
facilities, and to establish a means for constructing, maintaining, operating
and controlling the resulting facilities (wharves, docks, piers, slips, harbors
and warehouses)."[4]

A few months later, in September 1917, Wilmington authorities sought to
share in the booming economy induced by the war effort. Witness this front-
page story in a Wilmington newspaper, excerpted as follows:

> The most advanced step ever taken toward acquiring a developed riverfront for
> Wilmington will be possible should the Federal Government select . . . Wilm-
> ington . . . for one of its proposed three military warehouses.
>
>   . . . . Every man of power and influence in Wilmington and Delaware who
> can reinforce the efforts . . . by the Chamber of Commerce and Harbor Board
> should bring his most powerful arguments to bear upon the government agents
> to show them the wisdom of selecting Wilmington, on account of its admirable
> railroad facilities, its location right in the heart of the military industries of the
> East, its ample room for development . . . on the Delaware River where the
> channel is the proper depth for ocean going freight—better than any other
> point on the whole Delaware River for this purpose . . . where scores of big
> industrial establishments now engaged in making war munitions are now lo-
> cated.[5]

H. H. Richardson, special investigator of the Harbor Board, published a
report in December 1917 in which he estimated the business potential of the
proposed dock and terminal as follows:

> Using figures from the 1914 U.S. Census, he reported 310 manufacturing
> establishments in Wilmington and a total of 5.5 million tons of commodities

moving to and from Wilmington each year by all modes of transportation. He estimated that a new port could handle 50 percent of that tonnage. Now with American troops fighting in Europe, Richardson's appeal for Wilmington to take action took on a patriotic fervor. He wrote, "I have received letters [from U.S. government maritime officials] commending this Board for a most patriotic and essential duty as an aid to the government in winning the war, and as a splendid business opportunity for Wilmington to undertake immediately."[6]

In 1918, the Harbor Board developed a plan to proceed to construct wharfs and acquire land for piers and terminals. In 1919, the General Assembly approved construction of the port consisting of 105 acres on the bank of the Christina River near its mouth on the Delaware River, whereupon the Harbor Board purchased 101 acres at a price of $230,600 from the Lobdell Car Wheel Company and the city approved a bond issue of $2.5 million for the creation of the port.

With the assistance of the U.S. government, and especially the Army Corps of Engineers, construction of the Wilmington Marine Terminal began in 1921 and was completed in 1922. The port was officially opened in 1923. A channel twenty-five feet deep ran out to the Delaware River. The berthing area was 1,210 feet, capable of accommodating a number of ships at the same time. Three cranes with five- to thirty-ton capacity were purchased, enabling the port to handle shipments of 17,000 tons in its first year. Open storage consisted of ten acres, warehouse storage of 120,000 square feet, and transit storage of 48,000 square feet. The marine terminal was directly connected to all railroads that transited the city. Almost as soon as operations began, the volume of business began to increase exponentially. In short, a modern port had been created.

PRESSURES TO EXPAND THE PORT

Regardless of the massive postwar downturn in the world economy and the onset of the Great Depression of 1929, business at Wilmington's port continued to grow through the 1930s. The total cargo handled at the port grew from 17,000 tons in 1923 to 540,000 tons in 1938. A 1938 study that claimed it was "imperative" that the port's storage and wharf facilities be expanded forthwith was for naught, because the intervention of World War II postponed any such activity. But after that war, little was done to improve port facilities, and larger ships could not be accommodated because the Christina River channel connecting to the Delaware River had been dredged only to thirty-two feet, compared with much larger depths at Baltimore and Philadelphia ports. Nevertheless, record shipments reached 690,612 tons by 1951 and topped 850,000 tons in 1953.

Finally, the first major expansion of port facilities was completed in 1955 by virtue of a $2.3 million contract. This was followed by a $5 million expansion program in the early 1960s that extended the dock by one thousand feet and deepened the channel to thirty-seven feet, which accommodated larger ships and increased cargo to 901,422 tons in 1963. The impact on jobs was substantial, as the following report attested:

> The Harbor Board staff was now up to 100 permanent employees, plus 200 longshoremen and 1,200 employees of companies located at the Marine terminal. The impact on area employment was substantial, considering that approximately 2,500 more people employed by trucking firms, railroad companies, local merchants, taxicab and bus companies and contractors benefited from the success of the port. [7]

All assessments of the port's performance during the 1960s, however, were not positive. A comprehensive five-year study of its operations and facilities for the 1963–1967 period, completed in 1968, found that the existing facilities at the Philadelphia and Baltimore ports were

> capable of handling much more waterborne traffic than those at Wilmington. . . . The relative level of activity of the three ports for the first half of 1967 is summarized as follows:

Port	Number of Vessels	Millions of Tons
Philadelphia	6,493	24
Baltimore	4,853	22
Wilmington	190	1

> The implications are that the Wilmington Port will continue to be hemmed in from north and south by the two major ports unless it takes steps to broaden its economic base to the entire region. [8]

The principal recommendation of the study was the following:

> To ensure the continued growth and development of the Port and its consequent contribution to the area's economic development, a broader base of support is essential. Only the state can provide this means of industrial development support and the related support for necessary port facilities. It is therefore strongly recommended that a Delaware State Ports Authority be created to plan and manage the Port's long-range development and its consequent contribution to the economic development of the state. The City, therefore, should turn over the Port facilities and its operation to the Delaware State Ports Authority, once it is established. [9]

Nothing was done to turn the port over to the state during the 1960s or through the next two decades. Meanwhile, the port became the port of choice for importing certain commodities, such as fruit from South America, Fiat and Volkswagen automobiles from Europe, and meat from Australia. But the port experienced formidable obstacles including intermittent labor troubles, rotting piers, and facilities incapable of handling larger ships and containers. Progress was made over the years toward overcoming these obstacles. Cranes to handle containers were installed. One rotting pier was restored. A refrigerated warehouse was added. Still, the port continued to need an infusion of more money.

Another problem was an import–export imbalance. One study conducted in the 1970s noted: "Ninety percent of the terminal's business was unloading and storing commodities, but ten percent was in cargo exports." This meant that after unloading, ships sailed away empty. Ship owners who paid $5,000 a day to run a medium-sized freighter favored ports that could guarantee ships would be reloaded. [10]

In the mid-1980s, more than 80 percent of the port's business was still in imports. Throughout the 1970s and 1980s, discussion had revived about the state's involvement in the management of the port. Wilmington officials wanted to continue its management. New Castle County Executive Rita Justice wanted state management with the assistance of the county and the city. A consensus was developing, however, that future growth of the port would be thwarted were the port to depend solely on the limited resources of the city.

In 1991, a general decline in the nation's economy caused the port's profits to decline precipitously. By 1992, the port had posted a loss of $645,000, after eight years of growth. A University of Delaware study in 1996 recounted the dilemma facing Wilmington and the port, as follows:

> The Port of Wilmington had always been under the City of Wilmington. . . .
> Every year, if the Port ran a deficit, the loss was covered by City funds; but
> when the Port ran at a profit, the surplus went back to the City treasury. The
> City had never had any latitude for capital improvements, especially in recent
> decades when the costs of construction and equipment went beyond the re-
> sources of a City of 75,000 people. The ability of the City to borrow money
> was limited, and only Federal subsidies and direct capital from the State were
> able to keep the Port in business. As the surplus of Port revenues declined in
> the 1990s and as the City had its own financial problems, informal discussions
> began in 1994 about selling the Port. [11]

Meanwhile, two factors hastened the state's action to take over the port. The first was the fact that the state was $220 million richer in fiscal year 1995 by virtue of a windfall resulting from the decision of a federal court in January 1994. This decision settled a six-year dispute between the states of Delaware

and New York concerning certain intangible abandoned property that resulted in $220 million being awarded to Delaware. So the state of Delaware
had ample money available to purchase and improve the port. The second
factor was the potential departure of Volkswagen automobiles from using the
port for imports.

THE DIAMOND STATE PORT CORPORATION

After months of negotiation, the city of Wilmington and the state of Delaware agreed in June 1995 for the state to purchase the port from the city. The
state agreed to pay the city $4.5 million for the immediate purchase, as down
payment on $40 million owed over a thirty-year period, plus it agreed to
assume the city's $51 million in debts that had accrued for past port improve-
ments. Thus, the total cost of the purchase of the port over the succeeding
thirty years amounted to $91 million. The agreement was approved by the
Delaware State Legislature on July 1, 1995, and by the city council on
September 7, 1995, after which the actual transfer of the port to the state was
signed by Wilmington Mayor James H. Sills Jr. and Secretary of State Edward J. Freel. The General Assembly then enacted creation of the renamed
Diamond State Port Corporation (DSPC) within the Department of State.
DSPC was given "all power and authority necessary . . . to operate the Port,"
to pay no taxes, and to have its own personnel system separate from state
employees.[12]

Acquisition of Wilmington's port in 1995 represented the last local
government function given up to the state of Delaware during the 1935 to
1995 period. Beginning in 1935, when the state government assumed responsibility for all roads in the state, Delaware's small size and economy of scale
caused the state to take over many more local government functions, including care of the indigent, health administration, public education, welfare,
prisons, administration of elections, and Wilmington's municipal court.
Meanwhile, New Castle County gave up its airport to the Delaware River and
Bay Authority, an intergovernmental agency of Delaware and New Jersey.[13]

Funding in anticipation of the purchase of the port had been made available by the General Assembly's Bond Bill legislation for the fiscal year
ending on June 30, 1996. In addition, the Bond Bill allocated $25 million
from the state's Twenty-First Century Fund for port improvements.[14] After
the purchase, the state government continued to allocate substantial financial
support with, for example, an additional $20 million from the Bond Bill for
the fiscal year ending on June 30, 1999.[15]

In time, a large new cold-storage warehouse was constructed. Accordingly, many shiploads arrived containing fresh fruit from Chile plus meat and
seafood from New Zealand. The port became number one in the nation for

handling bananas from Honduras, Columbia, Costa Rica, and Ecuador. It also received pears, grapes, apples, and other fruits from Chile, making the Port of Wilmington a leading port for handling imported refrigerated fruit and concentrated juices. The Port of Wilmington had indeed become the Port of Delaware.

One of the most successful activities involving the port during the city of Wilmington's tenure had been the import of fruit, particularly from the Dole Fresh Fruit Company's operations in Latin America. The company had relocated its Chilean import center from Philadelphia to Wilmington in 1989. Dole sent fifty-seven ships to the port in 2009, from which its produce was distributed as far away as the Maritime Provinces of Canada and the states along the Mississippi River. Dole had about eight hundred employees at Delaware's port operations, occupying thirty-seven acres in 2010. DSPC sought to continue and improve this important business. Whereas Dole's contract was scheduled to continue until the end of 2011, with the option to extend until 2015, the company chose in May 2010 to sign a lease extension that could assure its business with Delaware through 2025.[16] But Delaware did not rely on Dole alone. Governor Jack Markell led a trade mission in August 2011 to Chile where he signed an agreement with Pacific Seaways, another Chilean fruit shipper, to ship to Wilmington a variety of fruits from dozens of companies, including Dole. The fruit is unloaded and stored in the port's 800,000-square-foot refrigerated warehouse. Then the fruit is transported to distribution centers and supermarkets in Canada and the United States.[17]

Companies began shipping dairy cows out of the port to the Middle East in 1987. That operation increased in 2011 to shipping 54,000 dairy cows to Turkey, Russia, and the Middle East, involving fifty to fifty-five huge livestock export ships each year. Federal regulations require a stopover of at least five hours for rest and health checks before a cow may board an export ship. Accordingly, Wilmington's City Council did not hesitate in June 2012 to approve an exception to its longstanding ban on keeping livestock within city boundaries by authorizing stays of cattle awaiting export up to ninety-six hours at a nearby "indoor inspection or resting facility." It was anticipated at the time that the new facility would make possible the loading of at least four thousand cattle on each ship. According to one port official, "All of these smaller staging areas could be eliminated. . . . We could gain an advantage over the ports that we compete with, mainly Galveston. The East Coast is easier for a ship to call on than [to go] all the way around to Galveston. We have an advantage of three to four days."[18]

In 2011, the port reported its highest general cargo tonnage since the state acquired the port in 1995 from Wilmington. It handled about four hundred vessels and 5.1 million tons of cargo—a gain of 26 percent from 2010. The port remained the continent's top port for importing perishable cargo, the largest banana port in the nation, and the second-largest banana port in the world, as well as the largest loading port on the East Coast for cattle exports, and the Delaware River's closest full-service port to the Atlantic Ocean.[19]

LOSING MONEY AND SEARCHING FOR A PARTNER

There was another portrayal of Delaware's port, however, that was not so glowing. A 2012 assessment found that state lawmakers had invested $177 million in the port since their 1995 purchase from the city of Wilmington. Nevertheless, the DSPC had lost money on the port's operations *every year* since 2002. The port had nine deteriorating berths on the Christina River, plus an auto berth pier stretching outward into the Delaware River for roll-on and roll-off deliveries. But the silt-prone Christina Channel required regular costly dredging and was still too shallow for the big ships that plied the forty-foot-deep Delaware River. Moreover, the auto pier was not usable for container cargoes.

Turning to the federal government for assistance was not adequate. In March 2012, DSPC formally requested that the federal government provide $20 million to support the replacement of Berth 5 and the rehabilitation of Berth 6, among the port's seven contiguous berths along the Christina River, because of deteriorating timber and steel piles. The total cost of the project would be $35 million, of which DSPC would contribute $15 million already authorized by the legislature's bond bill. According to the proposal:

> Weakening piles could lead to a collapse of the berths into the Christina River. Such a collapse could cause serious injuries, a concomitant environmental incident and closure of river traffic from the impact of debris. A collapsed area of the wharf would reduce the flow of cargo into and out of the Port of Wilmington, resulting in a loss of revenue and jobs. . . . Federal funding is necessary because the current economic climate prevents State and local governments from investing in the necessary long-term infrastructure projects.[20]

Meanwhile, the Army Corps of Engineers was already in the process of dredging the 103-mile main shipping channel of the Delaware River between Philadelphia and the Atlantic Ocean from its forty-foot depth to forty-five feet for deeper-draft ships. Added to this was the pressure to accommodate larger vessels pending from the widening and deepening of the Panama Canal originally scheduled for completion in 2014. None of the larger ships could navigate the shallow Christina River port.

Delaware authorities concluded in 2012 that it was timely and imperative to modernize the port. Aside from the auto berth roll-on, roll-off pier, it would be necessary to add a full-service berth on the Delaware River. However, DSPC chairman Alan Levin, who also was Delaware Economic Development Office (DEDO) director, estimated it would cost a potential $500 million to modernize and expand the port by building such a berth and supporting facilities on the Delaware River. That, said Levin, was more of an investment than the state alone could afford.

Accordingly, the state retained, under unreleased terms, a California-based financial consultant and financial advisor in 2011—BMO Capital Partners—to elicit and review proposals from possible private investors that could include joint operation of the port with the state or leasing all or part of the port to private investors. Governor Jack Markell said, "In the coming months, we will consider opportunities for a public/private partnership to expand and modernize the port, significantly increasing our capacity to handle global trade. . . . Doing so will not only protect those jobs currently at the port but will sow the seeds of future growth as we leap ahead of our competitors."[21]

WILMINGTON'S COMPETITORS

DSPC officials pointed to similar deals made by the Philadelphia and Baltimore ports. The Port of Philadelphia had long leased its marine terminal to various entities, including steamship lines and other companies. In fact, many financially distressed government-run ports nationally were considering similar leasing or partnership arrangements.

As recounted by Aaron Nathans of the Wilmington *News Journal*, a money crunch in 2009 at the Port of Baltimore led to a contract with a firm to run operations there for fifty years. Maryland Governor Martin O'Malley had informed the Maryland Port Administration that it would not have enough state money to upgrade the port in order to keep it competitive. So the port officials requested bids from potential private partners. Among bidders, the most lucrative was the proposal of Ports America, which took over operational control of Baltimore's port in January 2010, while the state continued to own the land the port was built on. Ports America reputedly was the largest terminal operator and stevedoring company in the nation, with operations in forty-two ports.

Nathans pointed out that the Baltimore port had an advantage over most other East Coast ports, including Wilmington's port. Whereas the depth of Baltimore's port had been fifty feet for over twenty years, the depth of Wilmington's port would not reach forty-five feet until dredging of the Delaware River would be completed, assuming its new berths could then be constructed to abut thereon. After upgrades by Ports America, including installation of the largest cranes in existence, Maryland officials claimed their privatization deal enabled Baltimore's port to be ready for the big ships that already pass through the Suez Canal to also pass through the expected widened and deepened Panama Canal and then head to the East Coast in 2015. Baltimore's port boasted 15 percent growth in cargo handled in 2011, the largest growth among all major ports in the nation.

By comparison, Wilmington's port had lost money on operations every year since 2002, with Delaware's state government providing regular infusions of taxpayer money for capital needs. In his article describing Baltimore's upgraded port, columnist Nathans reported:

> Skeptics have argued that all East Coast ports will be fighting for a share of the new business, and few will benefit all that much. Ports like New York/New Jersey, Miami, and Savannah, GA, also are working on improvements to benefit from the big ships. And West Coast ports and rail lines are expected to fight to keep their current business. But management and labor at the Baltimore port remain hopeful. [22]

Richard Norment of the National Council for Public-Private Partnerships commented that the Panama Canal work generated significant interest in partnerships among ports. He explained, "Keep in mind that this is a business, contractual relationship. The private sector is going to make a reasonable return. If the Port of Wilmington has been a financial black hole, loses money every year, it's not going to be very attractive, particularly when there are options from Miami all the way up the East Coast." [23]

In January 2012, in a series of articles in the Wilmington *News Journal*, journalist Jeff Montgomery revealed that in mid-2012, DSPC officials would be reviewing proposals from investors, but that the number and names of bidders were yet to be released. Montgomery cited one unnamed shipping expert who cautioned: "Wilmington and Philadelphia could find themselves in a spending battle for shares of a fixed or dwindling cargo pie, while Baltimore and other already-prepared metropolitan ports flourish after the Panama Canal becomes available to larger ships in 2014." Montgomery also quoted remarks of a Hofstra University professor of global studies, Jean-Paul Rodrigue, who warned:

> We have here a classic case of cross-jurisdiction competition where the respective actors want to capture the opportunities for their own backyard and may end up duplicating infrastructures and therefore not attracting enough traffic to justify both projects. . . .
>
> A key element would be to see if Wilmington is able to secure the commitment of a terminal operator, particularly one who deals at the global level. If terminal operators who are constantly looking for opportunities to expand their operations and who know the business well are not interested, then this does not augur well. [24]

After eliciting proposals from interested firms, the board of the DSPC chose affluent Houston-based Kinder Morgan in December 2012 as its exclusive negotiating partner to expand the port and operate it under a long-term lease agreement. DSPC's consultant, BMO Capital Partners, had ranked the proposals and rated Kinder Morgan as the top bidder. Kinder Morgan was the largest independent cargo operator in North America. Describing itself as mainly an energy and fuel transportation company, Kinder Morgan owned an interest in, or operated, about 74,000 miles of pipelines and 180 terminals that transported refined petroleum products, crude oil, and natural gas. Kinder Morgan had large petroleum storage facilities in New York Harbor, liquefied natural gas (LNG) terminals in Georgia and Mississippi, and handled coal in the Southeast. These facts spawned environmental concerns about the company's envisioned cargo at Wilmington, but the company's spokesman declined at the time to comment about energy as a new cargo line in its forthcoming formal plan.[25]

Seven weeks after Delaware named Kinder Morgan as its exclusive negotiating partner, it was disclosed on January 29, 2013, that a unit of Kinder Morgan had joined forces with Shell U.S. Gas & Power to export LNG from a Georgia terminal to countries around the world seeking abundant lower-priced natural gas, wrought by the recently developed fracking technology in the United States. This news only heightened the concerns of critics about Kinder Morgan's potential for transforming Delaware's port to become a predominantly gas-exporting facility.[26]

LEGISLATIVE INTERVENTION

The fact that Kinder Morgan was so heavily involved in fossil-based energy products, particularly LNG and coal, raised serious concerns. Many Delawareans still had fresh memories of Delaware's successful environmental protection effort, during the first decade of the twenty-first century, to invoke its Coastal Zone Act (CZA) to prevent British Petroleum (BP) from building an import LNG terminal on the New Jersey side of the Delaware River. Moreover, the fact that Wilmington's port was specifically exempted from the CZA could pave the way for Kinder Morgan to build large LNG or coal export facilities at Delaware's port. That the abundance of the nation's natural gas had become almost limitless, comparatively inexpensive, and cleaner than other fossil fuels meant that the use of gas in place of coal was growing exponentially in the United States. Accordingly, the nation's surplus coal was being exported to other nations. The involvement of Kinder Morgan, having a track record as one of the continent's largest gas and coal transportation and storage companies, was destined to arouse concerns about Delaware's port becoming a pollution-creating enterprise.[27] Green Delaware, a community organization concerned with environmental issues, pointed to "the extraordinary history of spills, leaks, explosions, and unacceptable operating practices of Kinder Morgan" and concluded, "However one looks at the proposed Port sale or lease, it doesn't look good."[28]

So it was not surprising that a move was initiated in the General Assembly to make sure that the legislature had a vote on any plan to lease the port to a private firm. Senator Robert Marshall, a Democrat and strong labor supporter from Wilmington, took the lead by declaring in mid-December 2012 that lawmakers would pass a bill providing for necessary legislative review. Although DSPC, as we have noted, had by law "all power and authority" to operate the port, DSPC Chairman and DEDO Director Alan Levin said it was unclear whether the General Assembly would have a vote, but that lawmakers would certainly be briefed. To this, Senator Marshall responded, "There's a distinct public policy question here of the legislature being an equal branch of government, and representing the taxpayer." Not knowing yet what sort of cargo Kinder Morgan planned to handle at the port, Marshall added, "We will only know if there are any significant implications regarding our environment after a public hearing and an airing of all the issues."[29]

Senator Marshall followed his "equal branch" remarks by writing legislation requiring the General Assembly's oversight of the port's privatization deal with Kinder Morgan. The Senate's Labor and Industrial Relations Committee, of which Marshall was chairman, then discussed the bill. DSPC Chairman Levin warned that such legislative action prior to a proposed contract with the company "could very well kill the deal." Meanwhile, Kinder Morgan sent a letter to DSPC's staff providing assurances that it would not convert the port "into a facility for the exclusive handling of coal or for use as an LNG terminal" and that "we fully expect to use the exact same management team, administrative staff and union employee base currently working at the Port."[30]

Kinder Morgan's assurances, however, did not allay expressed concerns about DSPC's prospective lease deal with the company. The Port of Wilmington Maritime Society, representing about sixty businesses doing work relating to the port, sent a letter in mid-January 2013 to Governor Markell saying that the society's businesses felt left out of the negotiation process. The letter, signed by the society's board, called for greater "transparency" and "the opportunity to take a more active part in the future of our port." Two companies at the port sent their own joint letter to DSPC Chairman Levin supporting the bill stating, "None of us are naïve or trusting enough to believe that a handshake or the verbal assurances that everything will remain 'status quo' will protect our businesses in the future."[31]

Meanwhile, Delaware's General Assembly passed Senate Bill 3 by a vote of eleven to nine, requiring that any transfer of control of the port to an outside entity be subject to a vote of the General Assembly. Testimony in the

House revealed support of the bill from union workers of the port. "We need you to protect us," said Julius Cephas, president of the local International Longshoremen's union. But representatives from Delaware building trade unions opposed Senate Bill 3, maintaining that such a law could jeopardize a deal that would affect many construction jobs at the port. Given the reluctance of the Markell administration for the General Assembly to have final authority over any port deal, a compromise amendment was struck in the House to have the General Assembly's joint Bond Bill committee of twelve members undertake such review authority, provided that should the General Assembly take no action within thirty days of the committee's review, the deal would be considered rejected. As amended, the bill was approved unanimously by the House, and the Senate approved the amended bill a few hours later, whereby the bill was signed into law by Governor Markell on February 5, 2013.[32]

Regardless of the toned-down, amended version of the law mandating review by lawmakers, Kinder Morgan officials thought the General Assembly's intervention could scuttle its negotiations with DSPC. John Schlosser, president-elect of Kinder Morgan, said, "We were very disappointed in the decision by the Legislature this past week, which we think may end up killing the deal." Rich Kinder, the company's CEO, added that "the legislation . . . seemed to be more intent on protecting union jobs than it is in the economic well-being of the port." Senator Robert Marshall retorted that their response "clearly indicates that they don't like anyone, elected or otherwise, having any review." DSPC chairman Alan Levin did not think Kinder Morgan was pulling out, saying, "They feel uncomfortable. They don't like being bashed. We're going to go through this until somebody says we're done." Simmons & Company energy investment analyst Mark Reichman considered it unlikely that Kinder Morgan would make great or quick changes at the port. He commented: "Terminalizing is a core competency for Kinder. It doesn't matter whether it's bananas or coal. It's something they know very well and they've been successful at. I sense that maybe in the community there is more a concern that, 'Is this a wolf in sheep's clothing. Is this going to end up being a big industry site for coal and liquefied natural gas and all that?'"[33]

James Young of Middletown was probably expressing the view of many Delawareans by writing in his letter to the editor of the Wilmington *News Journal*: "Thanks to our state legislators for acting responsibly. . . . The fact that the only proposal being considered is from an energy transportation company, which is heavily into building LNG terminals, should give citizens pause."[34]

KINDER MORGAN'S ENVISIONED PLAN

Kinder Morgan had yet to agree on a formal long-term lease contract with DSPC, which was likely not to happen until the end of the legislature's session in June 2013, pending the approval of the contract by the joint Bond Bill Committee. Kinder Morgan officials decided to outline their thinking about their prospective investment in the port with the Wilmington *News Journal* on February 1, 2013, and planned to address the DSPC board and the public at a later date.

At its meeting with the newspaper, as reported in its February 2, 2013, issue, company officials envisioned a $200 million investment in the port. It would add steel, scrap, ferro alloy, and liquid and solid fertilizer shipments, and two new mobile harbor cranes on the existing automobile berth on the Delaware River. Also envisioned was a new conveyor system to transport cargo from vessels that would free up existing Christina River port cranes for current port tenants. They anticipated that the company's first construction at the port, to accommodate new business, would include three bulk storage buildings, as well as a liquid storage facility. They disclosed that Kinder Morgan would not add LNG facilities at the port, nor did they have plans to add coal capacity, although they declined definitively to rule out shipping more coal. The port already handled about 100,000 tons of coal per year, and the company had already noted that the port's current infrastructure was not built to handle more coal. Kinder Morgan's director of business development was more specific at the meeting about projected expenditures at the port, paraphrased by journalist Aaron Nathans as follows:

> Kevin Golankiewicz said the company anticipates making at least $200.5 million in investments over time, while making lease payments of $142.5 million over 50 years—coming out to $2.85 million per year—to the port corporation. Also included would be a $16.5 million upfront payment. The balance would go toward maintenance expansion and physical improvements. . . . Physically expanding the port would be contingent upon getting enough new business, Golankiewicz said. Even without expanding onto the Delaware River, partnership between Kinder Morgan and the port would prove successful, although remaining on the Christina River would limit opportunities, he said.

In reporting the meeting, Nathans added that company officials emphasized that their first priority would be meeting the needs of existing tenants of the port, and that the company would "provide full employment to the current administrative staff for at least three years."[35]

Kinder Morgan's envisioned plan came under fire from critics at its mid-February public meeting with the DSPC board. Opponents generally complained that the company's projected expenditures were not enough to make necessary repairs, nor did its plan guarantee the port's expansion into the Delaware River.

DSPC needed about $156 million for infrastructure renovation, including replacing warehouses and cranes and repairing berths, just to assure the continuing operation of the port. The company pledged only $112.5 million for infrastructural improvements, however, and only $24 million over twenty years for maintenance, plus merely $5 million toward expansion—thus promising infrastructure funding far below the $156 million DSPC sought. Furthermore, Kinder Morgan had given no assurance that the port would be expanded into the Delaware River. DSPC Director Alan Levin initially had said that such expansion would cost approximately $500 million, much more than the state could afford. Hence, DSPC was thereby motivated to seek a wealthy partner to enable the port to remain competitive with other East Coast ports. Although the company acknowledged the "strategic value" of expanding the port to the Delaware River, it did not yet have the customers to allow it to make the assurance that it could pay for that expansion. After board members one-by-one repeated the message that the state could not afford to make the needed investments on its own, DSPC's board vice chairman, Secretary of State Jeffrey Bullock, said, "To those who say, 'do nothing, let things happen as they may,' we need to understand our responsibility to the taxpayers of the State."[36]

In his February 7, 2013, letter to the editor of the Wilmington *News Journal*, the president of the port's International Longshoremen's Local 1694-1 labor union, Julius Cephas, made it clear he thought that Kinder Morgan's stated intention to provide full employment to current port employees for "at least three years" was suspect. Cephas wrote: "Comparative long-term job creators? The long-term vision of Kinder Morgan is unclear, which makes for more public uncertainty. Buzzwords such as 'we will consider,' 'with concessions,' 'verbal assurances,' 'will not rule out,' and 'we intend to' are why this port deal needs public transparency and legislative oversight."[37] Two weeks later, Cephas was the author of an opinion-page column in the same newspaper attacking Kinder Morgan as an "oil pipeline giant . . . with a track record in the Northwest and beyond of pollution, labor and work-place safety violations . . . chosen as the 'preferred bidder' in a closed bidding process."[38]

On March 7, 2013, Kinder Morgan's president, John Schlosser, notified state officials that his company had "suspended" negotiations. Schlosser said the decision "while regrettable, stems from our concern that the leadership of Local 1694-1, principally Julius Cephas, is antagonistic to the point of making a productive relationship with our future work force impossible." He explained that the three-year pledge was "a starting point for our negotiations." DEDO Director Alan Levin plaintively asserted, "I think it's over."[39]

The conclusion was inescapable. The Kinder Morgan deal was dead. State officials had neither any backup plan to keep the port competitive nor any inclination to find another partner to save the port. Indeed, some state leaders concluded that the port in time was doomed. "If we don't grow," said one port board member, "I don't think the port will be operating in 10 years." House Speaker Peter Schwartzkopf said it would be a stretch for the state to come up with the $150 million needed to just maintain the port's current facilities over the next ten years. "I think the state of Delaware just shot themselves in the foot," he said.[40]

In another opinion-page column in the Wilmington *News Journal*, labor leader Cephas sought to have the last word, by explaining in part as follows:

> On March 7, Kinder Morgan announced that it was "suspending" its interest in the Port of Wilmington. That saved jobs; it did not eliminate them. Our focus was to ensure the viability of the port long-term and not sacrifice 30-year mortgages of working families for a three-year promise to protect the jobs for a select few. Our intent was to protect 30-year pensions and jobs and not accept a three-year promise that would see, at its end, a potential elimination of local job opportunities for residents that invest in this community. Our efforts in the state Legislature and the heroic efforts made on behalf of working families was to ensure that promises and commitments would be kept and not subject to the changing whims of a corporation committed more to its own bottom line instead of understanding that if our future and interest were tied together then we would all prosper together.[41]

Having successfully exerted the central effort to scuttle the Kinder Morgan deal, Cephas—in still another of his opinion-page columns—made this curious assertion: "The Port of Wilmington has the opportunity to double in capacity from the Panama Canal expansion in 2015."[42]

In January 2015, Cephas vowed to fight an arbitrator's ruling that supported the hiring of part-time workers at the port for previously full-time union jobs. Paul Cutler, the union's vice president, asserted: "Personally, I think it's a vendetta by the governor for the Kinder-Morgan deal."[43]

A DEAL WITH DOLE

Regardless of the failure to cement the deal with Kinder Morgan, the port still remained the major gateway for Latin American fresh fruit to reach one-third of the mainland U.S. population. But even this distinction was soon put in jeopardy by news that Dole, representing 30 percent of cargo tonnage at Wilmington's port, was seriously weighing a move to New Jersey's port of Paulsboro. Dole requested concessions from warehousing union members at Wilmington's port, including work rule changes and a proposed pay cut, about which the union's president, Julius Cephas, declined to comment.

"This is a big deal," said Alan Levin, chairman of the port. Should Dole leave, other fruit shippers would "follow suit," and "there would definitely be cutbacks on all staff, the management, administration, and the longshoremen side. This would really ripple through the whole community," Levin said. He added that DSPC was working hard "to make sure they don't go anywhere," and concluded: "We're optimistic." The trouble was, the CEO of the corporation that owned New Jersey's Paulsboro port also said he was "optimistic."[44]

Governor Markell traveled to Dole's headquarters in California on August 12, 2013. Two days later, the Wilmington *News Journal* reported that a deal had been clinched whereby Dole, the Port of Wilmington's largest tenant, had agreed to remain in Delaware for the next fifteen years. Details of the contract had yet to be finalized. It was known, however, that the port's Longshoremen Association had agreed to extend its 2011 pay cut through 2018. Julius Cephas commented:

> In the 15-year contract with Dole Food Co., officials stated they appreciated the "quality of the workforce" provided by the International Longshoremen. . . .
> But, the relationship with administration and organized labor still remains tenuous and sometimes not collegial. Relations with organized labor and administration can be greatly improved by appointing executive committee labor members . . . to sit on the board. Having port workforce expertise at the table to participate in vital decisions that impact port operations also improves transparency on all budgetary matters.[45]

Dole had been a tenant of the port for thirty-one years, leasing 37.5 acres there, importing diverse tropical fruits. DEDO's Alan Levin said, "Dole had other options for its business, but keeping Dole in Wilmington is a priority for the port and we worked hard to reach terms that would do that." State Senator Karen Peterson stated that losing Dole "would have been devastating," and added that the port is "one of the industries in Wilmington that has survived, as other industries went away." One of the terms in the deal made by DSPC, besides some price concessions to Dole, was that Delaware agreed to make capital renovations at the port to benefit Dole, including $34 million to be spent over three years involving cranes and cold-storage warehouses.[46]

For a long time, DSPC had sought federal government funding for the repair of its aging berths at the Port of Wilmington. On September 4, 2013, it finally became known that the U.S. Department of Transportation had granted $10 million to help renovate berths 5 and 6 at the port.

The total cost of the renovation would be $13.4 million, of which $3.4 million would come from capital funds allocated from the General Assembly's bond bill. "This funding is a tribute to the hard work of our federal delegation and the value that the maritime industry places on the Port of

Wilmington," said Governor Markell. He added: "The investments we make in the port will continue to be an integral part of our strategy to create jobs and grow Delaware's economy."[47]

CONCLUSION

In the final analysis, the Port of Wilmington was at its roots a commercial enterprise. The services it provided did not generate sufficient revenue to cover all of its operating costs and to generate a return on investment consistent with its need for future investment. No company could be expected to build the projected $500 million expansion in berths without an adequate flow of revenue to pay the bill. The Kinder Morgan fiasco told Delawareans just that. It was also questionable to expect taxpayers to carry the load when all of the other parts of the budget were short of funds. Unless the port could find ways to cover such costs, it faced a diminished future and might even be forced to close.

Any plan to make the port competitive and viable for the future would require the expansion of facilities to the Delaware River capable of handling the largest container vessels. With the Kinder Morgan deal dead, state officials had given up the idea of luring another large private-sector partner to make such an expensive investment. However, in July 2014, Julius Cephas and his longshoremen visited an undeveloped 170-acre landscape immediately south of the Delaware Memorial Bridge spanning the Delaware River that prompted them to envision just such an expansion of the port at that site. They enlisted the enthusiastic interest of New Castle County Executive Tom Gordon, who saw the site a plausible location for a public–private $400 million to $600 million venture to expand the port. "From everything I've seen, it would be one of the most productive ports on the East Coast," Gordon said. "The ships would be able to come directly from ocean to port and not have to travel up river. It would save a lot of money and a lot of time." Meanwhile, state officials apparently were kept in the dark. Governor Jack Markell said he hadn't been briefed about the project, but he was always interested in hearing more. DEDO Director Levin, who also chaired the DSPC, declined to comment. And Eugene Bailey, executive director of DSPC, acknowledged that he had heard no details about the proposal, but that he was interested in any idea to expand the port.[48]

Whether the proposed expansion will remain merely "pie-in-the-sky" wishful thinking, or will really move forward with or without the state government's intervention, remains to be seen, but progress is surely questionable. For example, the area in question would not enjoy the current port's Coastal Zone Act exemptions. Moreover, the mayor and city council of the nearby historic town of New Castle have been reported to be adamantly opposed. And finally, as editorials in the Wilmington *News Journal* have made clear, financing is the biggest question, and Delaware simply does not have the money to build either a new port or even an updated port.[49]

Not all news in 2015 about the port was negative. In February, it was announced that AutoPort Inc. will export Chrysler, Dodge, Jeep, and Ram cars and trucks through the Port of Wilmington to the Middle East beginning in March 2015, raising the prospect of rebuilding the port's once busy auto-shipping business and the possibility of involving thousands of vehicles annually.[50]

But the future of the port remains uncertain. Two years after the Kinder Morgan fiasco, in March 2015, DSPC directors were even considering "non-maritime uses" of some of the port's property. Alan Levin lamented: "We're not going back. That's clear from the Legislature. Until that changes, there's no reason to look at that. This is strictly to determine how to best use the land we have, the economic opportunities that are out there."[51]

NOTES

1. For Wilmington's unique financial constraints, see William Boyer and Edward Ratledge, *Delaware Politics and Government* (Lincoln: University of Nebraska Press, 2009), 130–32.

2. Gerard J. Mangone, ed., *Port of Wilmington: In the 21st Century* (Newark: Graduate College of Marine Studies, University of Delaware, January 1996), 1. For an early pictorial history of the port and its surrounding area, see Priscilla M. Thompson and Sally O'Byrne, *Images of America: Wilmington's Waterfront* (Charleston, SC: Arcadia Publishing, 1999), esp. 106–28.

3. Paul Dolan, *Government and Administration of Delaware* (New York: Thomas Y. Crowell, 1956), 332. See, also, William W. Boyer, *Governing Delaware: Policy Problems in the First State* (Newark: University of Delaware Press, 2000), 86, 99. Curiously, the book on Delaware government by Paul Dolan and James R. Soles virtually ignored discussion of municipal government in the state; see their *Government of Delaware* (Newark: University of Delaware, 1976).

4. See Cresap, McCormick, and Paget, Management Consultants, *City of Wilmington, Delaware: Future Development of the Port Terminal* (Volume I, Economic and Administrative Considerations, October 1968): III–1; and *Laws of Delaware*, Chapter 123, Volume 29 (April 12, 1917).

5. "Wilmington's Riverfront Dream May Be Realized if Government Locates Military Storehouse Here," *The Sunday Morning Star*, September 16, 1917, 1.

6. Forester and Company, *Delaware's Port of Wilmington, 75 Years of Personal Service, 1923–1998* (Wilmington: Diamond State Port Corporation, 1998), 3, 5.

7. Ibid., 27–28.

8. Cresap, McCormick and Paget, *City of Wilmington, Delaware*, Vol. 1, V–16.

9. Ibid., II–2, II–3.

10. Forester & Company, *Delaware's Port of Wilmington*, 38.

11. Mangone, ed., *Port of Wilmington*, 5.

12. See *Delaware Code Annotated*, Title 29, Chapter 87, Subchapter II, Sections 8780–89.

13. For discussion of the disposition of Delaware local government to give up functions to the state government, see Boyer, *Governing Delaware*, 99; and Boyer and Ratledge, *Delaware Politics and Government*, 120–23.

14. See the so-called "Bond Bill," Chapter 210, Vol. 70, Formerly Senate Bill No. 280, passed June 30, 1995, for fiscal year ending June 30, 1996, at p. 532, accessible at delcode.delaware.gov/sessionlaws/ga138/chp210.shtml#TopOfPage.

15. "Bond Bill," Chapter 378, Vol. 71, Formerly House Bill No. 750, for fiscal year ending June 30, 1999, at p. 1088, accessible at delcode.delaware.gov/sessionlaws/ga139/chp378.shtml#TopOfPage.

16. Aaron Nathans, "Welcome to 'Dole-aware," Wilmington *News Journal*, May 15, 2010.

17. Aaron Nathans, "Markell Heads to Chile on a Trade Mission," Wilmington *News Journal*, August 4, 2011, A8.

18. Jeff Montgomery, "City Could Get Some Country: Port Business Has Plans to Build 33-Acre Enclosed Livestock Site Near Southbridge," Wilmington *News Journal*, June 27, 2012, A1, A5.

19. See Jeff Montgomery, "Del. Eyes Partner for Port Growth, Shipping Industry Poised for Change," Wilmington *News Journal*, April 9, 2012, A1, A9; and Aaron Nathans, "Port Handled 26% More Cargo in 2011 than 2010," ibid., March 9, 2012, A10.

20. DSPC: Port of Wilmington, Upgrading Berths 5 and 6, March 19, 2012, 1, 18.

21. See, for example, Jeff Montgomery, "Officials Weighing Private Lease Offers for Port," Wilmington *News Journal*, January 20, 2012; Aaron Nathans, "Port Looks for 'Partnership,'" ibid., April 30, 2011; and Montgomery, "Del. Eyes Partner for Growth," ibid., April 9, 2012, A1, A9.

22. Aaron Nathans, "OPTIONS for Port," Wilmington *News Journal*, January 21, 2013, A8, A9.

23. Jeff Montgomery, "Discussion of Port Deal Resurfacing," Wilmington *News Journal*, November 23, 2012, A1.

24. Jeff Montgomery, "Deal Talks May Continue into Summer, Levin: No Deadlines on $500 Million Venture," Wilmington *News Journal*, May 26, 2012, A1, A7. See also Montgomery, "Proposals Come Rolling In," ibid., May 1, 2012, B1, B2; and Montgomery, "Input on Any Port Deal Is Sought," ibid., April 11, 2012, A1, A2.

25. Aaron Nathans, "Texas Giant Vies for Port Job," Wilmington *News Journal*, December 8, 2012, A1, A5.

26. Aaron Nathans, "Kinder Morgan in Deal," Wilmington *News Journal*, January 29, 2013, A6, A7.

27. See chapter 5, "Coastal Zone Protection," of our book *Pivotal Policies in Delaware: From Desegregation to Deregulation* (Newark, DE: University of Delaware Press, 2014).

28. Green Delaware, "The Port of Wilmington and Jack Markell and Kinder Morgan," www.greendel.org/2013/02/10/the-port-of-wilmington-and-jack-markell-and-kinder-morgan/ (accessed February 10, 2013).

29. Aaron Nathans, "Port Deal Draws Concern," Wilmington *News Journal*, December 15, 2012, A6.

30. Aaron Nathans, "Bill Giving GA Last Word on Deal Advances," Wilmington *News Journal*, January 16, 2013, A8.

31. Aaron Nathans and Jonathan Starkey, "Lease Deal Worries Port Group," Wilmington *News Journal*, January 17, 2013, A6, A7.

32. See Doug Denison, "Oversight Bill Advances," Wilmington *News Journal*, January 24, 2013, B1, B2; Denison, "Port Oversight Bill OK'd," Ibid., January 25, 2013, B1, B2; Senate Bill No. 3 As Amended, Act to Amend Title 29 of the Delaware Code Relating to State Government and the Diamond State Port Corporation, Delaware State Senate, 147th General Assembly, accessible at www.legis.delaware.gov/LIS/LIS147.NSF/vwLegislation/SB+3?Opendocument; and the 2014 proposal to increase the size of DSPC's board of fifteen members by adding six members all appointed by the General Assembly: Aaron Nathans, "Lawmakers Want More Say on Board, Proposal Would Add Six Spots All From GA," Wilmington *News Journal*, February 9, 2014, E1, E5.

33. Jeff Montgomery and Aaron Nathans, "Deal to Lease Port at Risk," Wilmington *News Journal*, January 31, 2013, A1, A2.

34. James Young, "Legislature Is Right to Keep Eye on Port Deal," Wilmington *News Journal*, February 5, 2013, A8.

35. Aaron Nathans, "Port Plan Includes Expansion," Wilmington *News Journal*, February 2, 2013, A1, A10.

36. Aaron Nathans, "Kinder Plan Critiqued," Wilmington *News Journal*, February 12, 2013, A6, A7.

37. Julius Cephas, "Go Back to Start Modernizing the Port," Wilmington *News Journal*, February 7, 2013, A10.

38. Julius Cephas, "Lessons for Strong Local Economy and Port of Wilmington," Wilmington *News Journal*, February 21, 2013, A13.

39. Aaron Nathans, "Port Lease Efforts Dead, Kinder Morgan Suspends Talks," Wilmington *News Journal*, March 8, 2013, A1, A2.

40. Aaron Nathans, "Port's Future at Risk, State Has No Backup Plan to Keep It Competitive," Wilmington *News Journal*, March 10, 2013, A1, A17.

41. Julius Cephas, "Port Union Acted to Save Worker Jobs and Pensions," Wilmington *News Journal*, March 17, 2013, A21.

42. Julius Cephas, "Investing in the Port of Wilmington Makes Sense," Wilmington *News Journal*, June 26, 2013, A10.

43. Quoted by Jeff Montgomery, "Port Union Vows to Fight Job Ruling," Wilmington *News Journal*, January 31, 2015, A12.

44. Aaron Nathans, "Dole May Be on Move, State Presses to Retain Top Port Tenant," Wilmington *News Journal*, July 28, 2013, E1, E3.

45. Julius Cephas, "Time to Look to Future for Wilmington Port," Wilmington *News Journal*, October 4, 2013, A10.

46. See Aaron Nathans, "State, Dole Reach Port Deal, Fruit Firm to Remain for Next 15 Years," Wilmington *News Journal*, August 14, 2013, A1, A2; Editorial, "Port Deal Will Pay Off for Dole and Delaware," ibid., August 15, 2013, A12; and Jeff Montgomery, "Delaware Works to Keep Chile Trade," ibid., January 21, 2015, A4.

47. Aaron Nathans, "Port Wins $10M Grant," Wilmington *News Journal*, September 4, 2013, A8.

48. See these articles by Maureen Milford: "Thinking Big: County Executive Gordon, Labor leaders, Want New Port of Wilmington on Delaware River to Attract Jobs, Ships," Wilmington *News Journal*, July 13, 2014, A1, A6, A7; "A Port Plan for 4,000 Jobs," ibid., October 17, 2014, A1, A7; and "Expansion Could Fuel Job Growth for Decades," ibid., October 18, 2014, A1, A10.

49. See these editorials: "Talk of New Port Raises Many Questions," Wilmington *News Journal*, July 13 2014, A10; and "Questions for the Propose Port Plan," ibid., October 20, 2014, A8.

50. Maureen Milford, "Wilmington Port Gets Auto-Export Boost," Wilmington *News Journal*, February 27, 2015, A4.

51. Jeff Montgomery, "Port of Wilmington Planning Bid Delayed, Directors Consider Non-Maritime Uses of Property," Wilmington *News Journal*, March 21, 2015, A6.

Chapter Three

Wilmington's Riverfront

Before the middle of the 1800s, Wilmington had become a hub of economic activity. Railroad cars and wheels were manufactured there. Its iron works produced steamboats, iron ships, yachts, paper mill rolls, and boilers. From 1870 to 1920, Wilmington was a booming city. Shipbuilding became a dominant industry, spurred by the Dravo Corporation. As we have noted, Wilmington's port then opened for business in 1923 and began to prosper. Dravo produced sub-chasers, landing craft, and many other vessels during World War II. The company became the state's largest employer. After the war, however, Wilmington's population began to decline. The city's population between 1940 and 1980 plummeted 38 percent. Dravo closed in 1965. The Riverfront became desolate. The Christina River was polluted. Scattered on its banks were brownfields, junkyards, and crumbling empty buildings, "the legacy of a once proud shipbuilding industry that had turned heavy industrial and gone bust."[1] In contrast, mills along the Brandywine River had long since ceased operating, preserving the river's natural beauty.

"A VISION FOR THE RIVERS"

Given the growing concern for Wilmington's waterfront, the General Assembly's Senate unanimously endorsed a resolution on June 24, 1992. It called for the governor "to appoint a blue ribbon task force to make recommendations concerning the future of the Brandywine and Christina rivers." Governor Mike Castle (1985–1993) signed Executive Order 109 on October 20, 1992, establishing a task force on the future of the two rivers. He named former Governor Russell Peterson and Dr. Arthur Trabant, University of Delaware's President Emeritus, as co-chairpersons. Two years later, Peterson and Trabant transmitted to then-Governor Tom Carper (1993–2001) the final report of the task force. In their transmittal letter to Carper, they wrote:

> These rivers constitute one of Delaware's most important assets. . . . [T]he Task Force members have defined the means of improving water quality, protecting and enhancing stream banks, providing public access to the streams, dedicating greenways, acquiring critical land areas, cleaning up the watershed, establishing Delaware's first urban wildlife refuge and rejuvenating the Wilmington waterfront. This last item is particularly exciting. A team of Delaware architects has produced a dramatic vision of what the waterfront could be like. It appears to us to be a practical way to make this area as exciting as San Antonio's River Walk and Baltimore's Inner Harbor and in the process create jobs and business opportunities, enhance the quality of life for Delawareans and provide an expanded tax base for Wilmington, New Castle County and the State of Delaware.[2]

Among the task force's many recommendations, the first four regarding riverfront development were the following:

> (1) Concentrate a variety of facilities and activities that will attract people to the waterfront; (2) Encourage pubic events . . . to create excitement, attract participants and generate a climate for economic development and investment. (3) Attract new entertainment facilities, such as theaters, restaurants and hotels. (4) Enhance the recreational aspects and amenities . . . to appeal to individual, family and corporate needs.[3]

On June 30, 1995, the General Assembly enacted legislation for fiscal year 1996 to implement major recommendations of the governor's task force concerning rejuvenation of Wilmington's Riverfront. Specifically, the new law declared:

> The General Assembly hereby authorizes the Governor to incorporate . . . a Riverfront Development Corporation . . . to promote the common good of the citizens of Delaware through the planning, development and management of programs and projects intended to foster, encourage and promote recreational, residential, commercial and industrial development and redevelopment along or in the proximity to the Brandywine and Christina Rivers as recommended in the report of the Governor's Task Force on . . . a Vision for the Rivers (1994).

The same law appropriated $4,500,000 for the Riverfront Development Corporation (RDC) to support the projects "identified . . . in *A Vision for the Rivers* (1994)" including "the development and construction of a publicly-owned convention/exposition center."[4]

An RDC-contracted study, by economist Dr. Simon Condliffe of the University of Delaware's Center for Applied Demography & Survey Research (CADSR), reported in 2007:

The Wilmington Riverfront has changed dramatically since 1996. Abandoned buildings and brownfield areas have been replaced by new commercial and residential projects. The major projects include Christina Landing [63 town-houses and 173 apartments], One River Place (AAA), the Barclays buildings, the Chase Center, the Shipyards Shops, the Riverfront Market, the Delaware Center for Contemporary Arts, the Delaware Theater Company, and the ING buildings. Since 1996 the riverfront has received over $850 million of invest-ment from public and private sources. Simultaneously, the riverfront has gen-erated revenue streams for city, county, and state governments, as well as being an economic engine for job growth. [5]

Among other findings of Condliffe's study for the period from 1996 to 2007, was the fact that the riverfront received $270 million in public funds—including funding from city, county, state, and federal agencies—of which the state contributed $213 million (plus $11.2 million from New Castle County, and $16.8 from the city of Wilmington), compared to $617 million provided by private investment. Riverfront employment totaled about three thousand jobs, plus approximately one thousand additional jobs supported by the impact of riverfront economic activity in Delaware. This rather glowing 2007 report concluded, "Riverfront activity is forecast to surpass $30 million in State revenue by 2012. . . . At this rate of growth, the state could expect to break even on its Riverfront investment by 2013." [6]

Unfortunately, Condliffe's optimistic forecast was never to come to pass, principally because his study's publication in April 2007 coincided with the onset of the nation's Great Recession. Five years later, the RDC again contracted with the university's CADSR to conduct a second study to ex-plore the fiscal impact of redeveloping the Wilmington Riverfront. The re-port of that April 2012 study was authored by economist Dr. Daniel T. Brown. According to Brown:

> Previous forecasts in Condliffe (2007) predicted that public revenues from Riverfront activity would be recovered by 2013. Estimates in this updated report differ for the following reasons: The previous report did not control for inflation. . . . Previous forecasts were based on gross activity instead of net activity. . . . The previous report assumed that future construction, land devel-opment, and employment would continue to grow at the same rates as had been occurring on the Riverfront until 2006. The deep economic downturn that began in late 2007 was unanticipated and adversely affected revenues to a large degree. . . . Most construction on the Riverfront came to a halt. . . . [7]

Brown's 2012 study stated that public funding on riverfront activity from 1996 through 2011 totaled $346 million of which the state of Delaware expended $306 million, or 89.3 percent of the total public funding, while receiving $173 million of revenues in return. But Brown recognized that "there are social benefits coming from the Riverfront development that do not translate into fiscal revenues." In this respect, he quoted a 2002 editorial written by two state senators, as follows:

> We've been asked if the Riverfront will turn a profit someday. Former Governor Peterson said it well when he told us the profits lie in the jobs it has created, the optimism it has fostered, and the renewal it has sparked. Will the Riverfront ever make money? Of course not. As Delaware Finance Secretary David Singleton aptly put it: "Will Rockford Park ever make money?" No, it won't. But aren't we fortunate to have places such as Rockford Park and the Wilmington Riverfront for the public to enjoy beauty and tranquility. The mountains of work involved have been eclipsed by the visible results. Even in these difficult times, we feel certain the Riverfront's best days are yet to come. [8]

Brown also noted in his 2012 study that, from 1997 through 2011, nearly 2,060 new jobs had been created in Delaware as a result of Riverfront activity. He predicted that "the state's Riverfront investment will equal revenues generated by the new Riverfront activity by 2016. Repaying the State of Delaware for all the spending on the Riverfront is anticipated to take an additional two to five years." [9]

Neither Condliffe's nor Brown's studies delved into the inducements that attracted particular major business entities to locate at Wilmington's Riverfront, which added jobs, wealth, and revenue. While the specific circumstances that induced various companies to locate at Wilmington's Riverfront differed significantly, and each of these companies was unique, commonalities included that they brought about dramatic change to the riverfront and the addition of new jobs to Delaware's labor force. The location of three such business entities illustrates this changed character: the entry of ING Direct USA in 2000, followed by AAA Mid-Atlantic in 2004, and Capital One in 2012 each deserves our attention.

ING DIRECT USA

The so-called ING Group is a Dutch multinational banking and financial services corporation headquartered in Amsterdam. ING stands for "Internationale Nederlanden Groep," which in English means International Netherlands Group. After the company was started in 1990, the market soon abbreviated its name to I-N-G. Its major businesses comprised several kinds of banking (retail, direct, commercial, and investment), insurance services, and asset management. ING Group was reported in 2008 to be one of the twentieth largest financial institutions in the world. In 2012, it was the world's largest banking, financial services, and insurance conglomerate in terms of revenue with gross receipts exceeding $150 billion per year. In 2013, ING

Group served over forty-eight million individual and institutional clients in more than forty countries, with a worldwide workforce exceeding 75,000.[10]

To expand its retail banking overseas, without creating a network of branches, the ING Group launched overseas direct banking businesses called ING Direct in Canada in 1997, followed soon in the United States, United Kingdom, Germany, France, and Australia. ING Direct featured no-frills, high-rate savings accounts that could only be accessed online, and that proved to be a successful ING Group venture. ING Direct entered the U.S. banking market in 2000, and established its corporate headquarters in a large, imposing new building at Wilmington's Riverfront. Its business model relied primarily on Internet banking for its more than 7.5 million American customers, who could easily access ING Direct representatives about their savings and checking account options online. While a number of U.S. banks also offered online services, ING Direct USA was unique in being one of the first banks in the U.S. to "unveil an eco-friendly and low-cost alternative" to traditional banks.[11] The conspicuous presence of prestigious ING Direct USA's impressive headquarters in Wilmington was greeted with enthusiasm—a major boost that served to invigorate riverfront development.

ING Direct USA, however, was a unit of what in time became a troubled Dutch ING Group holding company. ING Group ran into significant trouble during the onset of the Great Recession 2008–2009 credit squeeze and was forced to accept a Dutch government bailout. That deal in part required the sale of ING Direct USA.

CAPITAL ONE

Capital One Financial Corporation—a US-based financial services holding company—had been a November 2008 recipient of a federal stimulus bailout of $3.56 billion, which it repaid in June 2009. In June 2011, the credit card giant Capital One agreed to purchase ING Direct USA for $9 billion.[12]

In August 2011, Capital One announced that it would also buy HSBC's troubled credit card business in the United States, with 350 employees in New Castle, Delaware, for $2.6 billion. HSBC had been a British multinational financial services holding company headquartered in London. It was founded in 1991 by The Hong Kong and Shanghai Banking Corporation, hence its name: HSBC. By virtue of the fact that HSBC was at the center of the sub-prime mortgage-lending storm in 2009, it cut six thousand jobs in its U.S. finance arm, leaving only its credit card business to continue, which Capital One was poised to absorb.[13]

Having purchased ING Direct USA, and HSBC's credit card business in the United States, Capital One was induced in September 2011 to add approximately five hundred new jobs by 2013 in Delaware, mostly located at

ING's former building at Wilmington's Riverfront. State job-development incentives were offered to Capital One of up to $6.9 million, including a Delaware Strategic Fund grant of $5.6 million, plus up to $1.5 million for capital investments offered to its Wilmington facility.

While retaining all ING Direct USA employees, Capital One's new employees were expected to have an average salary of $130,000 and be in roles "heavily weighted in the manager level." Its five hundred new employees would bring Capital One's combined Delaware workforce to approximately 2,150. The deal would create the fifth largest bank in the country, albeit still much smaller than JPMorgan Chase and Bank of America.[14] Capital One's plans to expand its Delaware workforce were greeted with unstinting approval by Delaware notables, including Delaware Governor Jack Markell, Delaware Economic Development Office (DEDO) Director Alan Levin, and the state's entire congressional delegation of Senators Tom Carper and Chris Coons as well as Congressman John Carney.[15]

But not all Delawareans approved of the deal. For example, Executive Director Rashmi Rangan of the Delaware Community Reinvestment Action Council (DCRAC) simply did not believe Capital One's testimony at a hearing before Delaware Banking Commissioner Robert Glen, who approved the company's acquisition of ING Bank. A Capital One official testified that the company had given more than 4,200 grants and $60 million to nonprofit organizations since January 2009, and had made a ten-year commitment of more than $180 billion in new development lending, investments, and services to moderate and low-income borrowers. Noting that DCRAC "recognizes a foolish fantasy when it is paraded in public," Rangan declared that "when DCRAC asked Capital One to dedicate $18 million a year (one one-hundredth of its annual pledged commitment) for . . . the lower-income and traditionally underserved communities in Delaware, their nice Delaware attorneys told Commissioner Glen that our request was 'not necessary or appropriate.'" DCRAC's opposition alone may not have carried much weight against the merger, except for the fact that it was affiliated with the National Community Reinvestment Coalition that represented broader economic interests.[16]

Required approval by the Federal Reserve of Capital One's planned acquisition of ING Direct was uncharacteristically delayed, probably because the Fed's phone lines were flooded by consumer groups urging the rejection of the merger. For example, the National Community Reinvestment Coalition (NCRC) claimed that the merger would create the nation's fifth largest bank—hence another "too-big-to-fail" financial entity.[17] The deal was the first that the Federal Reserve reviewed under a provision of the so-called Dodd-Frank Act of Congress. In a September 2011 letter to Federal Reserve Chairman Ben S. Bernanke and Treasury Secretary Timothy F. Geithner, the NCRC maintained that the ING deal threatened the goals of the Dodd-Frank

Act, the financial industry's reform law enacted in 2009 amid the credit crisis and the Great Recession. That act required the Federal Reserve to consider whether mergers would result in "greater or more concentrated" risks to the nation's financial system. The Federal Reserve Board in the end approved the deal by a 5–0 vote.[18]

Regardless of the Fed's decisive vote, its consent came with conditions. Citing complaints against Capital One, the Fed ordered the bank to revise its internal controls concerning lending and debt collection. The board stated that it "expects Capital One will ensure that its risk-management framework and methodologies, including its compliance functions, are commensurate with its new size and complexity." Far from rubber-stamping the merger, it appeared in retrospect that the board was extraordinarily deliberate in its first test of overseeing its implementation of the Dodd-Frank law, which explained its unusual step of delaying approval of the merger in order to hold three public hearings. In the hearings, Capital One had moved to thwart criticisms that the merger would create "a sub-prime giant," posing a possibility that taxpayers might have to bail it out. A column in the *New York Times* reviewing the board's deliberations concluded:

> Capital One used the hearings to defend its record. While Wall Street banks deal in derivatives and other risky businesses, Capital One said it focused on mom-and-pop consumers, leaving it immune to the volatility of the investment banking business.
> The Fed appeared to agree. In a forty-page order, the Fed detailed its standards for systemically risky acquisitions. The Fed analyzed the size and complexity of Capital One and ING Direct, the interconnectedness between the banks and the broader economy, and whether competitors could easily step in to replace the bank should it encounter "severe financial distress." The Fed also examined how difficult it would be to unwind the combined banks should they show signs of collapsing. "These measures suggest that Capital One would be significantly less complicated to resolve than the largest U.S. banks and investment banks," the Fed said.[19]

In short, the legacy of the financial crisis loomed over Capital One's plan to purchase ING Direct USA. In the end, however, the Fed remained unconvinced that the merger of two midsized banks would cause another Wall Street crisis. Soon after the Federal Reserve's approval of the merger, the company was renamed "Capital One 360."

In July 2013, it was revealed that Capital One Financial Corporation had informed DEDO that it had decided to reverse its acceptance of the state's September 2011 offer of a $7.12 million incentive grant to the bank—a surprising action to say the least. Indeed, one banking consultant said, "I am fairly confident that no one else has done that as a financial institution." And a former Capital One manager said he had never heard of a bank turning down a grant. In a letter to DEDO Director Alan Levin announcing this decision, a Capital One attorney was somewhat vague, merely stating: "Capital One remains firmly committed to meeting our hiring and growth goals in Delaware. At the same time, we have seen changes in our economic relationship as compared to initial projections for the state. Accordingly, recognizing our role as a strong corporate citizen of Delaware, Capital One will forgo the various tax and other incentives." Reactions to this development varied. Delaware State Banking Commissioner Robert A. Glen conjectured that Capital One determined that by not accepting the state's grant, it retained flexibility in how it managed its Delaware workforce. DEDO Director Levin said, "They reiterated their commitment to hire 500 people, and that was our only concern."[20]

AAA MID-ATLANTIC

As we stated in our preface, Delaware is a very small state with a limited number of public affairs research institutes common in more populous states. Fortunately, an insightful New Jersey study of how the American Automobile Association (AAA) Mid-Atlantic chose to locate its headquarters at One River Place on Wilmington's Riverfront in 2004 sheds light on the fierce competition in the subsidy game that involved the four neighboring states of New Jersey, Pennsylvania, Maryland, and Delaware. This particular 2006 study, authored by policy analyst Sarah Stecker, was a product of the Economic Development Accountability Project of New Jersey Policy Perspective (NJPP), a nonpartisan organization established in 1997 to conduct research on and analysis of state issues.[21]

From this study, one can learn that Philadelphia-based AAA Mid-Atlantic in 2004 had a net income of $26.2 million, employed 2,600 people, operated in five states—comprising Delaware, Maryland, Washington, DC, and parts of New Jersey, Pennsylvania, and Virginia—and offered services to its 3.5 million members including roadside assistance, rental and leased cars, insurance, and financial instruments such as certificates of deposit and mutual funds.

According to the NJPP study, AAA's decision to move its headquarters to Delaware was preceded by AAA board members, then living in Delaware, telling public officials that AAA Mid-Atlantic was considering leaving Philadelphia, where it had been headquartered since 1901. Accordingly, Delaware state officials, including Governor Ruth Ann Minner (2001–2009), first approached AAA about moving to Delaware. Delaware officials and business leaders then courted AAA, as follows:

> One major event in Delaware's courtship of AAA was a special dinner two
> months before the club announced its move. On November 13, 2003, the

Delaware Economic Development Office (DEDO) and the Committee of 100, a Delaware business organization, hosted a dinner for AAA executives at the Brantwyn estate of the DuPont Country Club. The purpose of the dinner was to convince AAA to pick Delaware over other states. According to DEDO, the dinner also provided AAA with an opportunity for high-level interaction with other executives in Delaware; more than two dozen Delaware business leaders attended the event. Eight public officials, led by Governor Minner, also attended the dinner.[22]

To attract AAA Mid-Atlantic, Delaware gave it a $6 million Strategic Fund grant for its headquarters, creating 340 jobs in Wilmington, and a call center creating 360 jobs near Newark. A total of $2.4 million of the grant was contingent upon AAA employing 750 workers in Delaware for ten years, with the remaining $3.6 million designated for construction, infrastructure, and relocation. In addition, the city of Wilmington gave AAA a job creation grant of $1 million plus a five- to seven-year waiver of a local services tax. AAA Mid-Atlantic signed a fifteen-year lease on a $28 million building, owned by Commonwealth Group, for its headquarters on the Wilmington Riverfront. As owner/builder and leaser of AAA's headquarters, Commonwealth received $140,000 from the state for cleaning up the site (a "brownfield"), and ten-year property tax exemptions from both the city of Wilmington and New Castle County.

With respect to the "timing of events" that led to Delaware's Strategic Fund grant, author Stecker raised "some important questions," as follows:

> AAA Mid-Atlantic applied to Delaware for a subsidy on January 8, 2004, yet only eight days later AAA announced it was moving to the state. It was not until February 23, 2004 that Delaware's Council on Development Finance (CDF) okayed the package at a public meeting. Was the decision to move made independent of the desire for tax breaks—meaning Delaware taxpayers paid for something they might have gotten for free? Would AAA receive subsidies regardless of the contents of its applications or what might transpire at a public meeting?[23]

Without recounting details, policy analyst Stecker's account of the competition between Delaware and its neighboring states—which Delaware "won" by adding a net of seven hundred jobs by virtue of "AAA's moves"—tells us that Pennsylvania lost 554 jobs and Maryland lost four hundred jobs, whereas New Jersey gained a net of only eighty-four jobs.[24] But it is apparent from Stecker's study that she was clearly frustrated in obtaining information she sought because of the pervasiveness of secrecy she encountered, as her following comments reveal:

> This lack of information creates problems in evaluating how public money is spent, whether taxpayers are receiving good value and how corporate deci-

sions to relocate are really made. It is difficult to follow the decision-making process of a business engaged in the interstate tax break game when neither the businesses nor public officials involved in the negotiation will name the dollar value of the incentives. There is no way to answer questions such as whether the business moved to where it got the biggest incentive offer, or to what extent it might have played states against each other. This situation is repeated over and over again in multi-state business tax break negotiations in the region and around the country. . . .

Money is at the heart of the interstate tax break game. How much will state and local governments give out? How big are the offers businesses can round up? But the money is public money. So, the public should have ready access to tax break information—both on businesses that get tax breaks and on the process used to award these tax breaks. It is impossible to have an informed public debate about how taxpayer money is spent without available information. But often, such information is hard to get if it can be gotten at all. . . . The state of Delaware does not make information on the structure of its business tax break programs readily accessible, either online or by contacting Delaware directly. Delaware gave AAA subsidies from its Strategic Fund—what the state describes as its primary funding source for economic development projects. But the guidelines for awarding these subsidies, the subsidy application and information about the state board that approves or turns down subsidies are not available on the state's website. . . .

Not surprisingly, subsidized businesses are even less open with information than government officials. Despite AAA getting $8.1 million in state and local business tax breaks funded by public money in two states—this organization [CDF] will not give the public basic information about itself. . . .

On questions about its employees, AAA is close-mouthed with information up and down the pay scale. . . . Nor would it update the number of jobs at its headquarters. The State of Delaware also declined to provide wage information from AAA's subsidy application about jobs at the AAA headquarters. . . . A Delaware official wrote that the wage information is confidential financial data of AAA Mid-Atlantic and therefore cannot be given to the public.

Nor would AAA spokeswomen in New Jersey and Delaware provide updated job numbers for AAA operations in the two states. When asked how many jobs had moved from New Jersey to Delaware, a AAA New Jersey spokeswoman said to call AAA's Delaware headquarters. But the AAA Delaware spokeswoman said she couldn't give the number.[25]

Stecker concluded her study by remarking that it described "just one sliver" of everyday activities throughout the nation in the name of job creation and advancing good business: "With AAA Mid-Atlantic, New Jersey and other states in the region competed for an entity that moved its existing jobs from place to place without expanding its operations—and got paid to do it. While Delaware gave out the most money in this instance, the taxpayers from New Jersey or any other state could be in that position in the next round of this zero-sum game."[26]

THE HOTEL CONTROVERSY

Regardless of the recession, development of the riverfront appeared a great success in 2012. Overseen by RDC, a former polluted industrial wasteland had been transformed into a destination enjoyed by people of all ages. New features included a unique Christina River Walk adjacent to the Delaware Theatre Company, Frawley baseball stadium, restaurants, parkland, townhouses, condominiums, high-rise apartments, museums, a wildlife refuge, the Riverfront Market, several shops, and banks including Capital One 360, AAA Mid-Atlantic, and the Chase Center.

Construction of the Chase Center began in 1998. Originally a Dravo shipbuilding warehouse, it was transformed into an upscale exhibit center and banquet facility, and it notably expanded into a convention center and a multipurpose event facility. In December 2011, RDC sought funding to build a $36 million, 180-room Westin Hotel connected by a corridor to the Chase Center. Developing the riverfront had never been easy. RDC had always fought for needed support. Backed by the Buccini-Pollin Group (BPG)—the riverfront's longtime, foremost private developer—RDC's Executive Director Michael Purzycki proposed that the city of Wilmington provide $1 million, and the state of Delaware provide $2 million, of a total of $6 million needed in loan guarantees for BPG to secure a bank loan for the construction of the Westin.

After the plans became known, some hotel operators, industry experts, taxpayers, and lawmakers raised concerns. Members of the Delaware Hotel & Lodging Association wanted the same opportunity to receive public money. Wilmington's lame-duck mayor, James Baker, retorted: "So all you hotel owners just shut up." That remark, said an editorial, did Wilmington "a disservice."[27] Questions were also raised as to whether funding was within the scope of the state's recently created Infrastructure Fund. DEDO Director Alan Levin said that the hotel project did not "fit" Delaware's Strategic Fund. John H. Taylor, senior vice president of the Delaware State Chamber of Commerce and former editor of the Wilmington *News Journal*, referred to the hotel as "a no-brainer." He wrote: "The Buccini-Pollin group has done so much to develop downtown Wilmington and the riverfront area that both the state and city governments should be falling all over themselves to be the first in line to guarantee these loans."[28]

In a hearing before the General Assembly's Bond Bill Committee, RDC Director Purzycki said, "To my mind, it's the single most important project to occur on the Riverfront. Yet, for a variety of reasons, I think it's the single most misunderstood project in the Riverfront's history." Referring to developer BPG's quest for loan guarantees, Purzycki added, "This is not a publicly funded project. It never has been. What we have today is, we're asking the state and city for a little support for this private developer to finish this project."[29]

State lawmakers of both parties voiced their skepticism. For example, Senate Minority Leader Republican Gary Simpson said, "If it was a great deal, there wouldn't be any trouble getting financing through the traditional method." Democratic Representative John Kowalko added, "I don't know that I want to risk taxpayer money or the good rating of the state on that kind of venture."[30]

In the end, the state government refused to risk its support of a loan guarantee to help BPG developers finance the proposed hotel. According to Alan Levin, "The request for a letter of credit issued by the state is still a pledging of our assets. It's a pledge that requires the full faith and credit of the state. This is not something that this administration does, nor has done, for this type of venture, nor would we." Republican leader Representative Greg Lavelle approved, saying: "The state of Delaware is not a bank."[31] A *News Journal* editorial also agreed. It stated, "States are involved in economic development these days. . . . But the projects need to have a set of guarantees, often called 'claw-backs,' that return money to the state if the project is not completed, a number of workers are not hired or is canceled. There is still some risk involved, but the risk is tempered."[32]

Although the editorial seemed to signal the newspaper's approval of the state's denial of direct state aid for the hotel, a five-page "special investigation" appeared a week later with the banner headline "HOW DEALS GET DONE: Behind-the Scenes Negotiations for State Support of a Riverfront Hotel Shielded from Public Scrutiny—Until Now." The story purported to be grounded on documents acquired under the state's Freedom of Information Act, including more than one hundred emails that offered "behind-the scenes negotiations on behalf of a developer who has been a reliable contributor to city and state political campaigns." According to the story, "The newspaper has uncovered deals so tangled and opaque that even some of the officials who worked on the transactions struggled to provide complete explanations." Although the story was replete with negative and/or sinister wording (such as "fairness," "lack of transparency," "deals," "sudden about-face," "an uneven playing field," "more public disclosure," "political clout," "secrecy," "string-pulling," "shortcomings," "openness"), a different if unintended appraisal of the story is equally plausible. Such an appraisal reveals quoted emails and other exchanges among Michael S. Purzycky, Levin, Secretary of State Jeffrey W. Bullock, Governor Markell, BGP, city officials, and others that show that the issues involved were fully vetted by well-intentioned personages who were honestly doing their respective jobs without rancor or prejudice.[33]

In the midst of all this, the RDC fought and lost a legislative battle to retain the ability to use eminent domain as an economic development tool—seemingly a devastating blow. On May 18, 2012, within two weeks of the

Markell administration's decision to rule out the state's participation in providing direct financial aid for the Westin Hotel, the RDC approved a $9 million package of financial guarantees and land concessions that enabled BPG developers to obtain a commercial bank loan. The city of Wilmington contributed $1 million as part of the security package, but the Markell administration was finally off the hook. At the same time, RDC officials authorized the purchase and resale of the Delaware Department of Transportation (DelDOT) land needed for a nearby fifteen-screen cinema complex. Shortly thereafter, ground was broken for the construction of both BPG's hotel and cinema projects.[34]

As construction progressed on the new $37 million Westin Hotel, the hotel industry overall in Delaware continued to struggle. A longtime hotel in downtown Wilmington had been bought at a sheriff's sale in late 2011 by the Delaware College of Art and Design for student housing. In 2012, a Dover hotel company filed for bankruptcy, citing the opening of a new hotel at the Dover Air Force Base by the U.S. government, the nation's laggard economy, and overall competition. Hotel occupancy rates in the state remained flat in late 2012 at about 55 percent, when a minimum of about 60 percent occupancy appeared needed to be profitable. Room rates had still not recovered to 2006–2007 levels. RDC and state leaders, however, continued to support construction of the new Westin Hotel at the riverfront. Governor Markell considered it a "game changer," but was pleased the developers found a way to finance the project without direct state aid.[35]

CONCLUSION

Many economists consider winners and losers as intrinsic to the phenomenon of economic development. Whereas Capital One became a winner by purchasing the very successful ING Direct USA, and continued to be a winner by virtue of the Fed's decision that it was not "too big to fail," DCRAC on the other hand was a loser by failing to receive its sought-after $18 million from Capital One. And whereas Delaware became a winner by attracting AAA Mid-Atlantic to the riverfront, Pennsylvania and New Jersey were losers. Once the recession was under way, fiscal conservatives became winners in the sense that they were able to delay construction of a riverfront hotel—first proposed in 1992—until its construction began in 2012, when other area hotel leaders considered themselves thereby to be losers. When winners win more than losers lose, then economic development may be considered positive.

In assessing the development of the Wilmington Riverfront, it is important to emphasize its relationship to the economic development of Wilmington and the state of Delaware. In this respect, the factor of timing was undeniably significant. We noted that Condliffe's projection of the riverfront's development in retrospect proved to have been too optimistic in light of the onset of the recession. The recession, however, spawned the influence of economic "stimulus" moves. Ultimately, supporters of the economic development of Wilmington's Riverfront might claim to have been overall "winners," but public opinion has yet to decide that benefits have surpassed costs.

The 180-room Riverfront Westin Hotel opened in March 2014, and the $20 million thirteen-theater Penn Cinema Riverfront IMAX was up and running after December 2012. Besides the IMAX theater, riverfront developers could boast about the minor-league Blue Rocks' Frawley baseball stadium, the DuPont Environmental Education Center, the Delaware Theater Company, the Chase Center, Capital One 360, AAA Mid-Atlantic, other large and small businesses, various restaurants and shops, upscale condominiums and apartments, and river walkways.

There was even some buzz that the riverfront was on the cusp of becoming a "tourist mecca." One out-of-state visitor said in mid-2013, "Having been here years ago, when there wasn't much but dirt and some industry—seeing what it is now—it's a great revitalization of the waterfront."[36] However, nobody yet was touting Wilmington's riverfront as competing with Baltimore's Inner Harbor. After all, Wilmington was no Baltimore. Still, Baltimore's Inner Harbor remained an inspiration if not a model for Wilmington's riverfront. It was doubtful, however, that without substantial infusion of taxpayer money, the transformation of the riverfront would ever have happened.

While the riverfront became an economic development story, it was still an extremely compelling example of brownfield redevelopment. The economic benefits would have been difficult to realize without the tremendous remediation work required, and the partnership between the riverfront businesses, contractors, and state and city governments. This synergy produced amazing results, which aided the city of Wilmington financially and benefited the people of Delaware, who gained a new place to work as well as a place to play. Undoubtedly, there would be many more benefits to riverfront development in the future.

NOTES

1. Maureen Milford and Jeff Montgomery, "Development Projects Grew from Base of Tangled Deals," Wilmington *News Journal*, May 13, 2012, A6, A7. For a pictorial history of Wilmington's riverfront prior to World War II, see also Priscilla M. Thompson and Sally O'Byrne, *Images of America: Wilmington's Waterfront* (Charleston, SC: Arcadia Publishing, 1999).

2. See *A Vision for the Rivers: The Final Report of the Governor's Task Force on the Future of the Brandywine and Christina Rivers* (Dover: Department of Natural Resources and Environmental Control, October 11, 1994).

3. Ibid., 13.

4. See the "Bond Bill," Chapter 210, Vol. 70, formerly Senate Bill 260, passed June 30, 1995, for the fiscal year ending June 30, 1996, at pp. 535–36, delcode.delaware.gov/session-laws/ga138/chp210.shtml#TopOfPage (accessed May 15, 2012).

5. Simon Condliffe, *The Fiscal and Economic Impact of the Wilmington Riverfront* (Newark: Center for Applied Demography and Survey Research, University of Delaware, April 2007), 1.

6. Ibid., 3, 26, 31–32.

7. Daniel Brown, *The Fiscal Impact of the Wilmington Riverfront* (Newark: Center for Applied Demography and Survey Research, University of Delaware, April 2012), xviii, 5.

8. See ibid., 19, and his quote on page 21 of Patricia Blevins and Roger Roy, citing "Riverfront Will Progress Past Today's Setbacks," Wilmington *News Journal*, June 3, 2002, A9.

9. Brown, *The Fiscal Impact of the Wilmington Riverfront*, 26, 55.

10. See www.ing.com (accessed July 15, 2015).

11. David McMillin, "ING Direct," Bankrate.com, updated August 17, 2012, www.bankrate.com/finance/businesses/i/ing-direct.aspx (accessed May 6, 2013).

12. See "Capital One," www.capitalone.com/about (accessed July 15, 2015).

13. See "HSBC," www.us.hsbc.com/1/2/home/about/corporate (accessed July 15, 2015).

14. Aaron Nathans, "Capital One to Bring 500 Jobs," Wilmington *News Journal*, September 27, 2011, A1, A2.

15. See notables' statements quoted in Doug Rainey, "Capital One to Add 500 Jobs in Delaware," *Newark Post*, September 30, 2011, 1, 2.

16. Rashmi Rangan and James Angus, "Shame on Us for Believing Capital One's Empty Promises," Wilmington *News Journal*, February 3, 2012, A15. For other criticisms of Capital One's merger with ING Direct, see, for example, Tom Feltner, "Capital One Application to Acquire ING Direct, CRA and Systemic Risk Concerns and Recommendations," *Woodstock Institute*, September 2011.

17. Aaron Nathans, "Sale of ING Direct Delayed Again," Wilmington *News Journal*, February 14, 2012, A7.

18. Doug Williams and Ira Porter, "ING Merger Approved," Wilmington *News Journal*, February 15, 2012.

19. Ben Protess, "In Test of New Powers, Bank Merger Approved," *New York Times*, February 15, 2012, B3.

20. Wade Malcolm, "Cap One Declines State Incentive," Wilmington *News Journal*, July 30, 2013, A1, A5.

21. Sarah Stecker, *Mapping the Route to Dollars: AAA Mid-Atlantic's Four-State Tour* (Trenton, NJ: New Jersey Policy Perspective, July 2006).

22. Ibid., 7.

23. Ibid., 4.

24. Ibid., 3.

25. Ibid., 6, 9–10.

26. Ibid., 10.

27. Editorial, "Baker's 'Shut Up' Does Wilmington a Disservice," Wilmington *News Journal*, April 28, 2012, A8.

28. John H. Taylor, Jr., "Government Support for Riverfront Hotel is a No-brainer," Wilmington *News Journal*, January 26, 2012, A11. See also Maureen Milford and Jeff Montgomery, "City Asked for $1 Million Loan Guarantee," ibid., January 11, 2012, A1, A2; and Maureen Milford, "Troubled Hotel Firm Has $1 Million in Debts," ibid., February 17, 2012, B1, B2.

29. Jeff Montgomery, "Official Seeks $5M in Loan Guarantees for Hotel," Wilmington *News Journal*, February 28, 2012, A1, A2.

30. Jeff Montgomery and Maureen Milford, "Lawmakers Balking at Subsidies for Hotel," Wilmington *News Journal*, March 5, 2012, A1, A4.

31. Jeff Montgomery and Maureen Milford, "State Denies Money for Hotel," Wilmington *News Journal*, May 5, 2012, A1, A5.

32. Editorial, "Too Much Asked of the State in Hotel Proposal," Wilmington *News Journal*, May 6, 2012, A28.

33. See Maureen Milford and Jeff Montgomery, "How Deals Get Done." Wilmington *News Journal*, May 13, 2012, A1, A3, A7, A9.

34. Jeff Montgomery and Maureen Milford, "Hotel, Theater Deals OK'd," Wilmington *News Journal*, May 19, 2012, A1, A5. For more news about the cinema project, see Maureen Milford and Jeff Montgomery, "The Deal that Brought Back the Queen," ibid., May 14, 2012, A1, A8; Maureen Milford and Sean O'Sullivan, "Lawsuit May Derail Riverfront Cinema," ibid., July 14, 2012, A1, A2; Sean O'Sullivan, "Agreement Gets Cinema Work Back on Track," ibid., July 31, 2012, A1, A5; and Maureen Milford, "Railroad Files Suit on Land Concern," ibid., August 22, 2012, A1, A2.

35. Maureen Milford, "Struggle Continues in Quest for Guests," Wilmington *News Journal*, December 25, 2012, A1, A9.

36. Ryan Marshall, "At Awe with 'Tourist Mecca,'" Wilmington *News Journal*, May 6, 2013, B1, B2.

Chapter Four

Fisker Automotive

Beginning in the mid-twentieth century, the assembly of automobiles in Delaware comprised an industry that for sixty years was Delaware's second largest private employer, behind the DuPont Corporation. The General Motors (GM) Boxwood auto assembly plant opened in 1947 in Newport, Delaware. It closed during the Great Recession in the week of July 27, 2009, with 545 workers losing their jobs, down from a high of over 5,000 employees in 1986. The Chrysler plant opened in 1952 and peaked at 5,600 employees. When it closed its mammoth assembly plant in Newark, on December 19, 2008, the remaining more than 1,100 employees lost their jobs. [1]

Meanwhile, employment dropped during the recession in many other sectors of Delaware's economy. Accelerating job losses in such a small state were felt severely. Highest on incoming Governor Jack Markell's proactive agenda in 2009 was adding jobs by attracting, and keeping, employers. The prospect of attracting Fisker Automotive became a major focus of the Markell administration's Delaware Economic Development Office (DEDO).

ATTRACTING FISKER

Fisker Automotive was founded in August 2007 by Henrik Fisker and Bernhard Koehler in Irvine, California. Both Mr. Fisker and Mr. Koehler had worked for BMW in Munich. Later they worked for Ford in California. Fisker became director of Ford's Global Advanced Design Studio, and Koehler became his director of Business and Operations. The Fisker Karma was produced in Finland and made its appearance in Detroit in 2008. The Karma was an all-electric, plug-in, hybrid vehicle driven by two electric motors powered from a lithium-ion battery. Designed for the luxury car market, the Karma was first sold in the United States for $95,000 for the basic model, and $109,850 for the top model. In December 2011, these prices were raised to $102,000 and $116,000, respectively.[2]

Based in Anaheim, California, Fisker Automotive sought to build the Karma entirely in the United States, along with other electric plug-in hybrid vehicles. On September 18, 2009, Fisker Automotive received a conditional commitment for a $528.66 million loan from the U.S. Department of Energy (DOE). This total was divided into two parts: $169.3 million to complete work on the Karma in Pontiac, Michigan, and Irvine, California, and $359.36 million to support the so-called Project NINA design and production of Fisker's other electric plug-in hybrid vehicles. Of the number of DOE conditions precedent to its initial advancement of part of its loan to Fisker, foremost was the necessity for Fisker to acquire a U.S. site for production of its electric plug-in hybrid vehicles.

In March 2009, Governor Jack Markell had already introduced the Delaware Clean Energy Jobs Act that the General Assembly passed and the governor signed into law in July 2010. The act was aimed both at reducing the need for fossil fuels, by increasing previously established Renewable Portfolio Standards (RPS), whereby 25 percent of energy purchases would be derived from renewable sources by 2025, as well as adding thousands of clean energy jobs.[3] Attracting Fisker Automotive to establish its manufacturing headquarters in Delaware could be considered a major step in this direction. However, Delaware was competing with larger states—especially with California and Michigan—to provide the location for Fisker's NINA economic development project. When GM announced that it would close its Delaware plant, it also announced that it would close thirteen GM plants in other states. As a result of the recession, therefore, a number of idled or closed auto assembly plants were in populous states, with much larger tax bases, capable of offering greater incentive packages, than little Delaware.

Governor Markell had asked GM to leave equipment in place at the Delaware plant to help the state to attract another potential tenant. On August 24, 2009, Henrik Fisker and Bernhard Koehler visited Delaware with representatives of Motors Liquidation to look at the former GM plant. On September 1, Vice President and former Delaware U.S. Senator Joe Biden phoned Henrik Fisker to discuss Fisker's interest. Given assurances and a tentative offer of state incentives by the Markell administration, plus New Castle County's offer to abate the company's property taxes for five years, Fisker Automotive made it official. With government officials and hundreds of auto workers present, Fisker announced on October 27, 2009, his company's decision to purchase GM's former Boxwood plant for $18 million, thus meeting the first condition for qualifying for the federal DOE loan.[4]

On March 11, 2010, Bernhard Koehler signed for Fisker a DEDO "Delaware Strategic Fund Loan and Grant Application," submitted with a required check in the amount of $250.00. In the first space of the application form, the applicant is required to provide a detailed description of its project. Fisker's application stated the following:

> Fisker Automotive has selected the Wilmington Assembly Plant in Wilmington, DE to build affordable PHEVs to support its project NINA. Production is scheduled to begin in 2012. Fisker anticipates Project NINA to create/support 2000 factory jobs in Delaware and more than 3000 vendor and supplier jobs. Production vehicles will ramp up to 75,000–100,000 vehicles per year and >50 percent is to be exported. [5]

In an April 2010 memo to DEDO's advisory board—the Delaware's Council on Development Finance—DEDO Director Alan B. Levin formally proposed that DEDO offer Fisker the same amount as Fisker requested in its application, namely a total of $21.5 million, including a $12.5 million loan from the Delaware Strategic Fund, for the renovation of the Boxwood plant. The loan would be convertible to a grant provided the company reached its employment projections. Levin also proposed that DEDO honor Fisker's request for a $9 million Strategic Fund grant to offset utility costs in renovating the plant prior to vehicle production. According to Levin,

> The public announcement was one of the largest recruitment projects to come to Delaware, with the expectation of Fisker directly creating a combination of 1,495 production, engineering and managerial jobs at the idled plant. Fisker is expecting to create an additional 1,000 jobs from suppliers which will make the total Delaware workforce as a result of the project to be 2,495 jobs. Fisker is expecting to produce approximately 100,000 vehicles a year once production commences while the 3.2 million square foot Boxwood plant is capable of producing 300,000 vehicles a year. . . . It's expected that over 50 percent of the Fisker vehicles produced in Delaware will be exported, with most of them shipped to Europe where orders are already in place. The Port of Wilmington will play a very active role in the exporting of the vehicles as the basic infrastructure is already in place. [6]

Levin's memo concluded with the somewhat ebullient supporting recommendation by DEDO's staff, as follows:

> Fisker holds tremendous potential to rebuild the State of Delaware's automotive production industry and the necessary network of local suppliers. The proposed financing will assist Fisker in upgrading a facility that will produce world-class, fuel-efficient electric hybrid vehicles and indirectly supporting 1,495 factory and nearly 3,000 vendor and supplier jobs. Fisker's ability to raise $100 million in private equity in a recently sluggish venture capital environment and close to $528.66 million loan from DOE speaks to the promise the company holds and the quality of its leadership. Staff favorably recommends that the Council move to approve the proposed DEDO financing. [7]

It appeared a foregone conclusion that Fisker Automotive—armed with the DOE loan, its acquisition of the Boxwood plant, DEDO's backing for its Strategic Fund loan and grant, and its projection of over five thousand new Delaware jobs—could be certain that Delaware's General Assembly would do its part. This the compliant legislature did by unanimous enactment on June 30, 2010, of the fiscal year 2011 Bond Bill.[8]

ONGOING PROBLEMS WITH KARMA

As fiscal year 2011 was under way, Fisker announced on October 19, 2011, that it already had 120 workers at the Newport-area site, including contractors, and electrical and mechanical workers, engaged in refurbishing the former GM plant to build its second-line hybrid Nina. But an unpublicized glitch of sorts emerged, whereby company executives said production would not begin in 2012 as had been stated in its Strategic Fund application, but would be delayed a year until 2013.[9]

Two months later, in late December 2011, Fisker recalled 239 of its first-line Karma luxury sedans because of issues with its battery compartments in which misaligned hose clamps could cause coolant leaks, leading to a possible fire. Electric car analyst John Gardiner commented, "It's certainly not good for their company in their initial outing of the vehicle to have something come up so quickly. It's a little surprising that it's happening now and it wasn't caught before the vehicle was released."[10]

Within a week, Fisker spokesman Roger Ormisher assured Delawareans that the company's recall of the Karma would not delay production of its new hybrid electric car at its refitted former GM plant. "We're still on track," Ormisher said. DEDO Director Levin said, "They will survive this and will move forward." U.S. Senator Tom Carper rejoined, "This is a hiccup, not a heart attack."[11]

Nevertheless, it became known on February 7, 2012, that Fisker halted work and laid off twenty-six of its remaining workers at its Delaware plant because of a "cash crunch." The move resulted from DOE's decision not to release more money from its loan to Fisker because of the company's failure to meet DOE conditions. Ormisher stated that the loan conditions were confidential. He added that the company had received only $193 million of the $529 million DOE loan, mostly for the Karma, and that was in May 2011. "We can't keep going and going and going without that money," Ormisher said.[12]

Regardless of assurances to the contrary, it now became the perception of many Delawareans that Fisker was putting all of its eggs in its first-line Karma basket. A front-page banner headline in the Wilmington *News Journal* of February 13, 2012, posed the question, "CAN FISKER KEEP ITS

PROMISE?" The article noted that the first part of the federal DOE loan gave Fisker $193 million to develop its Karma luxury sedan. The second installment of $336 million was intended to support the development of its second-line Nina in Delaware. But that had been held up by the DOE because Fisker failed to meet certain undisclosed goals for the Karma. Fisker's response was to negotiate with the DOE to release the second part of the loan. The release did not happen because, as the article emphasized, politics entered the fray. The article recounted:

> That request has run head-on into the upcoming presidential election and the combat zone of partisan politics in the nation's capital, where the role of the federal government in aiding businesses with loans, subsidies or preferential tax status remains a red-hot issue. . . . President Barack Obama's administration faces increased scrutiny of any government aid targeted at creating so-called "green jobs" in the wake of the September bankruptcy of Solyndra, a solar-panel manufacturer that left taxpayers on the hook for a $535 million loan. . . . As the November general election nears, congressional Republicans have used Fisker's Karma hybrid as a weapon against Obama and Vice President Joe Biden. It also has drawn fire on the presidential stump in Iowa and New Hampshire.[13]

Two Republican, U.S. senators fired off a letter dated April 20, 2012, to the U.S. Department of Energy questioning why its loan was extended to this "troubled" auto company in the first place. Senators Charles Grassley of Iowa and John Thune of South Dakota asked in their letter what "technical expertise" the DOE used to evaluate the loan and how its estimates of job creation were determined. Their letter also asserted that "it would seem questionable how financing $100,000 luxury class automobiles would be the best use of taxpayer money."[14] DOE's response one month later was a three-page letter by David G. Frantz, acting director of the Department's Loan Programs Office. Frantz defended the Fisker loan by saying the department's review "was extensive—with rigorous financial, technical, legal and market analysis conducted over many months by DOE's internal professional staff, including qualified engineers and financial experts, and outside experts." But the DOE response did not satisfy the two senators. Senator Thune called it "evasive at best." Thune stated: "After promising to be the most open and transparent administration in history, it's unfortunate that with millions of taxpayer dollars at stake the Obama administration will not answer our specific questions."[15]

Within Delaware, politics also became a factor prior to the November 2012 election. Former U.S. Senator House Speaker Newt Gingrich, while visiting Vice President Joe Biden's home state of Delaware in April, took a shot at Biden by saying: "if the vice president can't deliver a little renegotiation for his own state, what's the point of having him?"[16] Moreover, Delaware's Republican candidate for governor, Jeff Cragg, challenged incumbent Democrat Governor Jack Markell, by claiming in July that government-funded jobs for Fisker "went to Finland. That's called outsourcing and it's especially galling when we take tax dollars . . . and we give them to private businesses to create jobs overseas." Markell's campaign spokesman, Jonathan Kott, responded that Republicans' criticisms of Markell were an attack on Delaware autoworkers. Kott said, "Even though Mitt Romney quit on American auto workers and Jeff Cragg is willing to quit on Delaware auto workers, Jack Markell and President Obama won't."[17]

It appeared that a March 17, 2012, *News Journal* editorial's earnest plea, "Let's try to do the impossible. Let's try to keep politics out of the discussion," was being ignored. The editorial continued: "So is Fisker a failure? Let's be realistic. No, not by a long shot. . . . The best bet is to follow the plan and regulations already in place. Fisker officials believe they will be able to meet the prescribed benchmarks. . . . What we shouldn't do is seize the moment for political opportunism."[18] One month later, an editorial in the same newspaper lamented the "sequence of recent company problems" that called for state officials to "step up monitoring of the Finland-based company's manufacturing problems."[19]

Why were these two successive editorials so different in tone? Two basic reasons for the difference were the interventions of the embarrassing performance of the Karma, followed by Fisker's management shake-up, to which we now turn.

KARMA'S EMBARRASSING PERFORMANCE

The distinctive feature of the Karma luxury sedan was its primary power source, namely its lithium-ion phosphate battery, along with a small internal combustion engine. The fact that Fisker had to recall all Karmas in late December of 2011 to replace the battery's coolant clamp was thereby a major setback for the company. It was feared that a leak of the coolant could have caused a short and possible battery pack fire. Accordingly, subsequent problems with the battery could be considered a near-disaster. But then the magazine *Consumer Reports* tried to test the Karma in March 2012.

Consumer Reports purchased a new $107,850 Karma sedan to test, only to find that the vehicle shut down even before the magazine could begin testing it. In its March 8 *Consumer Reports* issue, the magazine lamented: "We buy about 80 cars a year and this is the first time in memory that we have had a car that is undriveable before it finished our check-in process. It is super sleek, high-tech—and now it is broken."[20]

In response to the failure, Fisker later traced the problem to a fault in the battery pack. Fisker decided that the batteries in all 2012 Karma models had to be replaced free of charge. This was even worse news for the battery manufacturer—A123 Systems—for whom it would cost millions to replace the batteries. Shares of A123 Systems tumbled after the news was announced. Analyst Theodore O'Neill said that the replacement process was very expensive because each battery contained more than three hundred cells. Should just one cell be defective, according to O'Neill, the entire battery pack could be ruined. Thus, A123 Systems would have to replace a wide swath of batteries.[21]

The next incident of bad publicity for Fisker came in mid-May 2012 from Sugar Land, Texas, where an investigator from a county fire marshal's office linked a house fire directly to a Karma parked inside a garage. Fisker denied that the Karma's battery was a factor. "We are very confident that was not the source," Fisker spokesman Roger Ormisher said. "And the car was not plugged in. . . . There were three cars in the garage. The garage had a lot of combustible materials in it."[22] Regardless of Fisker's denial, it was reported on June 3, 2012, that Fisker Automotive was expanding its previous December's recall of the Karma "because of potential problems with the electric car's battery."[23]

Still another Karma fire was posted on the Internet on August 12, 2012, according to the following story:

> Similar to an incident last spring that left a model burnt to near smithereens and damaged its owner's house, the Karma . . . caught fire in a Woodside, CA parking lot while powered off. . . . As the story goes, the owner found the vehicle emitting smoke after returning from a grocery run, prompting a call to Fisker and then the local fire department, which arrived as it was already engulfed in flames. In a statement . . . Fisker has been vehement to note that the damage appears to be far from where the car's battery and sensitive electrical components are located. . . . All that said, it remains to be seen whether Karma's battery system, supplied by A123 Systems . . . had any role in igniting the car.[24]

As it turned out, the battery was not the cause of the fire in Woodside, California. An independent investigation determined it was a faulty cooling fan near the left front wheel that was to blame. Although the fan was not manufactured by Fisker, the incident caused the company to recall all 2,400 Karmas.[25]

In a leaked letter that Fisker sent to Karma owners, the company revealed still other apparent issues it was attempting to address. Among the issues were the day/night visibility of the control panel, slow boot-up of the computer-driven command center, the gas engine turning on when it shouldn't, side-view mirrors that would not deploy, and operation of the navigation system's voice that would not shut off.[26] With regard to the navigation system, *Jalopnik* posed this "fascinating philosophical question" on the Internet:

"Is it better to have no nav system at all, or a nav system where you can never stop the damn robot lady from asking you to make a U-Turn every 500 feet?"[27]

FISKER'S MANAGEMENT SHAKEUP

In mid-December 2011, Fisker Automotive announced the appointment of Tom LaSorda as its board vice chairman and strategic advisor to report directly to the company's chief executives including co-founders Chief Executive Officer (CEO) Henrik Fisker and Chief Operations Officer (COO) Bernhard Koehler. LaSorda was a recent past president of Chrysler and a longtime officer at General Motors. In his role at Fisker Automotive, LaSorda was expected to help guide the company's transformation from a start-up to a high-volume global manufacturer.[28]

Ten weeks later, in a major management shakeup, Tom LaSorda was named the company's top executive, replacing founder and company namesake Henrik Fisker as CEO. LaSorda promptly announced that it was no longer known when production of the second-line hybrid-electric sedans would begin in Delaware, thus dashing previous plans. Since payments on the DOE loan had been suspended, production in Delaware would depend on securing "alternate sources of financing," he explained. But he added that he "would never have taken the job if I didn't think the future of this company was bright."[29]

The company's top management shakeup continued in July 2012 when LaSorda replaced Fisker's incumbent chief financial officer with James Yost, who had thirty years of experience in the auto industry. This move was quickly followed by reassigning co-founder Bernhard Koehler from his post of chief operations officer to the new position of chief business development officer. Thus, since LaSorda came aboard, the company's two co-founders and top officers—Fisker and Koehler—had been effectively relegated to secondary background roles.[30]

The most jarring management change was yet to come: namely, the departure of LaSorda himself on August 14, 2012—in less than six months after he took over the helm of the company. Named to replace him as the new CEO was Tony Posawatz. LaSorda's departure was somewhat of a mystery, despite his assurances that he had always planned his tenure at Fisker to be on an interim basis until permanent leadership could be found. Senior analyst Aaron Bragman said that was news to him, and that losing LaSorda was "a blow to the company" that "was never billed as a temporary arrangement." On the positive side, Posawatz had successful experience developing Chevrolet's plug-in hybrid Volt at GM from its inception until it was brought to market in record time.[31]

Whether Posawatz's appointment as CEO was just the latest of the top management changes had yet to be determined. What was certain, however, was that Fisker's round of musical chairs, together with its murky past, could only stir the growing angst of Delawareans.

FISKER'S COMPETITORS

Americans had been slow to buy electric cars. But sales of GM's Chevrolet Volt plug-in hybrid compact car showed that Americans were willing to buy the Volt if prices were low enough. The Volt had been rated by the Environmental Protection Agency as the most fuel-efficient compact car with a gasoline engine sold in the United States. Moreover, it had won numerous awards, including the 2011 North American Car of the Year and the 2012 European Car of the Year. When a model of the Chevrolet Volt was first introduced in January 2007 at the North American International Auto Show, it became the first plug-in hybrid concept car ever shown by a major car manufacturer. Since sales of Volts began in December 2010, a total of 21,494 Volts had been sold in the United States through August of 2012.[32]

Sales of the Volt rose sharply in 2012 mostly because of GM discounts from a sticker price of $40,000 that reduced the cost to $30,000. On August 23, 2012, however, these caveats were reported:

Even so, electrics have a long way to go before they enter the mainstream and make money for car companies. Electrics and gas-electric hybrids account for 3.5 percent of US auto sales this year. GM is losing thousands of dollars on every Volt, raising the question of how long it can keep eating the steep losses.

For the foreseeable futures, carmakers will have to cut prices to move electric vehicles off dealer lots. The nonpartisan Congressional Budget Office says the cost of electric cars must drop to be competitive with gasoline-powered ones.

GM executives have conceded from the start that they were losing money on the Volt, and that was before the big discounts.

Now the losses could be even higher. It costs $60,000 to $75,000 to build a Volt, including development, manufacturing and raw materials. . . .

Much of the cost comes from an expensive combination of two power systems—electric and gasoline. With a sticker price of $40,000, minus the $10,000 the company pays in incentives, GM gets roughly $30,000 for every Volt. So it could be losing at least $30,000 per car. . . .

GM says the Volt has helped the company, even if it never makes a dime. The car has pulled in customers from rival brands, and helped Chevy wrestle at least part of the environmental halo from Toyota Prius. . . .

"Its prime purpose was to introduce a new generation of technology," says Lutz, the former [GM] vice chairman. "And at the same time . . . demonstrate to the world that GM is way more technologically capable than the people give it credit for."[33]

Fisker's Karma luxury sedan's chief rival, however, had not been the Volt, but rather the Tesla Roadster produced by Silicon Valley's Tesla Motors Inc. that, since 2008, had sold more than 2,250 Roadsters in thirty-one countries through March 2012. The Tesla Roadster was the first electric vehicle to use lithium-ion battery cells and had a base price of $109,000, roughly the price of the Karma. Indeed, it was the Roadster that inspired GM in 2007 to develop the Chevrolet Volt. In the August 2009 issue of *The New Yorker*, then–GM Vice Chairman Robert Lutz reminisced: "All the geniuses here at General Motors kept saying lithium-ion technology is 10 years away, and Toyota agreed with us—and boom, along comes Tesla. So I said, 'How come some tiny little California startup, run by guys who know nothing about the car business, can do this, and we can't?' That was the crowbar that helped us break up the log jam."[34]

Tesla Motors, in producing the Roadster and subsequent electric vehicle models, had experienced none of the grievous setbacks that plagued Fisker Automotive or Fisker's consequent failed quest for production of its autos at Delaware's Boxwood plant. Not only was Tesla Motors approved in 2009 to receive $465 million in interest-bearing loans from the U.S. Department of Energy (unrelated to federal bailout or economic stimulus funding), but also neither of its partial recalls in 2009 and 2010 involved its battery pack or main power system.[35]

Other possible competitors of Fisker Automotive on the horizon produced cars powered by hydrogen fuel cells. The following excerpts from an October 2012 issue of the Wilmington *News Journal* were illustrative:

> Nissan became the latest . . . to say it is ready to mass-produce cars powered by hydrogen fuel cells. Honda, Toyota and Hyundai say they will have fuel-cell cars—which create electricity on board to power the car—ready to go on sale by 2015.
> . . . After touting new fuel-cell powered cars at auto shows, auto makers stopped talking about hydrogen as they focused on plug-in electric cars.
> Now, with many consumers appearing to find that plug-in battery cars are too expensive and have too little range, hydrogen is back in favor.
> Automakers have been finding ways to cut fuel-cell costs and to make longer-range hydrogen tanks, and as they have, along came another boost: America's huge supply of natural gas. At present, almost all hydrogen used in cars is made by separating molecules in natural gas, and the shale boom has created huge reserves in the United States.[36]

Tesla's Fremont, California, factory employed 1,500 people in October 2012 producing Tesla's Model S sedans, with lithium-ion battery packs and electric motors, priced to sell from $57,400. Meanwhile, auto industry insiders speculated that Fisker Automotive was planning to seek a "strategic partner" to help it also produce an entry-level electric vehicle to rival the Chevy

Volt. But no mention was made that it might be produced at Delaware's idled Boxwood plant.[37]

While the 2012 Volt was leading by far all plug-in electric car sales in the United States, even at the expense of giant GM's bottom line, Fisker's Boxwood Road plant in Delaware remained absolutely empty for want of money. Fisker's CEO Tom LaSorda had cast the company's whole Delaware venture in doubt when he announced that the company might not build cars in Delaware if it could not secure additional funding from the DOE.[38]

Nevertheless, throughout 2012, Fisker officials somewhat blithely pushed a positive spin, issuing reassurances to Delawareans while also countering adverse publicity. In a TV interview on February 23, company co-founder and still-CEO Henrik Fisker had said his company "remains committed" to Delaware.[39] On May 29, Henrik's successor as CEO LaSorda issued a statement: "Pending completion of investment sourcing, we are poised to press ahead with further market expansion and development of our higher volume model, the Fisker Atlantic."[40] The Atlantic was the model that Fisker had said would replace the so-called Nina. However, a leaked internal company document showed that production of the Atlantic would not begin until well into 2014.[41] Local journalist Eric Ruth reported on September 6, 2012, the following:

> When it comes to the next model to hit the showroom floors, Fisker Automotive is apparently keeping its focus on the Atlantic rather than expend energy on modified versions of its first model, the Karma.
>
> Fisker spokesman Russell Datz recently told High Gear Media's Marty Padgett that the . . . models of the Karma are now "on the back burner."
>
> The first priority is ramping up production of the Atlantic, a smaller, high-volume model that Fisker wants to build in Delaware, Datz said.[42]

DEMISE OF A123 SYSTEMS

In the meantime, news about Fisker's troubled battery supplier appeared to be improving. Maker of Fisker's fire-prone lithium-ion batteries, A123 Systems, was on the verge of bankruptcy after replacing Fisker's expensive recalled batteries. A123 had been awarded a $249 million grant from the Department of Energy in August 2009 to help it build U.S. factories. About $123 million of that grant had been delivered before the company had fallen on tough times. Thereafter, A123 never posted a profit.

In May 2012, A123 Systems retained an outside advisor, news of which prompted a rise in its shares. In June, Reuters reported that the firm was set to hire four hundred workers at its manufacturing center in Michigan. And in August 2012, A123 seemed to have struck a deal with the Wanxiang Group Corporation whereby the Chinese auto parts company would infuse A123 with $450 million of cash to acquire 80 percent of the battery maker, thus saving A123 from financial disaster while giving Wanxiang a majority stake in the company.[43]

However, that deal was called off on October 16, 2012, apparently because A123 was unable to obtain clearance by the Committee on Foreign Investment in the United States, which reviews transactions involving foreign corporations that could affect national security. Moreover, the fact that the deal with Wanxiang, a Chinese company, occurred during the height of the 2012 presidential campaign was obviously a factor. A123 Systems had posted its revenue high of $159.15 million in 2011. But the company overall had been in the red since 2001. During 2006–2011, it had lost $877.7 million, including a loss of $269 million in 2011 alone through August. Its battery pack failures, forcing Fisker Automotive's costly recall in early 2012, caused A123 to scramble to stay afloat. Accordingly, A123 filed for Chapter 11 bankruptcy protection in October 2012, whereupon the American company Johnson Controls Inc. moved to buy the assets of A123 Systems in a transaction valued at $125 million.[44]

It soon became apparent, however, that the Chinese company—Wanxiang—would pursue legal action to acquire A123 assets. U.S. Bankruptcy Judge Kevin Carey gave interim approval in November 2012 for A123 Systems to borrow $50 million from Wanxiang and for A123 to sell its assets at a December 6 auction, when bidders would include both Johnson Controls and Wanxiang.[45]

Because Fisker's sole battery supplier was A123 Systems, and A123 applied for bankruptcy, Fisker meanwhile patiently awaited the December sale of A123's assets. According to Fisker CEO Tony Posawatz, "Because we have no batteries, there's no production right now. Inventory is starting to get a little low. We'd like to restart production as quickly as possible. We should know the outcome of the auction by the middle of December."[46]

At the December 11, 2012 auction, Judge Carey approved the sale of A123 to Wanxiang, which outbid three other companies including Johnson Controls. The sale excluded A123's business with the U.S. government and its military contracts. That portion of A123 was to be sold to Navitas Systems, a small Illinois energy company, thus addressing potential U.S. national security concerns. Although Johnson Controls appealed the court's decision, it appeared that A123's existence had come to an end.[47]

FISKER FLOUNDERS

Without its battery maker, Fisker had virtually halted production of its cars. During a presidential debate in October 2012, Republican nominee Mitt Romney made specific reference to the Obama administration's $529 million loan to Fisker, the stalled electric carmaker. Romney told Obama, "You don't just pick winners and losers. You pick losers."[48]

There was no question that Fisker's two most grievous problems were cash and technology. Needing support for both, the company made known in October 2012 that it sought a strategic partnership. Investors conjectured that Fiat/Chrysler might be a prime candidate for helping out Fisker Automotive.[49] Two months passed without any such partner coming forth. In December 2012, Fisker CEO Tony Posawatz announced that Fisker hired investment bank Evercore Partners Inc. to search for a strategic partner to help manage Fisker's production costs. Meanwhile, Fisker could not resolve its problem of obtaining batteries, given the bankruptcy of A123 Systems. Nor did Fisker have the money to engineer its second model, the Atlantic, at Delaware's Boxwood plant. Acknowledging that Delaware state officials had little impact on Fisker negotiations or next moves, DEDO Director Alan Levin said, "We're still in wait and see right now."[50]

As Fisker Automotive was enduring the end of a very bad year, it not only was still facing a cash crunch, but it also had not produced a car since July of 2012. Industry analyst Rebecca Lindland, of HIS Automotive, commented:

> If you're not producing your product, you're in a world of hurt. They're not making product, and their battery, basically the motor of their car, isn't being produced either. That's two strikes against them.
>
> Finding an automotive partner could be really tough. You're looking at a stalled company. Getting a stalled company up and running again is even more costly than starting a new company.
>
> Resiliency is something that's really tough to measure. But at some point, we have to start seeing positive news from them in order to believe in their long-term viability.[51]

While Delaware still awaited Fisker's fate, Fisker announced in November 2012 that it would introduce its Karma to China, with its Asia operation likely to be headquartered in Shanghai.[52] Unfortunately, Fisker ended 2012 with only more negative news. Indeed, to top off its series of setbacks, Superstorm Sandy swept floodwaters through the port of Newark, New Jersey, in early November, destroying 338 parked Karmas awaiting shipment to dealerships throughout the region—a haymaker estimated at a $34.8 million loss. To make matters worse, Fisker's insurer denied the company's claim for the loss, whereupon Fisker embarked in January 2013 on suing that insurer.[53]

BANKRUPTCY

As 2013 was under way, faint hopes for better news about Fisker Automotive creating jobs in Delaware did not materialize. Indeed, resignation and even despair appeared to govern the fate of the Boxwood Road plant. It was reported on March 14 that Henrik Fisker, co-founder of the company bearing his name, abruptly resigned as its executive chairman.[54] The next day, a Wilmington *News Journal* poll reported that 85 percent of respondents predicted that Fisker would go bankrupt and be unable to repay its grants from the state.[55]

By mid-2013, Fisker still had found neither a partner nor buyer. It had fired three-quarters of its staff and was teetering on the edge of filing for bankruptcy. The DOE had not given any sign that it would ever release any of the balance of its conditional loan to the company. And if and when Fisker should file for bankruptcy, it was questionable that Delaware's state government could claw back any money it had granted to Fisker. A sizable portion of Fisker's sordid saga was the main feature story in the Sunday *News Journal* of May 13, 2013. A front-page banner headline was: "How Delaware Bought a [drawing of a lemon]."[56]

Meanwhile, even though the Boxwood plant continued to remain empty, it appeared that Delaware taxpayers were still paying its utility bills in mid-July 2013, which had totaled more than $400,000 alone from April through December 2012.[57]

As could be expected, Delaware was awash in playing the blame game. For example, Michael Begatto, executive director of the Delaware Public Employees Council 81, the public employees' union, blamed Governor Jack Markell for Fisker's demise, as witness these excerpts from Begatto's mid-2013 opinion column:

> If you had a choice of where you could wisely invest taxpayers' funds to gain a decent return, where would you place the money? Gov. Jack Markell placed his reliance on Fisker Automotive for an investment of $26 million. . . . As we know . . . in the terminology of the market, it "tanked."
>
> . . . Sadly . . . state employees today make less than when Gov. Markell came to office. . . . Gov. Markell has not proposed one increase in wages or benefits since he has come to office, proposing instead only reductions.
>
> . . . If you see Gov. Markell . . . ask him if investing in Delaware State employees would . . . produce more than the "Fisker experiment."
>
> Also, the next time someone asks you what type of investment should Delaware seek to further its economic interests, suggest a guaranteed investment with a great return —Delaware State employees.[58]

After months of efforts, Fisker Automotive had failed to attract any bidders to buy its remaining assets. The final demise of the company appeared certain when the U.S. Department of Energy announced in September 2013 its intention to auction the balance of the department's $192 million Fisker loan to the highest bidder offering "the best possible recovery for the taxpayer." Nary a mention was made of any remaining Fisker obligation to build cars in Delaware or to repay any portion of Delaware's state grant of more than $20 million to the company. Governor Markell plaintively remarked, "At least there's now a path forward. There's considerable uncertainty, but at least there's direction."[59]

The final chapter of Fisker Automotive's odyssey occurred when the hybrid carmaker finally filed for Chapter 11 bankruptcy in Delaware in November 2013. That move all but killed Delaware's chance to claw back any of Delaware taxpayers' money given to the ill-fated company, and left in limbo the future of the Boxwood auto plant.[60] In December 2013, the bankruptcy judge ordered an auction for the assets of Fisker Automotive, which was won by a bid of $149 million from the U.S. arm of China's largest auto parts supplier—Wanxiang America.[61]

In the end, it was reported that Fisker's Boxwood auto plant property was sold in March 2014 by Wanxiang America to its affiliated real estate holding company for $18 million, the same price Fisker had paid for it in 2010, and that Wanxiang had indicated on its new Fisker web page—thenewfisker.com—it was considering restarting the brand name using the Delaware plant for mass production. It was also reported that New Castle County and the state of Delaware each received $270,000 in real estate transfer taxes for the property.[62]

CONCLUSION

It appeared that the state government might never recover any of the taxpayer money paid to Fisker Automotive, or even any of its total payments of $7.4 million for electricity and heating utilities that accumulated over the months to maintain the empty Boxwood plant in the vain hope that Fisker someday could reopen it.[63]

The state of Delaware had chosen to follow a highly concentrated strategy in 2009 by investing $21.5 million in Fisker. The facts that Delaware at the time had more than 25,000 unemployed residents, and had recently experienced the closings of its two auto assembly plants, had surely combined to focus the state's vision too narrowly. Moreover, that the federal DOE would loan start-up Fisker $500 million probably served to close the deal, making Delaware's risk seem worth taking. Still, cautionary notes should have been sounded, given the fact that the market during the recession for high-cost electric plug-in hybrid luxury automobiles was then unknown.

At the same time, there was well-established competition. Models were due out from General Motors, Toyota, Nissan, and others, making the competition more intense for a small market. In addition, Tesla was well ahead in the production timeline for a similar high-end vehicle like Fisker's. With no established dealer network and a product produced only in Finland, it would seem that red flags were waving warnings even well before the decision to invest was made.

Perhaps this experience suggests that a portfolio strategy is needed in cases of economic development where smaller sums are invested in a bundle of companies, especially if those companies are start-ups. If Delaware does not have the necessary resources and thus is forced to put "all its eggs in one basket," maybe the answer to investing in a start-up should be, "No, thank you."

Meanwhile, the Boxwood plant remained empty over a year after Wanxiang reportedly had bought the plant in March 2014. In April 2015, after Democratic Governor Markell and state development officials, who pled to Volvo Cars to invest in Delaware, were ignored, Republican state legislators introduced a "right-to-work" law. The proposed legislation would have allowed state officials to establish right-to-work zones within which it would be illegal to require workers to join unions and pay dues as a condition of employment. It was suggested that the change could help entice a manufacturing company to move to Delaware and use the defunct Boxwood plant. Regardless of the fact that twenty-five states had passed right-to-work laws, and Delaware Republican legislators and business groups supported the proposal, Democratic lawmakers who controlled the legislature declined to support it.[64]

NOTES

1. See, for example, Maureen Milford, "End of the Road," Wilmington *News Journal*, July 13, 2009; Andrew Eder, "Delaware's Auto Industry Vanishes in GM Bankruptcy," ibid., June 2, 2009, A1; Eric Ruth, "As GM Plant Closes, Doors Open for Few Opportunities," ibid., June 2, 2009, A7; Andrew Eder, "Chrysler's Stamp on Delaware History Comes to End Today," ibid., December 19, 2008, A1.

2. "Fisker Karma," in www.caranddriver.com/fisker/karma (accessed July 15, 2015).

3. The General Assembly passed the bill on June 29, 2010. See "Governor Markell Signs Landmark Clean Energy Jobs Package," Press Release, Governor's Office, July 28, 2010.

4. See the timeline, "How Delaware Landed Fisker Automotive," Wilmington *News Journal*, September 23, 2012, A16.

5. Copy of Fisker Automotive's application to the DEDO, signed March 11, 2010, archive.delawareonline.com/assets/pdf/BL18754344.PDF. Among the items "redacted" (meaning crossed out or blank) from this copy were: the company's email address, estimate of annual minimum wages, and independent auditor's report of its financial statements.

6. Copy of Memorandum from Hon. Alan B. Levin to The Council on Development Finance (CDF), April 14, 2010, 3, archive.delawareonline.com/assets/pdf/BL18754344.PDF.

7. Ibid., 7. Note that the section entitled "Financial Analysis" has been "redacted" on pages 4 and 5 from this memorandum.

8. Without mentioning the Fisker appropriation, the Bond Bill for FY 2011, adopted June 30, 2010, allocated $30,437,400 to DEDO's Strategic Fund, thus more than enough to fund Fisker's request; see Section 1 Addendum—Fiscal Year 2011 Capital Improvement Project Schedule. See HB500 Delaware General Assembly at www.budget.delaware.gov/fy2011/capital/11capbudact.pdf.

9. Jonathan Starkey, "Fisker Pushes Nina Production to Mid-'13," Wilmington *News Journal*, October 20, 2011, A10.

10. Jonathan Starkey, "Fisker Issues Karma Recalls," Wilmington *News Journal*, December 30, 2011, A1, A2. Former Secretary of State Colin Powell and former Vice President Al Gore were among early Karma owners; Starkey, "Fisker's $100,000 Hybrid Lands a Role in Sitcom," ibid., September 28, 2011, A10.

11. Jon Hurdle, "Fisker Plant in Delaware on Track Despite Karma Recall," WDDE 91.1 FM, January 6, 2012, www.wdde.org/21486-fisker-delaware-plant-karma-recall (accessed September 14, 2012).

12. See Eric Ruth, "Fisker Slows Work at Former GM Site," Wilmington *News Journal*, February 7, 2012, A1, A5; and Angela Greiling and Jeff Feeley, "Fisker Stops Work On Car Factory after U.S. Blocks Loan," *Bloomberg Businessweek*, February 7, 2012.

13. Eric Ruth and Chad Livengood, "Can Fisker Keep Its Promise?" Wilmington *News Journal*, February 13, 2012, A1, A5.

14. Jonathan Starkey, "Two Republican U.S. Senators Question Fisker's Federal Loan," Wilmington *News Journal*, April 24, 2012, A1, A5.

15. Jonathan Starkey, "Senators: US Skirts Inquiries on Fisker," Wilmington *News Journal*, May 19, 2012, B1, B2.

16. Jonathan Starkey, "Gingrich Blames VP Biden for Fisker Stall," Wilmington *News Journal*, April 20, 2012, A1, A7.

17. Jonathan Starkey, "GOP Targets Fisker Loans," Wilmington *News Journal*, July 20, 2012, A1, A2. See also Starkey, "GOP Challenger Attacks Markell's Job Investments," ibid., July 18, 2012, B1, B9.

18. Editorial, "Let Fisker Plan Follow Supervised Course," Wilmington *News Journal*, February 15, 2012, A10.

19. Editorial, "Fisker's Troubles Can't Be Ignored, Yet . . . ," Wilmington *News Journal*, March 17, 2012, A8.

20. See, for example, James R. Healey, "Consumer Reports 100K Fisker Karma Dies on Arrival," *USA Today*, March 9, 2012; and Cori Anne Natoli, "Karma Credibility Hit," Wilmington *News Journal*, March 16, 2012, A6.

21. Eric Ruth, "Batteries in 2012 Karmas Faulty," Wilmington *News Journal*, March 27, 2012, A1, A2.

22. Eric Ruth, "After Fire, Fisker Fends Off Accusations," Wilmington *News Journal*, May 18, 2012, A1, A6.

23. Staff and Wire Reports, "Fisker Expands Karma Recall," Wilmington *News Journal*, June 3, 2012, A25.

24. Joe Pollicino, "Fisker Karma Owner Returns from Grocery Run to Find Hybrid EV on Fire," *Engadget*, August 12, 2012, www.engadget.com/2012/08/12/fisker-karma-hybrid-ev-second-fire/ (accessed September 4, 2012).

25. Eric Ruth, "Fisker Issues Recall after Fire," *Wilmington News Journal*, August 21, 2012, A6, A7.

26. Eric Ruth, "Fisker Tackling More Bugs in Its Karmas," Wilmington *News Journal*, August 24, 2012, A8.

27. Jason Torchinsky, "Leaked Document Shows Fisker Has More Issues Than Fiery Cars," *Jalopnik*, August 22, 2012, jalopnik.com//fisker-karma/ (accessed September 4, 2012).

28. Jonathan Starkey, "Former Chrysler Executive Hired by Fisker," Wilmington *News Journal*, December 16, 2011, A9.

29. Jonathan Starkey, "New Chief Executive Named at Fisker," Wilmington *News Journal*, February 29, 2012, A1, A6.

30. See Eric Ruth, "Names Ford, Dana Veteran as Its New CFO," Wilmington *News Journal*, July 4, 2012, A10; and Eric Ruth, "Fisker Automotive Reassigns Second of Its Founders," ibid., July 26, 2012, A10.

31. Eric Ruth, "Fisker: New Leaders But What Direction?" Wilmington *News Journal*, August 19, 2012, E1, E3.

32. Sean Szymkowski, "And Now, a Chevrolet Volt VS Nissan Leaf Sales Update," GM Authority, gmauthority.com/blog/2015/03/and-now-a-chevrolet-volt-vs-nissan-leaf-sales-update/.

33. Tom Krishner, "GM Offers Big Discounts to Boost Volt Sales," Wilmington *News Journal*, September 23, 2012, A21.

34. Tad Friend, "Elon Musk and Electric Cars," *The New Yorker*, August 2009.

35. "Tesla Motors," see Department of Energy, Loan Programs Office, energy.gov/lpo/tesla.

36. Chris Woodyard, "Fuel Cells Get a Fresh Look; Hydrogen in Vogue with Electric Cars Pricey," Wilmington *News Journal*, October 7, 2012, E5.

37. See Bloomberg News, "Tesla Gets $10M Grant for Electric SUV," Wilmington *News Journal*, October 12, 2012, A12; and Eric Ruth, "Report: Fisker Will Build Model to Rival Chevy Volt," ibid., November 15, 2012, A8.

38. Jonathan Starkey, "Fisker Plant 'Absolutely Empty,'" Wilmington *News Journal*, April 17, 2012, A1, A10.

39. Doug Williams, "Fisker Says Commitment to Del. Plant Unwavering," Wilmington *News Journal*, February 14, 2012, A6.

40. Eric Ruth, "Fisker Pushes the Upside," Wilmington *News Journal*, May 30, 2012, A10, A11.

41. Eric Ruth, "Blog: Fisker Atlantic Production Off Until 2014," Wilmington *News Journal*, May 20, 2012, E1.

42. Eric Ruth, "Good News for Del.: Fisker Says Atlantic Is a Priority," Wilmington *News Journal*, September 6, 2012, A6.

43. See the following news stories by Eric Ruth in the Wilmington *News Journal*: "Fisker Battery Maker Retains Advisor," May, 22, 2012, A8; "Fisker Battery Maker Has Good News at Last," June 8, 2012, A12; and "Fisker's Troubled Battery Supplier Grasps at Lifeline," August 10, 2012, A10.

44. See, for example, Patrick Fitzgerald, Mike Ramsey, Mike Spector and Ryan Tracy, "Battery Maker Files for Bankruptcy," *Wall Street Journal*, October 16, 2012; Bill Vlasic and Matthew L. Wald, "Maker of Batteries Files for Bankruptcy," *New York Times*, October 16, 2012; Thomas Content, "Johnson Controls Bids on Battery-Maker A123's Assets," *Journal Sentinel*, October 16, 2012; Eric Ruth, "Fisker Supplier Is Saved," Wilmington *News Journal*, October 17, 2012, A12, A13; and Craig Trudell, Bloomberg News, "A Bumpy Road for Battery Maker," ibid., October 21, 2012, E1, E5.

45. See Carla Manin, Bloomberg News, "Fisker: Delay A123 Asset Auction," Wilmington *News Journal*, October 30, 2012, A11; Phil Milford and Dawn McCarty, Bloomberg News, "More Snags for A123," ibid., November 6, 2012, A6; Bloomberg News, "A123 Sets $50M Loan from China's Wanxiang," ibid., November 7, 2012, A20; and Bloomberg News, "A123 Receives Court OK for Dec. 6 Asset Auction," ibid., November 9, 2012, A7.

46. Bloomberg News, "Fisker Awaits A123 Sale to Resume Making Karmas," Wilmington *News Journal*, November 12, 2012, A12.

47. See Bill Vlasic, "Chinese Firm Wins Bid for Auto Battery Maker," *New York Times*, December 10, 2012, B1, B9; Associated Press, "Wanxiang Wins Bid for A123," Wilmington *News Journal*, December 11, 2012, A6, A7; and Dawn McCarty and Michael Bathon, Bloomberg News, "Johnson Controls Appeals A123 Bankruptcy Sale," ibid., December 18, 2012, A6.

48. Dialogue Delaware, "Is Fisker A Loser? That's a Stretch, Gov. Romney," Wilmington *News Journal*, October 7, 2012, B1.

49. See the following Wilmington *News Journal* articles by Eric Ruth: "Fisker Automotive Ready to Reach Out for Help," October 2, 2012, A2; "Report: Henrik Fisker Pessimistic about U.S. Loan," October 7, 2012, E1; and "Chrysler Could Be Fisker's Savior, Columnist Argues," October 9, 2012, A8.

50. See Jonathan Starkey, "Fisker's Boxwood Plans Remain Stalled: Troubled Company Looks for Financial Partner," Wilmington *News Journal*, December 12, 2012, A1, A5; and Mike Ramsey and Sharon Terlep, "Its Battery Drained, Fisker Hunts for Partner," *Wall Street Journal*, December 8-9, 2012, B1, B4.

51. Jonathan Starkey, "Del. Awaits Fisker Fate," Wilmington *News Journal*, December 26, 2012, A2, A3.

52. Eric Ruth, "As Delaware Waits, Fisker Sets Course for China," Wilmington *News Journal*, September 17, 2012, A7.

53. See Cori Anne Natoli, "Sandy Ruins 338 Karmas," *Wilmington News Journal*, November 11, 2012, E1, E4; and Eric Ruth, "Fisker Fights for $30M Claim," ibid., January 3, 2013, A8, A9.

54. Aaron Nathan, "Fisker Exits His Startup: Co-founder Resigns Over Firm's Strategy," Wilmington *News Journal*, March 14, 2013, A10, A12.

55. "Poll Results: "What Do You Think Will Happen at the Boxwood Road Plant?" Wilmington *News Journal*, March 13, 2013, B1.

56. Jonathan Starkey and Nicole Guadiano, "How Delaware Bought a [drawing of a lemon]: Early Warnings o ver Loan to Fisker Emerge after Delaware Bet Big on Hybrid Automaker," Wilmington *News Journal*, May 5, 2013, A1, A16, A17. See also, for example, these articles by Jonathan Starkey: "Fisker 'Teetering on the Edge," ibid., March 29, 2013, A1, A7; "Fisker Fires Most of Staff: Bankruptcy Likely for Automaker," ibid., April 16, 2013, A1, A5; and "So Why Is Fisker Still Standing?" ibid., May 12, 2013, E1, E4.

57. Jonathan Starkey, "Taxpayers Foot Utilities Bill for Fisker," Wilmington *News Journal*, August 10, 2012, A1, A2.

58. Michael A. Begatto, "Investing in Fisker vs. a Guaranteed Success," Wilmington *News Journal*, June 4, 2013, A9.

59. Jonathan Starkey, "US Plans to Auction $164M Fisker Loan," Wilmington *News Journal*, September 18, 2013, A1, A2.

60. See Jonathan Starkey, "Bankruptcy Puts Fisker Plant in Limbo," Wilmington *News Journal*, November 27, 2013, A12, A13.

61. Aaron Nathans, "Winning Bid for Fisker $149M," Wilmington *News Journal*, February 15, 2014, A1, A10.

62. Aaron Nathans, "Fisker Plant Property Sold for $18 Million," Wilmington *News Journal*, March 25, 2014, A4.

63. Aaron Nathans, "Taxpayers Foot $7.4M Fisker Utility Bill," Wilmington *News Journal*, December 4, 2013, A1, A2.

64. See these articles by Jonathan Starkey: "Republicans Target Unions," Wilmington *News Journal*, April 8, 2015, A1, A7; and "Democrats Bury GOP Right-to-Work Legislation," ibid., April 30, 2015, A16.

Chapter Five

Bloom Energy

At the time when Henrik Fisker announced on October 27, 2009, his company's intention to purchase GM's former Boxwood Road plant, the former Chrysler assembly plant in Newark that occupied 272 acres had remained closed since it had shut down the previous December. However, President Harker of the University of Delaware (UD) revealed on November 23, 2009, that UD, after twenty months of negotiations and discussions, had officially acquired the adjacent Chrysler site. The purchase price of $24.25 million had been approved by the U.S. Bankruptcy Court in New York. "This is an historic day for the University of Delaware," Harker said. "We foresee great economic development and community infrastructure initiatives on the site that will have a tremendous positive impact on the city of Newark, the state and the region." The initial objective of the property, according to Harker, would be to develop a research and technology campus that would feature faculty research and the creation of businesses. [1]

On June 9, 2011, California-based Bloom Energy of Silicon Valley announced plans to build its East Coast fuel-cell manufacturing plant at UD's science and technology campus, thus making a major stride toward realizing UD objectives. Delaware notables from business, government, and academia were ecstatic. Governor Jack Markell took major credit. He disclosed that the state had been working on the deal to attract Bloom for fourteen months. "Some of the world's largest companies have chosen Bloom energy to power their growth," he said, "and now Bloom has chosen Delaware as the best site for their expansion." [2]

According to Bloom's Vice President of Business Development Joshua Richman, Bloom had turned down more generous offers from other states in deciding to base its East Coast expansion in Delaware. "Delaware at that time was not anywhere on our map," Richman said. Former businessman

Markell rejoined, "We think it should be on your map. We need to show companies that we understand their industries better than any other state would." Delaware's success in attracting Bloom was a consequence of personal contact and state incentives.[3]

When Governor Markell appointed Collin O'Mara as secretary of Delaware's Department of Natural Resources and Environmental Control (DNREC) in 2009, O'Mara became at twenty-nine the youngest state cabinet official in the nation. Prior to joining Markell, O'Mara had served as the clean tech strategist for the California city of San Jose, during which time he helped the city attract more than fifty clean technology companies, which created more than three thousand new jobs. Perhaps the one individual most instrumental in attracting Bloom Energy to Delaware, DNREC Secretary O'Mara in a visit to Silicon Valley in 2010 had suggested Delaware to Joshua Richman.[4]

Millions in state incentives were made available to help attract Bloom. Bloom would receive $11.2 million once it hired nine hundred employees. The state could claw back portions of this amount should that target not be met. A strategic fund grant of $3.3 million also would be paid to the company should its suppliers account for hiring another six hundred workers, a grant that also could be clawed back if it failed. The state pledged to pay a maximum of $1.5 million for outfitting the Bloom plant to be constructed on about fifty acres of the university's 272-acre science and technology site. In addition, UD would receive $7 million from the state to help it develop that former Chrysler facility.

All told, the terms offered Bloom totaled slightly more than the approximately $20 million incentives given Fisker with claw-backs. But unlike start-up Fisker Automotive, Bloom Energy's fuel-cell technology was well established. Indeed, Bloom manufactured a technology that at least twenty UD professors were already researching, constituting another—albeit intangible—incentive for a future Bloom–UD partnership.[5]

Regardless of the multiple incentives offered Bloom, two related issues still remained. One consisted of the fact that Bloom fuel cells used a fossil fuel—natural gas—rather than renewable energy. The other issue consisted of a complicated and convoluted deal involving Delmarva Power, its customers, and the state's Public Service Commission (PSC). Resolving these related issues would generate over time the most lucrative and generous of the multiple state incentives inducing the company to establish Delaware as the hub of its East Coast expansion. Each of these issues merits explanation.

THE RENEWABLE ENERGY ISSUE

Governor Jack Markell came into office in January 2009. In March, the Governor's Energy Advisory Council submitted to Governor Markell its comprehensive "Delaware Energy Plan 2009–2014." In the introduction of the plan, Council Chairman David Hodas of Widener University School of Law stated:

> This energy plan represents the emergence of a new generation of energy policy that will begin to move us from a fossil fuel dependent society to a sustainable energy future.
>
> Energy from the sun and wind, although currently more expensive to use than fossil fuels, do not go up in price. . . . According to the U.S. Energy Information Agency, in 2006 [the most recent year such data was available] . . . Delaware ranks last in the nation in renewable energy production; overall, less than .05 percent of our energy came from renewable sources. We are so low, that the next lowest state, Rhode Island, with a population slightly larger than Delaware's, generated more than 50 times the amount of electricity from renewable energy than did Delaware. . . . This Energy Plan for Delaware faces these challenges directly. . . . The plan's recommendation, if implemented, will propel our transition to a state powered by efficient use of renewable energy—a green future. [6]

Among the many recommendations of this comprehensive 2009 plan of 115 pages was for the governor to consider an increase of the so-called Renewable Portfolio Standard (RPS) that called for an increasing percentage of electricity sold in the state to Delmarva Power customers to come from renewable energy sources. The plan noted that the RPS was first established by the 143rd General Assembly wherein the percentage of electricity required from renewable sources started at 2 percent in 2007 and increased each year to 20 percent in 2019. [7] However, the 144th General Assembly increased the RPS schedule to start at 5 percent effective in 2010, increasing each year to 25 percent in 2025. [8] Enforcement of the RPS in Delaware was divided between the State Energy Coordinator and the PSC. [9] Of interest is this observation from the 2009 plan: "Currently, twenty-four states and the District of Columbia have RPS policies in place: four others have nonbinding goals for adoption of renewable energy. The more aggressive requirements are California, which has a requirement of 20 percent by 2010, and Oregon and Illinois, which both have requirements of 25 percent by 2025." [10]

A main problem for Bloom's entry into Delaware was the fact that its fuel cells used natural gas. Instead of burning the gas, Bloom fuel cells used an electrochemical reaction to convert the gas into electricity, which was allegedly much cleaner than other uses of natural gas. By any standard, however, natural gas was not a renewable energy source. A UD professor of engineering stated, "Calling these [Bloom] boxes 'renewable' stretches credibility." [11]

Bloom's use of natural gas, therefore, could not be considered within the then-current RPS schedule of Delaware's law that required Delmarva Power to sell to its customers an increasing percentage of electricity that came only from renewable energy sources.

Accordingly, the only path forward for Bloom Energy was for Delaware to change its law to accommodate Bloom by making an exception for natural gas for fuel-cell use. This the General Assembly did forthwith in record time. A fast-track strategy had been in the works even before Bloom Energy publicly announced on June 9, 2011, that it would build its East Coast plant at UD. The State Senate by a vote of 18–2 passed legislation on June 16, 2011, allowing Delmarva Power to dedicate electricity generated by fuel cells using natural gas toward Delmarva's RPS. The State House of Representatives did the same by a vote of 35–4 on June 23 to send the bill to Governor Markell. Both senators who voted against the bill were from Kent County, one senator who abstained was from Sussex County, all four representatives who voted against the bill were from Sussex County, and all seven were downstate Republicans. The fast-track legislation thus flew through the General Assembly only two weeks after Bloom's announcement.[12]

Democratic Governor Markell and his staff defended their decision to declare Bloom's fuel cells a "renewable" power source. They rationalized that Bloom's use of natural gas would help grow a cleaner energy industry while generating at least nine hundred jobs in the state. DNREC Secretary O'Mara offered the following politically charged spin of how Bloom Energy fit into Delaware's clean energy future:

> From an environmental perspective, the technology is exceptionally clean. It uses an electrochemical reaction rather than combustion, which produces virtually none of the unhealthy smog-forming, ozone-depleting, and acid rain-causing pollutants, and significantly fewer carbon emissions than even the cleanest and most efficient natural gas plants.
>
> Specifically, compared to coal or natural gas-fired generation, Bloom's technology produces 99 percent less nitrogen oxides, only trace amounts of sulfur dioxide, 66 percent less carbon dioxide than coal-fired plants, and 17 percent less carbon dioxide than combined-cycle natural-gas plants.
>
> . . . In addition to providing significant environmental benefits, Bloom will be able . . . to put several hundred people to work manufacturing the fuel cells.
>
> . . .These workers will join the growing cluster of more than 50 Delaware energy efficiency companies, 600 Delawareans currently employed in the solar industry, and hundreds more jobs that will be created by leading clean-tech manufacturers like Fisker Automotive.[13]

It was no accident that not a single Democratic legislator questioned or voted against the law that redefined natural-gas-powered fuel cells as renewable. But critics abounded. They disagreed with changing the definition of "renewable," noting that short-term gains in job creation might be at the expense of long-term sustainable solar and wind businesses. As a matter of fact, Delmarva Power by law was required to buy 25 percent of its power from renewable sources by 2025. Now that natural gas had been defined by law as renewable, Delmarva could thereby diminish its purchases from solar and wind power sources. Dale Davis, president of Delaware's Solar Energy Coalition, worried about the precedent; he rhetorically asked: "Why don't we declare clean coal renewable, or nuclear?" Vice President of the American Wind Energy Association Peter Kelley asserted, "Renewable means it never runs out." Neil Sullivan, director of the Colorado Fuel Cell Center, admitted: "Natural gas came out of the ground. That's not really renewable."[14]

One could add that production of natural gas in the United States also appears limitless. Increasingly, natural gas is produced by the controversial process of "fracking." Environmentalists have claimed that hydraulic fracturing entails blasting a combination of water, chemicals, and sand deep into the earth, releasing huge quantities of natural gas, but also releasing wastewater into streams and rivers from which drinking water is often derived. Hence, rightly or wrongly, the claim is made that natural gas cannot credibly be cleaner when, paradoxically, its production by fracking entails pollution.

A COMPLICATED AND CONVOLUTED DEAL

In addition to the $16 million in state financial incentives allocated for Bloom Energy to put its East Coast fuel-cell factory on the site of Newark's former Chrysler assembly plant, Bloom set another very complicated condition for coming to Delaware—the last part of the incentive package announced by Governor Markell in June 2011. Besides Bloom's plan to construct its 200,000-square-foot plant in Newark, Bloom and Delmarva Power planned to locate two clusters of "Bloom Boxes"—one at Delmarva Red Lion substation on River Road in New Castle County, plus a smaller one next to Delmarva's Brookside substation in Newark. Together, these clusters would generate thirty megawatts of electricity to be added to the grid.

The most controversial aspect of this arrangement would require that these fuel cells be paid for by Delmarva's three hundred thousand customers with an unpredictable surcharge over a period of twenty-one years. During the life of that project, Delmarva customers would pay more were Bloom to receive less than it anticipated for its power on the open market, and pay less if the price of the power was more—hence the unpredictability of the surcharge. Delmarva officials estimated that the average monthly surcharge paid by a Delmarva residential customer would range from $1.04 in 2014 to a high of $3.45 in 2018 before declining thereafter. DNREC Secretary O'Mara estimated the total annual average amount gained from the surcharge would be $4 million to $5 million. The aggregate amount collected from Delmarva customers during the twenty-one years would be about $158 million. By adding the amount brought in by Bloom from the open market, the estimated total accruing to Bloom during the life of the project would be a whopping $751.3 million. Accordingly, this power generation deal appeared to represent the largest economic incentive for Bloom Energy, precisely because of the guaranteed total revenue the company would receive.[15]

Delaware required the Bloom–Delmarva deal to be approved by the state's PSC to become effective. Bloom requested in August 2011 that PSC issue its approval by October 18, 2011, so that its first fuel cells could be up and running by December 2012. However, during the interim before a PSC hearing could be held, proponents and detractors of the deal were locked in a divisive controversy seldom experienced in Delaware public affairs.

PUBLIC CONTROVERSY OVER THE DEAL

As the October 18 deadline approached, the PSC scheduled three late September public hearings to elicit public comment about the Bloom–Delmarva application. A few days prior to the hearings, John A. Nichols of Middletown authored an op-ed in the Wilmington *News Journal*, which served as an opening salvo claiming "the proposed fuel cell cost[s] at least two to three times more than combined cycle natural gas." He continued, "It is difficult to learn much about Bloom's finances. . . . However, it seems reasonable to conclude, if Bloom had a viable business plan, they would head directly to Wall Street instead of using the political system to secure capital the private sector seems unwilling to provide. . . . This is a sweetheart deal for Bloom and a lousy deal for the ratepayers."[16] Residents from all three Delaware counties voiced concerns at the PSC hearings about the Bloom deal. One New Castle County resident called it a "foolish boondoggle," and another termed it a "no brainer that fails." One Kent County farmer said he already spent $54,281 on electricity each year and was wary of added costs. A Sussex County resident claimed that the electric rate surcharge that would be passed on to Delmarva Power customers would be a burden that the poor and middle class could ill afford.[17]

Besides representatives of the Markell administration, UD, and Delmarva Power, who spoke in favor of the plan, the hearings were tantamount to opening a "Pandora's Box" of multiple criticisms of the proposal. According to the *News Journal*, even the report of PSC's own consultants—New Energy Opportunities Inc., La Capra Associates Inc., and Birch Tree Associates, LLC—appeared to be very critical of the plan, reported as follows:

> Gov. Jack Markell's plan is filled with risks, the consultants said, most involving the linkage of incentives to build the factory to higher electric bills Delmarva customers would be paying for twenty-one years.

In fact, the way the Delmarva deal is written now, ratepayers could be left on the hook to continue paying a surcharge for two decades even if the factory in Newark is never built, closes prematurely or never ramps up to full production and employment, the report prepared for the Public Service Commission says.

The project allocates risk in a way that is "highly favorable to the . . . company and unfavorable to ratepayers," the consultants wrote, noting that tens of millions of dollars are riding on what they viewed as a questionable business plan for sale of Bloom's fuel-cell generators in East Coast markets. . . .

There is a risk that the factory could be built but operate at a low level because of unfavorable business conditions, and that risk "appears to be high," the consultants wrote. And that would probably suppress employment at the factory, they wrote.

East Coast business conditions are less favorable for Bloom, the consultants said, because subsidies here are lower than in California.

If the factory closes prematurely, Bloom would be required to pay a termination fee to the state. But that fee would be a fraction of the amount that would continue to be collected by the surcharge on electric bills, the consultants wrote.

In the event of a bankruptcy, the state may not even get the termination payment because there's no security money put away for this purpose, the consultants said. . . .

"At bottom, it is very uncertain as to whether the market in the Northeast for Bloom Energy's fuel cells will be sufficiently robust to sustain a Bloom Energy manufacturing facility operating at its peak capacity," the consultants wrote.[18]

Governor Markell responded that the risks identified by the consultants that Bloom might not meet its sales or employment goals would not happen. "The surest way to fail," Markell said, "is not to pursue jobs in the first place."[19]

Joining those opposed to the Bloom Energy deal were two senior officers of the Caesar Rodney Institute, a conservative think tank. In an op-ed column, they charged that the deal completely ignored "the jobs that will disappear due to higher electricity prices," a fact that "defies common sense and experience." They concluded: "If a private project cannot muster in the capital markets without massive government subsidies, it makes no sense to simply forge ahead while putting the taxpayers at risk."[20]

As the October 18 deadline for the PSC decision approached, three last-minute developments illustrated that criticisms of the Bloom Energy plan were having an effect. First, a *News Journal* editorial pleaded that "Bloom Must Make the Case for State Deal."[21] Second, three state lawmakers sent a letter urging the PSC to delay its decision by at least a week so that the central issue could be more fully considered, namely that "ratepayers should not be required to pay for something that they are not receiving."[22] Finally, and most important, Bloom announced an agreement whereby it would pay the state as much as $41 million if the factory was not built.

An article in the *News Journal* summarized Bloom Energy's offer of new financial pledges to better insulate Delaware taxpayers and electricity users from risks. In a filing with the PSC on October 13, Bloom agreed to the following:

> If the plant isn't built by the end of 2013 and a surcharge on Delmarva Power electric bills is already in place, Bloom would pay a $41 million penalty fee. That fee would be backed by an "unconditional, evergreen letter of credit, surety bond." . . .
>
> The state also would have a senior claim on half the value of the factory should Bloom go bankrupt.
>
> The new proposals address concerns raised about the complicated Bloom Energy incentive deal by a team of consultants to the PSC staff. . . .
>
> Under the amended deal, . . . if Bloom does not occupy the factory by December 31, 2013, and the first third of the electric project is built, Bloom would pay the state $41 million. . . .
>
> The $18 million in Delaware Economic Development Office incentives can be "clawed back" if employment lags.
>
> . . . Bloom and DEDO are finalizing an additional agreement in which Bloom would be obligated to spend $36 million on payroll each year. If it does not, Bloom would repay DEDO the difference.
>
> Bloom and the state arrived at that figure by multiplying 900 jobs by an average salary of $40,000.[23]

PSC APPROVES BLOOM DEAL

After a day-long hearing on October 18, 2011, in a packed House Chamber in Dover's Legislative Hall, the PSC unanimously approved the Bloom deal. Much of the hearing consisted of statements by Markell administration officials, Bloom officers, and representatives of Delmarva Power.[24] But a number of critics voiced their opposition to the proposal. Indeed, though the votes by each of the PSC commissioners were cast approving the proposed deal, they did so with some apprehension or reservation, as the following account demonstrates:

> When commissioners finally voted at about 6 p.m., they weighed whether the proposal met the requirements laid out in a law passed by the General Assembly this summer, including whether it uses innovative technology and has economic benefits. The commissioners had the right to say that customer costs outweighed the benefits, but declined to do so.
>
> James Lester, one of the five PSC commissioners, said the new financial assurances from Bloom were crucial in winning his vote. "A week ago, this never would have flown," Lester said.

Commissioner Chairwoman Arnetta McRae, who was presiding over her final meeting, said she had "lingering concerns about how pricing will evolve for consumers." But she said no one made a strong enough case to drive this home.

Commissioner Dallas Winslow said the proposal would provide economic development benefits for the state. But he also said asking the PSC, which typically sets rates on utility bills, to decide the merits of an economic development project was awkward. "I hope we don't see another situation like this again," Winslow said.

The other commissioners, Joann Conaway and Jeffrey Clark, said they had reservations but felt the benefits outweighed them. "Risk and opportunity go hand in hand," Clark said. . . .

After the vote, Lester opened a large binder that had been sitting on his desk containing letters from the public. A few sheets toward the front, he said, came from supporters. He then grabbed the rest with an open fist. These, he said, were those challenging the plan. But "at least now we have some assurances if they [Bloom] leave," Lester said.[25]

Now that the PSC had approved the Bloom deal, nothing appeared to be in the way for construction of Bloom's factory and the Delmarva clusters to begin. Indeed, UD announced in early January 2012 that it was preparing the site at its Science and Technology Campus for the construction of the Bloom factory. In fact, after clearing many of the buildings at the former Chrysler site, work had already begun in mid-December, with UD's Wilmington contractor, Eastern States Construction, handling the removal of concrete, footings, and asphalt for Bloom's fifty acres. "The site will be delivered to Bloom in advance of its March 1 date to begin its construction activities," UD promised. "And they'll begin site work immediately thereafter. Their goal is to be up and running by Spring of 2013 and be in full operation by September of 2013."[26]

The cost to the university of clearing the Bloom site was $1.4 million, to be paid by the state economic development funds, according to UD Vice President David Singleton. President Harker added that UD gave Bloom a "no-cost ground lease" in exchange for those state funds. Singleton explained that Bloom, as the new campus's first tenant, was playing an important anchor role for future prospective tenants.[27]

The no-cost ground lease was just another gift Delaware was giving to Bloom. In April 2012, the state announced that it was dedicating an additional $7 million to ready the site for Bloom's arrival on campus, in lieu of the amount it had already appropriated in 2011 from the state's strategic fund. The $7 million was transferred to UD from the New Jobs Infrastructure Fund, a $55-million cash and bonding authority conceived in 2011 by Governor Jack Markell as a means to stimulate job creation. UD announced that its contractor, 1743 Holdings LLC, had already demolished all the old buildings on the new campus, leaving only concrete slabs. It remained for the holding company to bring electricity, water, data, and phone lines to the Bloom factory site.

The electric power needed for Bloom's factory was to be supplied by the city of Newark's municipal electric system, which would require a massive peak energy capacity of three megawatts that could increase to nine megawatts once Bloom ramped up full production. The city planned to increase the electric supply to its southern end by installing a new electric substation near the factory. Its estimated cost was projected to be at least $2 million, a cost likely to be absorbed not by Bloom but by city ratepayers. Thus, Newark ratepayers would also be required to foot the bill from the city to deliver electricity to the Bloom factory.[28]

Bloom's subsidies from Delaware amounted to only a small fraction of the California subsidies it had garnered. In 2010 alone, Bloom and its customers claimed $215.8 million, or approximately two-thirds of a California state subsidy fund devoted to alternative on-site generation. Its California customers included Walmart, Staples, Adobe, and Coca-Cola.

The proof of Bloom's success in Delaware would depend entirely on its ability to find East Coast buyers—a concern a number of knowledgeable Delawareans had voiced.

On April 30, 2012, Bloom Energy finally "broke ground" on its new "Bloom Energy Manufacturing Center" at UD in a ceremony featuring Bloom CEO KR Sridhar, UD President Harker, Governor Markell, other state officials, and Delaware's congressional delegation. Sridhar announced that Bloom's new East Coast customers would include Owens Corning, Urban Outfitters, Delmarva Power, Washington Gas, and AT&T. "That's really where the proof is—in the pudding," Governor Markell said. Sridhar made it known that Apple also would use Bloom fuel cells at its North Carolina data center.[29]

SETBACKS

The so-called groundbreaking ceremony on April 30, 2012, really did not involve driving ceremonial shovels into the ground. Instead, Bloom and state officials merely unveiled a sign reading "Future Site of Bloom Energy." The ceremony also did not mean that the Bloom Energy factory would be in the process of construction any time soon thereafter. Indeed, Bloom had stated in 2011 that it intended to break ground on the project at the end of that year. Then, in May 2012, Bloom Vice President Joshua Richman said that the company would begin its work at the site in June or July of 2012. Although he added that Bloom would not release detailed plans for construction, he nevertheless said: "The underlying message . . . is that everything is on schedule. There have been, and are, no delays." Meanwhile, Delmarva customers were already on track to begin paying for the project that May. [30]

Governor Jack Markell had announced the Bloom project on June 9, 2011. On that day, he envisioned 350 new construction jobs to be created in 2011, followed by manufacturing beginning in mid-2012, establishing as many as 1,500 permanent high-tech jobs. Nearly five months after the groundbreaking ceremony, and roughly a year after lawmakers and the PSC had quickly cleared a path for Bloom to manufacture fuel cells at the Newark site, the Bloom factory had not yet begun to rise. On September 23, 2012, it was reported that Republican Representative Greg Lavelle of New Castle County voiced his disappointment that the jobs had not yet materialized. [31]

The only movement toward construction of the factory during the remainder of 2012 was the announcement by Bloom in early November that it had hired the Buccini-Pollin Group to build its manufacturing facility. The Buccini-Pollin Group (BPG) had been the most active developer in Wilmington for over ten years. Its contract would be a lease arrangement whereby BPG as the contractor would own the Bloom building and Bloom would be a long-time tenant. Some observers questioned whether this arrangement would void Bloom's prior promise to pay the state $41 million should construction of the factory not be completed by the end of 2013, because BPG would be its owner and thereby responsible to construct the factory. Bloom also announced that it appointed a Delaware human resources director "to ramp up our hiring." And the company posted two Delaware jobs for engineers on its website. [32]

Otherwise, 2012 ended with no progress made toward the actual construction of Bloom's factory. The "Future Site of Bloom Energy" sign was the only outward physical change noted by passing observers in 2012. It was not entirely clear what reasons had caused the delay in completing Bloom's factory. But Geoff Sawyer, Governor Markell's deputy chief of staff, pointed to a lawsuit against the Bloom deal filed in the U.S. District Court of Delaware as a main reason. "We would be weeks, if not months, ahead of where we are today if not for that lawsuit," Sawyer said. [33]

John Nichols, a citizen activist from Middletown, had been unrelenting in his opposition to the Bloom deal from its inception. In May 2012, he challenged the Coastal Zone Act Permit issued earlier that month for the twenty-seven-megawatt Bloom cell cluster outside New Castle to provide electric power to the regional grid. Nichols claimed that DNREC failed to consider all environmental impacts. In June, the Coastal Zone Industrial Control Board dismissed Nichols' challenge, but that did not stop Nichols. [34]

Nichols next teamed up with FuelCell Energy Inc. of Danbury, Connecticut, to bring suit against Governor Markell and members of Delaware's PSC, seeking to invalidate the surcharge for Delmarva Power ratepayers that would subsidize the two energy generating clusters operated by Bloom's subsidiary. The lawsuit of June 20, 2012, filed in the U.S. District Court of Delaware, called for "Declaratory and Injunctive Relief," alleging that the 2011 amendments to Delaware's Renewable Energy Portfolio Standards Act ("REPSA") were motivated by:

> economic protectionism; . . . discriminate against and deny out-of-state companies equal competitive footing with the in-state "crony company" favored by Delaware government officials; . . . force a unique, discrete class of Delaware consumers to subsidize this discrimination through higher electricity bills; and unconstitutionally burden interstate commerce.

Accordingly, the plaintiffs claimed that the REPSA as applied violated both the Dormant Commerce Clause (which forbids states from passing laws that excessively interfere with interstate commerce) and the Equal Protection Clause of the Fourteenth Amendment of the U.S. Constitution.[35]

A spokeswoman for Governor Markell responded: "Mr. Nichols is a litigant who wants to stop a project that will bring hundreds of good manufacturing jobs to Delaware. He is hardly in a position to comment on the productivity of Delaware's economy. The Bloom project is on track."[36] David McBride, an attorney representing Governor Markell and the PSC, told the court that FuelCell Energy had never indicated any interest in doing business in Delaware, and "cannot be heard to complain of being denied 'equal competitive footing' when it had yet to place its foot on the competitive playing field." McBride said that it would be a "travesty" for the court to blow up the Bloom Energy deal with no assurance that FuelCell Energy would step in. The judge gave no indication before the end of 2012 when or if he would rule.[37]

RISING COSTS

During Governor Jack Markell's campaign for a second term in the fall of 2012, his Republican opponent, Jeff Cragg, hammered Markell for his administration's efforts to attract big employers like Fisker Automotive and Bloom Energy. Cragg charged that the Markell administration spent time and tax dollars attempting to "pick winners." Instead, "Fisker had never manufactured a car or made a profit; Bloom had never made a profit. We blew it," Cragg said. Markell responded to Cragg, "If you had your way, that [Delaware City] refinery would be rusting right now. You've joined the ranks of Sarah Palin and others who are fighting against American workers."[38] In the end, Markell won a second term resoundingly, leading the Democrats' ticket by garnering over 70 percent of the vote.

But Cragg's charge that Bloom had never made a profit was not completely without merit. Although Bloom Energy's financial information as a private company had been confidential, the technology blog GigaOM reported in August 2012 that Bloom Energy was only "halfway" to becoming profitable. The article's author, Katie Fehrenbacher, wrote that Bloom "needed lots of capital to scale up manufacturing."[39] Three months later, in mid-November 2012, *Fortune* magazine reported that it had obtained Bloom's financial information, which revealed that Bloom had an approximate $32 million loss during the third quarter of 2012. *Fortune* reported that "the figures seem to confirm much of the Bloom skepticism, including the part about each box costing more than it costs to buy. Moreover, at this burn rate, Bloom would be out of cash within a year." Bloom Chief Financial Officer Bill Kurtz told *Fortune* that on a "pro-forma basis Bloom has become a gross margin positive in 2012 and is on track with our goal to be profitable in 2013." And *Fortune* also reported in May 2013 that the total funding of Bloom Energy had reached $1.1 billion.[40]

The fuel-cell clusters installed at two sites near Delmarva Power to generate power for sale to the regional grid, at Delaware ratepayers' expense, constituted a setup designed to subsidize the cost of building Bloom's factory at UD's Newark site. The question remained whether Bloom Energy's Delaware business venture would become profitable in the future.

Bloom officials announced that actual construction of their factory began in January 2013.[41] They showed off the shell of their new factory on April 19. Less than three months later, in July 2013, they actually delivered Bloom Energy's first fuel cells, manufactured at its still partially constructed Newark factory, to the cluster installed at Delmarva Power's site near New Castle. Accordingly, these so-called Delaware-made "Bloom Boxes" began generating power for sale to the regional electricity grid, thereby garnering additional surcharge revenue from Delmarva customers. Moreover, the factory at the time had only fifty full-time workers, though the firm had been expected in 2011 to hire nine hundred workers within two years.

Whereas Delmarva officials had estimated in 2011 that the average monthly surcharge paid by a Delmarva residential customer would be $1.04 in 2014, such a customer was expected to pay $2.07 in July 2013 as part of the subsidy approved for the state's Bloom deal. Hence, the controversial Delmarva surcharge, calculated monthly by a formula based on electricity market conditions, had already been exceeded by about 100 percent of the 2011 estimate. According to the Wilmington *News Journal*:

> Rep. John Kowalko, D-Newark, criticized the "spiraling upward cost to the ratepayers" for the electrical project, which was established as a financial incentive to woo Bloom to Delaware. He said he worried costs would increase further still as the size of the electrical project builds toward its full capacity. . . .

> Kowalko said it is premature for Bloom to charge Delamarva rate-payers
> for boxes produced at the new factory, since employment there is but a fraction
> of the 900 promised jobs.[42]

State Representative Kowalko was prescient to say the least. The controversial surcharge that Delmarva Power customers paid each month for the Bloom Energy project continued to soar beyond anyone's expectations.

Residential electricity consumers paid an average monthly surcharge that rocketed from sixty-seven cents to $3.83 over the year from September 2012 to September 2013, a surcharge not yet to have been found on their monthly electricity bills.[43] The average surcharge continued to increase to $3.98 by October 2013 and to $4.37 by November 2013, up from $1.08 a year before. No slowing to the surge was in sight. Instead, the Bloom surcharge was reported to top $5 on February 4, 2014, and hovered near $6 just one month later.[44] Republican State Senator Greg Lavelle said his constituents did not understand why the surcharge was going up when electricity prices were going down. "There is confusion, concern, and disappointment in the public over this," he said.[45] A typical residential customer in March 2015 was expected to pay a surcharge of $4.34 for his or her May 2015 bill, still high but below the record high of $5.83 set for typical customers in May of 2014.[46]

CONCLUSION

In retrospect, the Bloom Energy deal remained complex, to say the least. It employed mechanisms not usually found in economic development. In general, most economic development strives to generate positive returns in jobs, income, and income taxes. In this case, however, economic development was conflated with environmental policy and negative results. The special legislation permitting natural gas to be considered a renewable energy continued to strain credulity, with the entire cost of Bloom's residency in Delaware having been shouldered by ratepayers independent of any benefits to offset that burden.

Over a twenty-year period, this strategy portended job losses that far exceed anything Bloom Energy was likely to produce. Even toward the end of 2014, its promise of creating nine hundred jobs by the end of 2016 appeared to be a pipe dream. Relative to its agreement with the state, Bloom Energy had only hired 208 full-time employees instead of its promised three hundred by September 2014, and it promised to hire six hundred by a year later and nine hundred by a year after that—targets that seemed unlikely to be met.[47]

Not only were taxpayers likely to pay more with the grants given to Bloom, but also their utility rates already had become far higher than they had been without Bloom.[48] Taxpayers had been given the privilege of buying very expensive electricity with no discernible return. In fact, the true cost of that privilege was grossly underestimated from the beginning. An initial surcharge cost expected to be $1.04 per one kilowatt hour had exploded to nearly $6 in early 2014. For some consumers, the surcharge cost per month became nearly $30; compared with those who had taxpayer-subsidized solar power, for whom the cost was nominal.

A June 2014 class action lawsuit against Delmarva Power and its parent company Pepco Holdings Inc., on behalf of all Delmarva customers, alleged that Bloom Energy servers were not as energy efficient as claimed. The suit alleged that Bloom was using more natural gas than allowed under the permits with DNREC, asserting: "Delmarva knowingly and recklessly concealed or suppressed knowledge that Bloom servers consumed more natural gas and therefore, emitted more carbon dioxide than allowed under the permits with the intent to deceive its electricity customers into believing that using Bloom servers created cleaner electricity in exchange for a higher electric charge."[49] DNREC's response in July 2014 was that it erred in not updating its permit to Bloom as the project grew larger, and therefore it would reissue a new Bloom Energy electrical project permit allowing its fuel cells to consume more natural gas.[50]

In September 2014, Governor Markell announced that Bloom Energy's plant in Newark, not those in California, was producing "pretty much all" of its servers. Sam Jaffe, principal research analyst of Navigant Research in Colorado, commented: "It is impossible for an outsider to measure how much production is going on at Bloom, because it is a private company that closely guards its secrets." Noting that most of Bloom's customers were in California, but that its customer base was in Japan as well, Eric Wesoff of Greenwich Media added that, as for the reason Bloom was building in Delaware, "I can only think that it's continued subsidies, incentives, and perhaps a less expensive workforce. . . . There's no obvious answer."[51]

The various changes wrought by Bloom Energy's presence in Delaware redirected income that could have been used to purchase goods and services in the state's economy. Clearly, the mixing in this instance of two different policies—economic development policy and energy policy—was counterproductive.

NOTES

1. See "UD Officially Acquires Chrysler Property in Newark," *UDaily*, University of Delaware, November 23, 2009; and "Research Campus Proposed for Former Chrysler Site," *UD Messenger*, University of Delaware, Vol. 17, No. 2 (2009).
2. "Bloom Energy Plans," *UDaily*, University of Delaware, June 9, 2011.
3. Eric Ruth, "Fuel Cell Firm Coming to Former Chrysler Site in Newark; 1,500 Jobs Expected," Wilmington *News Journal*, June 9, 2011.

4. Penny Atkins, "Delaware's Deal with Bloom Energy Looks Like No Bargain," Wilmington *News Journal*, September 27, 2011, A14.

5. See Editorial, "Manufacturing Deal Gives State, UD a Big Boost," Wilmington *News Journal*, June 10, 2011, A12; Wade Malcolm, "UD, Bloom Find Perfect Match with Each Other," ibid., October 10, 2011, A11; and Wade Malcolm, "UD Hopes to Get Additional $7M," ibid., July 25, 2011, B1, B2.

6. The Governor's Energy Advisory Council, *Delaware Energy Plan 2009–2014* (Dover: State of Delaware, March 26, 2009), 6–7.

7. SB 19 Amended by HB 1 An Act to Amend the Delaware Code to Increase the Renewable Energy Portfolio Standard. Approved July 24, 2007, accessible at legis.delaware.gov/LIS/LIS144.NSF/vwLegislation/SB+19?Opendocument.

8. SB 119 An Act to Amend Title 26 of the Delaware Code Relating to the Renewable Energy Portfolio Standards. Approved July 28, 2010, accessible at legis.delaware.gov/LIS/LIS145.NSF/vwLegislation/SB+119?Opendocument.

9. See, *Delaware Code*: Title 29, Ch. 80, Subchapter II, The Delaware Energy Act; and Title 26, Chapter 1, Subchapter III–A. Renewable Energy Portfolio Standards, delcode.delaware.gov/title29/c080/sc02/index.shtml and delcode.delaware.gov/title26/c001/sc03a/index.shtml.

10. Governor's Energy Advisory Council, *Delaware Energy Plan 2009–2014*, 72.

11. Letter to the Editor by Charles Boncelet, "Bloom Energy Subsidy Reeks of Desperation," Wilmington *News Journal*, June 26, 2011, A19.

12. See Chad Livengood and Jeff Montgomery, "Senate OKs Bill to Boost Bloom," Wilmington *News Journal*, June 17, 2011, B1, B2; Chad Livengood, "House Panel OKs Bloom Bill," ibid., June 23, 2011, B1; and Chad Livengood, "House Clears Way for Surcharge to Subsidize Bloom," ibid., June 24, 2011, B2.

13. Collin O'Mara, "Bloom and Delaware's Energy Future," Wilmington *News Journal*, September 9, 2011, A13.

14. Aaron Nathans, "'Bloom Boxes' a Blow to Clean Energy," Wilmington *News Journal*, September 9, 2011, A1, A6.

15. See, e.g., Aaron Nathans, "Delmarva Customers' Cost in Bloom Deal Varies Wildly," Wilmington *News Journal*, August 20, 2011, A1, A5.

16. John A. Nichols, "Subsidizing Fuel Cells Is a Bad Deal for Delawareans," Wilmington *News Journal*, September 23, 2011, A15.

17. See Eric Ruth, "NCCo Residents Face off on Bloom Deal," Wilmington *News Journal*, September 29, 2011, A1, A7; Aaron Nathans, "Kent Residents Question Bloom Energy Deal," ibid., September 28, 2011; and Molly Murray, "Bloom a Hit; Subsidy Plan Isn't: Sussex County Residents Express Support for Jobs But Not Delmarva Surcharge," ibid., September 30, 2011, A8, A9.

18. Aaron Nathans, "Big Reward but High Risk: Bloom's 900 Jobs Put Delmarva Customers on Hook to Pay," Wilmington *News Journal*, October 9, 2011, A1, A10.

19. Ibid., A10.

20. David Stevenson and John Stapleford, "Case for Bloom Is Undermined By the Numbers," Wilmington *News Journal*, October 14, 2011, A15.

21. Editorial, "Bloom Must Make the Case for State Deal," Wilmington *News Journal*, October 9, 2011, A30.

22. Copy of letter to Delaware PSC Chairperson Arnetta McRae from State Representatives Greg Lavelle, Lincoln Willis, and Dan Short, October 17, 2011, accessible at www.delawarestatehouse.com/pdfs/101811_Lawmakers_Ask_PSC_to_Protect_Ratepayers_in_Bloom_Energy_Deal5.pdf.

23. Aaron Nathans, "Bloom Agrees to Financial Collateral: Company Will Pay Penalty Fees if the Deal Falls Through," Wilmington *News Journal*, October 14, 2011, A1, A2.

24. See Jim Hilgen, "Public Service Commission Gives Bloom Energy Deal Its Approval," *WDDE 91.1 FM, DFM News*, October 18, 2011, www.wdde.org/18847-bloom-hearing-delaware (accessed December 11, 2012).

25. Aaron Nathans, "PSC Approves Bloom Energy Deal," Wilmington *News Journal*, October 19, 2011, A1, A14. That known Delaware critics of the Bloom plan far outnumbered its

supporters was evidenced by letters to the editor of the Wilmington *News Journal*. For example, of eight letters in its October 15, 2011, issue, seven opposed the plan.

26. See Aaron Nathans, "Work Begins at Bloom Factory and Generator Sites," Wilmington *News Journal*, January 6, 2012, A10; and LeAnne Matlach, "Bloom Energy to Build on Chrysler Site in March," *WDEL 1150am–Video*, January 23, 2012, www.wdel.com/story.php?id=40348 (accessed January 30, 2012).

27. Aaron Nathans, "Former Auto Plant Ready for Bloom to Take Root," Wilmington *News Journal*, February 26, 2012, C1, C3.

28. See Wade Malcolm, "Bloom Executives Receive a Warm Welcome from Newark Officials," Wilmington *News Journal*, May 1, 2012, A1, A2; and Aaron Nathans, "Bloom Subsidy Hikes June Bills," ibid., May 21, 2012, A10.

29. See Aaron Nathans, "Bloom Factory Set to Put Down Roots," Wilmington *News Journal*, April 29, 2012, E1, E5; Bloom Energy Press Release, "Bloom Energy Expands to East Coast," April 30, 2012, www.bloomenergy.com/newsroom/press-release-04-30-12/ (accessed October 2, 2012); and Martin LaMonica, "Bloom Energy Today Opens Plant in Delaware . . .," *CNET News*, April 30, 2012, www.news.cnet,com/8301-11386_3-57434037-76/apple-data-center-helps-fuel-bloom-energy (accessed October 2, 2012).

30. Aaron Nathans, "Bloom Factory Won't Rise Soon in Newark," Wilmington *News Journal*, May 13, 2012, E1, E4.

31. Aaron Nathans, "Bloom Factory a Year Behind First Timetable," Wilmington *News Journal*, September 23, 2012, A9.

32. Ibid.

33. Aaron Nathans, "Bloom Picks Firm to Build Newark Plant," Wilmington *News Journal*, November 11, 2012, E1, E4.

34. See Aaron Nathans, "NCCO Resident Challenges Permit for Bloom Project," Wilmington *News Journal*, May 25, 2012, A16; and Aaron Nathans, "Appeals Panel Affirms Permit for Bloom Cell Cluster," ibid., June 15, 2012, A12, A13.

35. See John A. Nichols and FuelCell Energy, Inc. v. Jack Markell et al., U.S. Dist. Ct. of Delaware (June 20, 2012), www.greentechmedia.com/articles/read/lawsuit-accuses-bloom-energy-delaware-of-cronyism; Aaron Nathans, "Markell, PSC Sued over Deal," Wilmington *News Journal*, June 22, 2012, A14; and Aaron Nathans, "Court Test for Bloom Deal," ibid., November 15, 2012, A8.

36. Aaron Nathans, "Bloom Picks Firm to Build Newark Plant," Wilmington *News Journal*, November 11, 2012, E1, E4.

37. See Randall Chase, "Judge Eyes Challenge to Delaware Bloom Energy Deal," *Yahoo! News*, November 15, 2012, news.yahoo.com/judge-eyes-challenge-delaware-bloom-154744849.html (accessed January 8, 2013); and Aaron Nathans, "State Counters Lawsuit Contesting Bloom Subsidy," Wilmington *News Journal*, September 7, 2012.

38. Doug Denison, "Candidates Square Off, Governor Hopefuls Discuss Fisker, Bloom," Wilmington *News Journal*, October 17, 2012, B1, B2.

39. Aaron Nathans, "Bloom Energy is 'Halfway' to Becoming Profitable," Wilmington *News Journal*, August 20, 2012, A10.

40. See Aaron Nathans, "Bloom Energy's Financials Revealed: Still in Red," Wilmington *News Journal*, November 18, 2012, E1; and Aaron Nathans, "Report: Bloom Energy Raises $140 million more," ibid, May 15, 2013, A8.

41. Aaron Nathans, "Bloom Projects Advance," Wilmington *News Journal*, January 10, 2013, A8.

42. See Aaron Nathans, "Future on Display, Bloom Unveils Factory . . . ," Wilmington *News Journal*, April 20, 2013, A6; and Aaron Nathans, "Bloom Makes First Fuel-Cell Servers in Del.," ibid., July 13, 2013, A1, A2.

43. See Aaron Nathans, "Bloom Subsidy Spikes Early, Delmarva Surcharge Grows as Anticipated Newark Jobs Languish," Wilmington *News Journal*, August 25, 2013, A1, A20, A21. Note that the PSC in May 2014 finally approved surcharges to appear on Delmarva Power monthly bills; see Aaron Nathans, "PSC Approves Detailed Delmarva Bills," ibid., May 6, 2014, A6.

44. See these articles by Aaron Nathans in the Wilmington *News Journal*: "Bloom Surcharge Tops $5, Lawmakers Ask Why Surcharge Is So High," February 4, 2014, A6, A7; "Record Bloom Energy Delmarva Surcharge Hovers at Near $6," March 5, 2014, A1, A6; and "Why the Bloom Energy Surcharge Increased," March 19, 2014, A8.

45. Aaron Nathans, "Bloom Charge for Delmarva Customers Soars, Monthly Rate Has Quadrupled Since Last Year," Wilmington *News Journal*, September 28, 2013, A1.

46. Jeff Montgomery, "Delmarva Surcharge for Bloom Energy Rises," Wilmington *News Journal*, March 19, 2015, A16.

47. Aaron Nathans, "Bloom Employment in Newark Misses Benchmarks," Wilmington *News Journal*, November 2, 2014, E1.

48. Note that in 2006, Delmarva Power Company had imposed a 59 percent increase in electricity rates, as discussed in William Boyer and Edward Ratledge, *Pivotal Policies in Delaware: From Desegregation to Deregulation* (Newark: University of Delaware Press, 2014), chapter 10.

49. Aaron Nathans, "Lawsuit Attacks Bloom Box Energy Claims," Wilmington *News Journal*, June 30, 2014.

50. Aaron Nathans, "DNREC Says It Erred on Permit for Bloom," Wilmington *News Journal*, July 9, 2014.

51. Aaron Nathans, "Markell: Bloom Using Del. to Build Most Units," Wilmington *News Journal*, September 6, 2014, A4.

Chapter Six

Delaware City Refinery

According to Delaware historian John Munroe, Tidewater Oil, which was later to become Getty Oil, moved from Bayonne, New Jersey, to Delaware City in New Castle County, "because Delaware offered tax advantages as well as the opportunity to build a new largely automated plant at a point to which tankers could conveniently bring foreign petroleum."[1] The Delaware City refinery was established in 1956 and began production in 1957. It was the largest refinery to be built in the nation when it began operating (with a 140,000 barrel-per-day capacity at the time). The refinery since then has had a checkered history, remnants of which have persisted well into the twenty-first century.

FROM GETTY TO STAR ENTERPRISES

In 1967, Tidewater merged with Getty Oil, which operated the Delaware refinery until 1984. Situated on a property of over five thousand acres, about one-half the area of the city of Wilmington, Getty Oil's huge petrochemical complex dwarfed everything in the vicinity and vitally affected the health and life of residents of nearby Delaware City (population 2,024 in 1970). A 1983 study—based on 1978 data—found that Delaware City's hospitalization rate was 53 percent higher, and its mortality rate was 36 percent higher, than New Castle County's average rates.[2] Moreover, it was Getty Oil refinery's emissions of sulfur particulates that convinced Governor Russell Peterson to initiate Delaware's renowned Coastal Zone Act (CZA) of 1970.

Texaco bought Getty in 1984 and ran the refinery until 1988, when Star Enterprises took over. Star was a company formed when Saudi Aramco bought half interest in the enterprise. The refinery's operations became a product of Saudi Arabia's petroleum empire, whereby its national oil company—Saudi Aramco—owned not only a large share of the Delaware City refinery, but also 50 percent of the refinery's crude oil imports of almost thirty million barrels transported in 1992 to the refinery by ships from Saudi Arabia.

Meanwhile, no pollution site in Delaware through the 1990s was the subject of more complaints than Star Enterprises's refinery. Complaints from nearby, and even more distant, residents appeared to accelerate, most often concerning intermittent foul odors, such as the smell of rotten eggs, onions, and urine. At times residents also complained of sulfurous fumes, soot, and irritation of their eyes and throats.[3]

In August 1990, the refinery released hydrogen sulfide gas, which required hospitalization of twenty-three of the 640 Star employees, four of whom had to be revived from cardiac arrest. State investigators claimed that the gas released could have caused the death of nearby Route 9 motorists. Delaware's Department of Natural Resources and Environmental Control (DNREC) Secretary Toby Clark declared the refinery an "imminent danger."[4]

A breakdown of a refinery unit usually was found to have been the source of complaints. The refinery company claimed to have spent millions in pollution abatement systems, upgrades and replacements. Nevertheless, in 1995, Delaware's state government sued Star over more complaints. For example, doctors at Christiana Care Hospital linked respiratory problems suffered by patients and staff to Star emissions. Star agreed to pay the state $175,000 to install special devices to closely monitor its refinery's emissions, whereupon the state dropped its suit. But still more emissions, accidents, and complaints ensued, which led the DNREC to assign one of its engineers to be a full-time monitor at Star and other chemical plants located in the area.[5]

MOTIVA

The Star refinery's name was changed to Motiva Enterprises in 1998 to signal operation of the refinery by a joint venture between Star (Saudi Aramco) and Shell.

Motiva's operation of the refinery became most controversial, mainly because of the catastrophic explosion of an acid tank on July 17, 2001, which killed one worker, injured eight others, and caused massive environmental damage. The explosion caused other storage tanks to release their contents, as well. Approximately 1.1 million gallons of spent sulfuric acid spilled into the streets of the refinery, of which 99,000 gallons were released into the Delaware River, killing many fish and crabs. A federal investigation revealed that Motiva was at fault for not heeding or responding to repeated warnings over the previous decade from inspection reports of corrosion and leaks in the storage tanks.[6]

Motiva failed to participate in good-faith efforts during settlement negotiations in the wake of the explosion. As a result of a federal–state civil lawsuit, Motiva paid a $12 million penalty, was forced to fund a series of environmental projects worth a total of $7.5 million, and had to reimburse the U.S. and Delaware governments over $170,000 for its cleanup costs. Another federal penalty cited Motiva's "willful violations," which Motiva settled for a total of $132,000. Moreover, Motiva pleaded "no contest to criminally negligent homicide and assault charges" brought by Delaware's attorney general, for which the company paid $296,000 in penalties. In September 2003, Motiva agreed to pay $36.4 million to the widow and family of the worker who was killed. Finally, as part of a criminal plea agreement in 2004 with the U.S. Department of Justice, Motiva pleaded guilty to "endangering its workers," for which it was ordered to pay a $10 million fine.

Delaware Governor Ruth Ann Minner (2001–2009) commented: "While nothing can erase the human and environmental impacts resulting from this event, we have made a number of changes on a state level as a result, including the enactment of Delaware's Above Ground Storage Tank Act and our enforcement action requiring enhancements to the refinery's mechanical integrity program." Delaware Attorney General Jane Brady added: "Motiva's conduct was inexcusable. Nothing we do can undo the harm to the workers and their families but I trust all companies will take a lesson from this . . . and realize that we will not tolerate this type of behavior in Delaware."[7]

Notwithstanding severe criticisms of Motiva by Delaware public officials, the Delaware City refinery represented an important business that contributed significantly to Delaware's economy. As if to deflect continuing criticisms, while improving its public relations, Motiva contracted with the Center for Applied Demography & Survey Research (CADSR) of the University of Delaware to conduct a study of the company's economic impact in Delaware. CADSR assigned the study to economist Dr. Simon Condliffe, who released his report in October 2002. The first paragraph of his report stated that Motiva commissioned the study, the purpose of which was to measure the economic impacts of the Motiva refinery, and that the study was not intended to be an audit of Motiva's operations, its management, or an assessment of the desirability of the refinery. Dr. Condliffe's major findings in his study of twenty-five pages were condensed in his executive summary as follows:

> The operation of Motiva Enterprises . . . Delaware City Refinery (DCR) has an estimated total economic impact of $379 million per year to Delaware. The DCR has a total employment of 3,227 within the state, and a wage and salary impact of $186 million per year.

Direct employment at the DCR includes 675 workers, plus an additional
155 . . . workers at the facility's power plant and a further 32 at the distribution
center. A varying number of contractors are also employed at the refinery. The
primary maintenance contractor . . . has a core of 250 building-trades union
contractors at the facility.

The refinery's intermediate purchases, and the expenditures from the direct, indirect, and induced employment and income, generate additional employment for the state.

Petroleum refining is a high productive industry. Output per employee is
over $2 million.

The refinery generates direct and indirect and induced state and local
government fiscal revenues of $50 million per year.

The average salary at the refinery is $65,813, which is 31 percent higher
than the Delaware median income of $50,359 (Census 1999 in $2002 dollars).

The refinery supplies products to several manufacturers in the state, and
supplies gasoline to 90 percent of the state's gas stations through exchange
agreements with other petroleum companies.

Retirees of the DCR received pensions from Motiva. . . . Over 200 DCR
retirees reside in the state.

The DCR is a secure source of heating oil and propane for the agricultural
industry in the state. In winter conditions, the DCR is a supplier of propane for
the state's poultry farming (chicken coop heating) and grain farming (drying
operations). [8]

Among other findings, Dr. Condliffe reported that New Castle County received approximately $900,000 in property taxes annually from Motiva,
which in part funded schools, and that Delaware City received $159,000 in
property taxes annually. [9]

Of all the owners of the Delaware City refinery, Motiva would prove the
most controversial, not only because of its 2001 accident, but also because of
the many federal and state violations of emission regulations and lawsuits the
company thereafter experienced. Indeed, days before a contempt trial in October 2007, long after Motiva had departed Delaware in 2004, Motiva together with its predecessor corporation Texaco, settled a unique long legal battle
that had lasted nearly twenty years with two environmental groups—the
Delaware Audubon Society and the Natural Resources Defense Council. For
repeated violations of water pollution permits and court orders, Motiva and
Texaco agreed to fund $2.25 million in environmental projects in the Dela-
ware City area. [10]

PREMCOR, VALERO, AND PBF

Premcor Inc., one of the nation's largest independent petroleum refiners,
purchased Motiva's Delaware City refinery complex in 2004. The purchase
price was $435 million and the assumption of $365 million of tax-exempt

bonds issued by the Delaware Economic Development Authority (DEDA). In a press release, Thomas D. O'Malley, Premcor's chairman and CEO, said, "This transaction, which will increase our crude oil processing capability by approximately 30 percent, represents a major step forward for Premcor. We are extremely pleased to have the opportunity to acquire the most technologically complex refinery on the East Coast."[11]

In November 2004, within months after Premcor's takeover, Delaware's state government approved the largest air pollution control agreement in the state's history. DNREC's agreement called for Premcor to spend an estimated $200 million to upgrade its smokestack and abide by a new cap on emissions. DNREC projected that Premcor would thereby reduce emissions of sulfur dioxide by almost 30,000 tons, equivalent to about 97 percent of Premcor's then-current sulfur dioxide output.[12] However, Premcor, and its Delaware City refinery, was sold only ten weeks after it signed its agreement with DNREC.

On April 25, 2005, Valero Energy Corporation agreed to buy Premcor, Inc. for $6.9 billion in cash and stock to become the largest U.S. petroleum refiner. Included in the sale was not only Premcor's Delaware City refinery but also Premcor's plants in Tennessee, Texas, and Ohio.[13]

However, Valero's tenure at the Delaware City refinery was not profitable. With the onset of the nation's economic recession, Valero issued a public statement in November 2009 abruptly closing its Delaware City refinery, reportedly because of "weak economic conditions, high local costs and chronic maintenance problems." Valero's chief spokesman explained, "We've had potential buyers come in and look at the plant, but we've never had any viable offers for that property. We've looked at other alternatives besides shutting the refinery down. We talked about operating it without certain units that were specific money losers. Not even that was viable." Operating costs at the refinery had averaged about $1 million a day since January 2009. Officials of the Delaware Economic Development Office (DEDO) estimated that the closing of the refinery could cost the state's economy $882 million in lost wages and income to suppliers and workers in jobs supported directly and indirectly by the refinery.[14]

The closing of the Delaware City Refinery came amid a radical decline in the number of U.S. refineries over a period of twenty-two years. The number dropped from 204 in 1989 to 125 in 2011.[15] During the three years from 2009 to 2012 alone, a total of eighteen refineries in the United States and Europe were shut down, according to industry analysts.[16]

Valero's abrupt shutdown of its refinery happened within Jack Markell's first year as Delaware's governor, coincident also with the first year of the nationwide economic downslide. Governor Markell (2009–present) actively sought to fill the resulting job void of some 550 workers by seeking another company to purchase Valero's dormant plant. He became involved in negotiations between Valero and Switzerland-based PBF Energy, Europe's largest independent petroleum refiner. He pressed the two companies to negotiate and pledged $45 million in state assistance for a deal between them. As an incentive to PBF, the state committed a $20 million loan from its Strategic Fund.[17] The state also promised that PBF's loan agreement would convert to a grant from the state should the company spend in excess of $100 million and support six hundred full-time jobs in Delaware for five consecutive years.[18]

PBF Energy announced its purchase of the refinery from Valero in June 2010 for $220 million. After eighteen months of the refinery remaining shuttered, PBF spent $465 million in restoring the plant. PBF then announced on October 7, 2011, the successful restart of the refinery, to be known as the Delaware City Refining Company. Among others attending the ceremony to celebrate the restart was Governor Markell, who said: "This reopening is the culmination of two years of teamwork. First [is] to find a new owner for this great facility. Then, through tens of thousands of hours of labor by over a thousand people, to bring the refinery from shuttered to in-service. Now, hundreds will report to work here each day, better able to support their families and their neighborhood businesses."[19]

One year later, on October 11, 2012, the refinery manager of the Delaware City Refining Company, Herman Seedorf, reported that the restart of the refinery had led to the rehiring of nearly five hundred employees ("the company hired back those who wanted to be hired back"), plus the hiring of three hundred contactors. He added that operation of the refinery created a total of three to four thousand jobs.[20]

BILLION-DOLLAR EXPANSION PLANNED

Whereas the Delaware City refinery was purchased in June 2010 and restarted in October 2011, PBF Energy meanwhile also purchased in December 2010 the Paulsboro refinery thirty-five miles to the north in New Jersey. Both refineries converted heavy crude oil, the Delaware City refinery with a capacity of 190,000 barrels per day and the Paulsboro refinery with a capacity of 170,000 barrels per day. On December 21, 2011, PBF announced its so-called PBF Clean Fuels Project plan to construct over three years a hydro-cracker and hydrogen plant at its Delaware refinery that would process streams from both of its refineries. PBF claimed the project would "reduce the sulfur content by 99 percent in approximately 65,000 barrels per day" that would certainly make Delaware City and Paulsboro "world class refineries," and ensure their long-term survivability. Governor Markell hailed the announcement. He stressed that the investment "will mean hundreds of thousands of man-hours during construction, as well as additional permanent jobs at Delaware City." But PBF's announcement included this somewhat pro-phetic caveat, as events would prove:

> This project is contingent upon the issuance of timely and appropriate Federal
> and State environmental and other permits that will not increase the cost to
> build or operate the project, as well as acceptable labor agreements that will
> ensure that the project can be built in an efficient and cost effective man-
> ner. . . . It is imperative, however, that we are able to swiftly move with the
> government agencies to get the appropriate permitting in place. [21]

One of the factors driving PBF's expensive plan was projected federal regulations requiring the burning of ultra-low-sulfur fuels. Moreover, PBF Energy President Michael Gayda stated that PBF recognized that the public wants low-sulfur products, and PBF's plan "is really an opportunity to make more valuable products from the same crude oil or even lower-value crude oil." Delaware's CZA, however, might stand in the way because PBF's pro-ject could be the type of expansion that would cause a full Coastal Zone review. Noting that his company was wary of delays in seeking permits, Gayda said, "We're not going to make major commitments until we have greater certainty on the permits. So if the permits get tied up or delayed or it becomes a case of too many conditions on the permits, we will not have invested so much money that we can't reverse course." [22]

An editorial in the state's leading newspaper lauded PBF's billion-dollar announcement, especially the prospect of a big boost in construction jobs, and expressed the view that "delays should be avoided" in the permitting process and environmental reviews. But praise of the proposed billion-dollar project was destined to end. Without any publicity, PBF Delaware City Re-finery Company officials decided in mid-2012 to postpone its $1 billion plan to expand its ultra-low-sulfur-oil production, not because of the barbs and criticisms of environmental advocates, but rather to shift its major investment to a very profitable "crude-by-rail" effort.

SHIFTING TO CRUDE-BY-RAIL

In December 2012, PBF Energy—comprising the refineries at Delaware City, Paulsboro, New Jersey, and Toledo, Ohio—filed with the U.S. Secur-ities Exchange Commission (SEC) to offer $512 million of common stock to public stockholders, the sale of which would finance, in part, investment needed to modernize and streamline refinery operations. The SEC filing revealed significant information about the Delaware City refinery such as, for example, the steps PBF took to reduce $200 million in annual operating expenses in Delaware City and its heavy investment to create an extensive rail yard to enable it to bring in much less expensive crude oil from Canada and North Dakota instead of relying on importing higher-priced oil from overseas as in the past. Early in the twenty-first century, an extraordinary transformation in the availability of crude oil in Southern Canada and in North Dakota, together with recently developed extraction technology, caused the Delaware City refinery in 2012–2013 to completely shift from importing expensive crude oil from overseas to reliance on so-called crude-by-rail deliveries. Inexpensive Canadian crude oil from Alberta and Saskatchewan was being extracted by strip or pit mining of heavy tar-sand crude. Meanwhile, in North Dakota, heavy crude was being produced by fracking, similar to fracking methods used for extracting natural gas from shale. At the same time, the Delaware refinery was the only heavy crude refinery on the East Coast, making it uniquely and routinely capable of processing the thick, high-sulfur, acidic crude extracted from Alberta's tar-sand fields.

PBF's filing with the SEC also revealed plans to lease about 2,400 rail cars for transporting the crude oil, whereby the Delaware City rail yard would have the capacity to unload 110,000 barrels a day. Some of the oil transported to Delaware would be shipped by barge to PBF's Paulsboro refinery. Finally, PBF reported profits in the SEC filing of $539.8 million during the first nine months of 2012. Accordingly, PBF achieved a remarkable turnaround from a few years before when refineries throughout the nation were closing, including several within the northeast such as, as we have noted, Valero's Delaware City refinery.[23]

In February 2013, nine western and midwestern state governors requested that President Obama approve the construction of the Keystone XL oil pipeline from Canada. At the same time, a coalition of sixty environmental organizations urged newly appointed Secretary of State John Kerry to block the Keystone XL pipeline to save the country from increased pollution and health risks. However, a U.S. State Department report issued in March 2013 appeared to support approval of the pipeline. The draft report found no significant environmental impact would be generated along the pipeline's proposed route from Western Canada to Texas refineries along the Gulf Coast. Republican Speaker of the House John Boehner hailed the report, claiming there was no longer a reason to block the pipeline. But environmentalists claimed the report failed to account for climate risks. Daniel Gatti of the Environment America group, citing a Washington rally in February attended by 35,000 pipeline opponents, said, "Americans are already suffering from consequences of global warming, from more powerful storms like Hurricane Sandy to drought conditions currently devastating the Midwest and Southwest."

The State Department analysis showed, nevertheless, that shipping oil by railroad would release more greenhouse gases that would contribute to global warming than would be released by use of the Keystone XL pipeline. Regardless of State Department analyses, President Obama in late February 2015 vetoed a bill that would have approved construction of the controversial pipeline. In early March, the Republican-controlled Senate failed to override the veto. Senate Majority Leader Mitch McConnell said: "The President's veto of the bipartisan Keystone bill represents a defeat for jobs, infrastructure, and the middle class."[24]

Meanwhile, this still unresolved dispute only bolstered the Delaware City refinery, which was planning to invest substantially to expand its capacity to about 210,000 barrels per day, driving PBF to complete the East Coast's premier rail facility and depot, and to add about 3,600 rail cars, or in other words to depend on what was tantamount to a "pipeline by rail."[25] In the final analysis, shipping oil by rail to the high-value markets on the East Coast was more profitable than shipping oil to the Gulf Coast and refined products back to the East Coast.

It was likely that even if the possible construction of the Keystone XL pipeline proceeded, that would not hamper the initial progress of PBF's Delaware City refinery, primarily because the amount of heavy crude oil in the Canadian and North Dakota fields far exceeded the capacities of U.S. refineries. Moreover, very few of the nation's refineries were equipped to process heavy crude, and the Delaware City refinery had already proved its unique and routine capability in that respect. In February 2013, PBF Energy officials took notice of how profitable the previous year had been. The company's CEO reported, "Our East Coast system, on a cash basis, was profitable not only for the fourth quarter but for the entire year. That's in spite of having a truly bad half of the year, when the East Coast lost money." Noting that the Delaware City refinery had a huge market advantage with its opening of a premier rail terminal for low-cost heavy crudes from the West, PBF Chairman Tom O'Malley added: "Everything we see says to us the movement of heavy crude by rail, particularly if you can get bitumen [heavy oil] into the complex—and we can—that's something that's around for the next decade. We are making investments and signing agreements in Canada to source that crude as we speak. That's a long-term perspective." O'Malley concluded that the company's financial performance should continue to improve, with 2013 looking "like a great year for our industry."[26]

ENVIRONMENTAL CONCERNS SURFACE

The granting of Delaware permits was the responsibility of the state Department of Natural Resources and Environmental Control. Secretary Collin O'Mara pledged that DNREC's entire hearing process regarding permits would remain. However, two state permits would be required—a Coastal Zone Permit and an air emission control permit that could also involve water and solid waste reviews. The question O'Mara was considering was whether the two permits could be combined, whereby they would be announced to the public at the same time and have the same public hearing. Brenda Goggin of the Delaware Nature Society stated, "We have a concern if the Coastal Zone Permit were to be combined with the air permit, because the Coastal Zone program is so unique. They would be placing the public in a very difficult position."[27]

The CZA of 1971 banned new heavy industries from Delaware's coastal zone, namely land bordering on the Delaware River, Delaware Bay, and Atlantic coast. Since existing plants in the coastal zone were exempted or grandfathered in, their expansion required a case-by-case permit review that any new pollution had to be offset by environmental controls and mitigation. Environmental advocates, however, had good reason to be especially concerned about PBF's pending air permit process. A citizen-led air pollution study had compared chemical and soot levels near and in Delaware City both before and after the reopening of PBF's refinery in 2010. Data from the study by the so-called Delaware City Environmental Coalition showed increases in sulfur dioxide and dust after the refinery's start-up. The greatest increase was in a known carcinogen, benzene, found around Clinton Street in Delaware City. This finding was especially troubling insofar as Delaware City already had a new cancer rate per 100,000 residents that was 32 percent higher than the rest of the state and 46 percent higher than the national average.[28]

In January 2012, the Delaware City Coalition had complained to DNREC of a power failure at the refinery inducing flaring, which released thousands of pounds of sulfur dioxide and other pollutants, made noticeable when flames from flare towers illuminated low clouds over the refinery. Most vexing for nearby frightened residents was the disabling of PBF's community information line by a power failure, leaving them uniformed about the emergency and without knowledge of the severity of the problem.[29]

In June 2012, the Delaware Chapter of the Sierra Club—one of Delaware's largest environmental organizations—also cautioned against streamlining review processes for PBF refinery permits. Amy Roe, the conservation chair of the chapter, said, "We do not see added value to expediting a highly complex project review and are concerned that doing so would overwhelm the public and may impinge upon the public's time to review and understand the project, as well as impact opportunities to provide meaningful input."[30] A few weeks later, in July, Roe sent a notice to chapter members summoning them to a special Sierra Club forum on fish impacts by the Delaware City refinery. The notice stated:

> The Delaware City Refinery utilizes water withdrawn from the Delaware River as part of its once-through cooling system. As part of this process, enormous quantities of fish are killed as they are impinged and entrained against the

intake screens which are more than fifty years old and have never been updated with advanced technology that represents the industry standard of best practice. The refinery also releases heated water back into the river, which changes the thermal characteristics of the river ecosystem, impacting the health and vitality of the Delaware River's aquatic environment. Complicating the environmental and economic impacts of fish impingement, entrainment and thermal pollution, the Delaware City Refinery is operating under a permit that expired in 2002. The Delaware City Refinery's fish impacts . . . not only impact the river and its ecosystem, but also recreational value of the Delaware River and Bay and the livelihoods of commercial fishermen. [31]

Meanwhile, the Delaware Chapter of the Sierra Club posted an article online entitled "Delaware City Refinery" that stated in part the following:

The Delaware City Refinery has had numerous spills and permit violations to date. For example, in 2011 alone, the Refinery violated its air emissions, wastewater and solid waste landfill permits 29 times. . . . The main contaminants released into the environment are benzene, toluene, ethyl benzene, xylene, and other petroleum hydrocarbons compounds, including MTBE. Metals and chlorinated hydrocarbons have contaminated the soil, groundwater and sediments.

The article concluded by listing induced health effects as including colon cancer, leukemia, liver damage, euphoria, dizziness, and loss of memory. [32] The president of the Delaware Audubon Society also evinced concern about the refinery's emission of pollutants. [33]

One may note that regardless of PBF's previous announcement that its $1 billion plan would significantly reduce the sulfur content of its oil production, there appeared no instance in which a Delaware environmental organization advocate had voiced anything favorable about the plan. Another example of this occurred in October 2012, after PBF plant manager Herman Seedorf made public that state economic development officials approved a $10 million grant to PBF earlier in the year to help fund converting the plant's combustion turbines to run on natural gas instead of synthetic gas. Seedorf said the state's expenditure of millions of dollars was critical in helping PBF to restart the refinery. That this move also was made to reduce the refinery's emissions of nitrogen oxide and sulfuric dioxide evoked no notice or praise from any Delaware environmental advocate. [34]

With the advent of importing large quantities of heavy crude oil by rail at the Delaware City refinery, criticisms by environmentalists tended to shift from the refinery plant itself to its train deliveries. Moreover, critics were not confined to environmentalists alone, but also included neighbors, police, and others affected by such deliveries. Although the Delaware City refinery had always depended on railway tank cars for some movements, deliveries by rail of huge volumes of heavy crude by railway tank cars started arriving at the refinery in 2012 from the Upper Midwest and Canada. According to PBF Energy officials, 150,000 barrels or even more were expected, via four trains with up to 240 cars each, to arrive daily by the end of 2013. This phenomenon was attributable to the availability of low-cost oil, which in turn was wrought by technological advances in extraction.

Only months before the train deliveries began, PBF had taken over the failed Valero refinery amid a global recession that caused refineries in Europe and the United States to shut down. Herman Seedorf, PBF's manager of the Delaware City refinery, commented: "We were thinking, 'What are we going to do? How are we going to make this a viable business?' You know what? The Holy Grail appeared to us, and the Holy Grail was this burgeoning supply of crude oil reserves in the center of our country and in Canada." Amy Roe of the Delaware Chapter of the Sierra Club was not sanguine about PBF's "Holy Grail." At a community meeting near the refinery of more than 150 people to discuss new concerns, Roe said, "We're very concerned about the rail project and what it means for pollution at the Delaware City refinery, the impact that the pollution will have on the Delaware River and nearby communities, and the connection between this project and the Canada tar sands."[35]

New Castle County Police Chief Kevin McDerby complained at the community meeting that train movements at times had blocked police responses in emergency situations. Others cited instances of slow-moving, lengthy crude-carrying trains causing long delays at highway crossings. A resident who lived close to a track for crude oil deliveries complained of excessive noise. "Why," he asked, "would they need to blow their horn thirteen times in one minute?" A woman whose property was adjacent to the tracks spoke of tank cars speeding in the middle of the night, shaking the house, clanging and squeaking, and often waking up her and her family: "The house is rocking. That's disturbing. I worry about foundation problems." She added that some days a train would sit on the track idling for several hours.[36]

THREATENING PBF'S SURVIVAL?

As winter 2013 turned into the spring of that year, the concerns of environmentalists escalated, becoming strident and somewhat threatening to PBF. A high-stakes campaign of sorts was launched as the refinery faced imminent filings for state and federal renewal permits. A May 24 email letter addressed to Delaware Sierra Club members from Michael Marx, the club's "Beyond Oil Campaign Director," stated in part as follows:

> Delaware has some of the highest cancer and asthma rates in the country, yet refinery officials want permits to increase air pollution as they begin processing even more tar sands--the same toxic goo Keystone XL would carry. . . .

It's time for public health to come before private profit. The refinery is making money hand over fist—it does not need any more special breaks from the state. . . . Toxic tar sands should stay in Canada's ground, not in Delaware's air. . . . *Take Action!* [original emphasis][37]

Meanwhile, PBF Energy announced its intention to raise its intake of crude oil by rail from 150,000 barrels a day to as much as 180,000 barrels a day at its Delaware City refinery by early 2014—an increase to a total of 100,000 barrels per day of light shale-oil arriving from North Dakota alone. Much heavier crude from Canada was expected to reach 80,000 barrels per day in 2014. Accordingly, it was estimated that PBF's Delaware City rail hub would require expansion to accommodate the 30,000 barrels-per-day increase, amounting to forty more tank cars arriving daily in Delaware. The operation would entail a forecasted increase of two or three more oil trains arriving daily in Delaware. Of the total of 180,000 barrels of crude oil by rail shipment to the Delaware refinery each day, 45,000 barrels would move north daily on the Delaware River to PBF's Paulsboro, New Jersey, refinery by virtue of a new barge loading dock completed in May 2013 at its nearby Delaware City site. PBF officials bragged that its Delaware City refinery had become the East Coast's "destination of choice" for Midwestern and Canadian crudes.[38] These figures were likely to greatly increase by the first half of 2014. In response to a planned expansion of heavier Canadian sand crude oil, PBF announced on October 1, 2013, that Delaware City's rail capacity would rise to 205,000 barrels per day, more than double the amount that PBF had forecasted when it first announced its crude-by-rail plan in early 2012. That estimate was predicted to increase to 210,000 barrels per day by the end of 2014—requiring the arrival of about 350 rail carloads daily. As steady increases were reported, concerns over rail safety gained traction.[39]

On June 4, 2013, DNREC reported that more than 263 tons of sulfur dioxide had been released without a permit by PBF's Delaware City refinery during a thirteen-day period in the previous January, after a breakdown in a major recovery and pollution control unit of the plant. The state considers any industrial site that emits one hundred tons or more of sulfur dioxide during an entire year to constitute a "major" pollution source subject to closer regulation. DNREC reported that the refinery had also exceeded limits for emissions of ammonia, hydrogen sulfide, hydrogen cyanide, and carbon monoxide.

As if on cue, the violation notice surfaced the day before DNREC's scheduled public hearing for the refinery's required state air quality permit, and also for review of the refinery's federally mandated Title V air permit, established by Congress in 1990 to reduce air pollution emissions nationally. Amy Roe, conservation chair for the Sierra Club's Delaware chapter, gasped, "We are alarmed." Delaware's Sierra Club was joined by the Delaware Audubon Society, and the Green Party of Delaware, among others, calling on DNREC to require installation of continuous, "real-time" air pollution monitoring along the refinery's fence line, as well as to expand emergency response plans, and to clarify rules for reporting problems, mishaps, or spills at the refinery's rail loading and unloading areas.

PBF complained, with an unsigned letter to refinery employees, stating that "every permit and every approval we receive gets focused opposition from a small but loud minority of activists whose ultimate objective is to shut the refinery down and eliminate all the jobs and other positive benefits of our facility." PBF's spokesman, Michael Karlovich, said a rally was planned at the refinery for employees, contractors, and other "friends of the plant" on the afternoon of the hearing, after which buses would be available to transport those who planned to attend the hearing in Delaware City. "Having the public participate in a public hearing on a topic that means so much to so many working families should be perceived positively by all," Karlovich said in an email. David Carter, conservation chair for the Delaware Audubon Society, said that PBF's call for a rally reflected a pattern of "corporate bullying and an apparent attempt to pack the hearing." He asked, "Do good ethical corporate stewards sponsor rallies against citizen groups?"[40]

The next day, DNREC's public hearing was attended by an unprecedented crowd of about 1,800 to discuss the renewal of an air pollution permit for PBF's Delaware City refinery. Environmentalists numbered a few hundred, while the remaining attendees consisted mostly of PBF employees, family members, contract workers, and supporters. The crowd filled Delaware City's fire company hall, with the overflow listening from an outside lot where a line of state troopers separated the two sides to maintain order. "We are not here to demand that the refinery be shut down and we are not here proposing that the state deny the refinery a . . . permit," said Sierra Club leader Amy Roe, "What we are asking for and what we have always asked for is that the refinery obey the law." A PBF manager, Arthur Jensen, countered that environmental groups had misled the public about the refinery. "I find the false and misleading information about the refinery to be personally offensive because it so incorrectly portrays who we are," Jensen said, "The very large voluntary turnout from the refinery at this public hearing is strong evidence of how we want to set the record straight." Among various other speakers was a woman from Wilmington who said the refinery needed to do more to keep the public informed. "You say I'm misinformed? Then inform me," she said.[41]

After the hearing, the Sierra Club Delaware Chapter and the Audubon Society shifted their strategy from making pollution claims to mounting moves against PBF's steadily growing crude-by-rail unloading operation, as well as its barge loading operation sending 45,000 barrels of crude oil daily from the new rail yard to the Paulsboro plant in New Jersey. Specifically, the environmental groups challenged DNREC Secretary Collin O'Mara's ruling that Delaware's celebrated CZA of 1971 was not violated by PBF's operations. The environmental groups appealed his ruling. They contended that PBF built its rail unloading complex outside the refinery's recognized boundaries and that its barge loading operation violated the Coastal Zone Law's ban on new "bulk transfer" facilities. O'Mara ruled that the Coastal Zone Law did not apply because the rail unloading operation was an existing industrial use that did not expand plant operations. He reasoned that the rail complex was transportation infrastructure that did not expand the refinery's actual manufacturing. Rather, it was a facility similar to a new road built within an industrial site. PBF officials maintained that the rail delivery complex was crucial to its profitability and dismissed the environmental groups' appeals as being "without merit." They claimed that activists had made "specific references" in Internet postings to wanting the refinery shut down. Governor Jack Markell and Attorney General Beau Biden considered activists' challenges about Coastal Zone Law violations to be serious enough to retain Max B. Walton, an attorney with much experience in coastal zone issues.[42]

Representing the Sierra and Audubon organizations, on the other hand, was Kenneth T. Kristl of Widener University's Wilmington-based Environmental and Natural Resources Law Clinic. PBF Energy spokesman Michael Karlovich asserted that the Delaware City refinery "followed everything DNREC said must be done to obtain the applicable permits. . . . Trying to prevent our ability to receive North American crudes at a time when they are integral to our sustainability is tantamount to wanting to shut the refinery down."[43] Indeed, he later explained, the company's operations were a matter of survival for both PBF refineries, and were "the only way we can compete in the global market place."[44]

In the meantime, outsiders joined the dispute. The General Assembly's House of Representatives passed a resolution calling upon the Norfolk Southern Railway to reduce inbound rail crossing delays and excessive noise caused by idling refinery trains near residences.[45] The president and CEO of the Delaware State Chamber of Commerce warned in a newspaper opinion column that "the after-the-fact legal analysis seeks to declare the refinery's operations illegal and shut down its business is the ultimate jobs killer. It will not just kill the jobs at the Delaware City Refinery it will kill the thousands of jobs related to the refinery."[46] Seeking to answer these claims in a follow-up opinion column, the president of the Inland Bays Foundation emphasized the adverse impacts of the refinery on the aquatic resources of the Delaware River Estuary. He concluded with what Governor Jack Markell had stated in one of his campaign speeches: "'When I get the chance, Gov. Russ Peterson's Coastal Zone Act is the kind of legacy I promise you that I will seek to leave.' I surely hope that the Governor keeps this promise."[47]

Another opinion column soon appeared. This one was contributed by the president of Delaware's Building and Construction Trades Council. He claimed that the American Civil Liberties Union had joined the activists, who "will stop at nothing." He characterized their challenges to the refinery permits as "astonishing . . . antics," that "threaten our livelihood." He claimed that the new refinery owners were "more committed to safety, the environment, and reliability than prior owners."[48]

Here, then, was a classic "jobs-versus-environment" political conflict with both sides and their lawyers girded to convince the state's Coastal Zone Industrial Control Board to fatefully choose between them in its hearing scheduled for July 16, 2013. The day before the hearing, Governor Markell's office released a statement noting that the CZA "never prohibited the construction of a rail facility. Although the refinery has substantially reduced emissions in all categories, its opponents now want to limit its access to North American crude by arguing the rail loop which is more than two miles inland, is a prohibited docking facility."[49]

The day after the board's hearing, the front page of the Wilmington *News Journal* blared in bold capital letters this banner headline: "REFINERY CAN CLAIM VICTORY IN ROUND 1." It so happened that the board did not consider the merits of either side, but instead unanimously decided that the environmentalists supporting the appeal lacked standing to challenge the state's key permit related to the refinery's crude-by-rail unloading operation. The board ruled that the sixteen Delaware Sierra Club and Audubon members supporting the appeal failed to prove specific personal harm or jeopardy regardless of their affidavits claiming such harm. The refinery's lead attorney said, "Belief and concern is clearly not enough. There must be a specific basis that there is actual harm." Still pending was another Coastal Zone Board hearing to consider a challenge to the refinery's barge loading operation. Although some contemplated possible appeals to Delaware courts, costs of such litigation could be a deterrent. Nevertheless, Amy Roe warned, "I don't think we're considering this [the Board's decision] a defeat. . . . We'll regroup and think about next steps on this."[50]

Regardless of the state's successful defense of PBF's new rail hub from the challenge posed by environmental groups, DNREC fined PBF Energy the week after the hearing a total of $529,000 in environmental penalties and fees for pollution releases, reporting failures, and other violations that the Delaware City refinery had accumulated since it restarted the plant. Foremost among the violations cited was the thirteen-day period in January 2013 during which the refinery released 263 tons of sulfur dioxide and other hazardous pollutants. DNREC Secretary Collin O'Mara acknowledged that the PBF operators had made "significant improvements" over preceding owners of the refinery and had operated the refinery "in a more responsible way," but they "still have had emissions above and beyond where they should have been. Even though the overall emissions are down significantly, we still need to hold them accountable."[51]

CONCLUSION

It may be a truism that criticism of oil refineries by environmentalists may never end, precisely because refineries by definition engage in a dirty business. The bottom line for many environmentalists, moreover, is that they dislike all forms of energy produced by fossil fuels, and especially oil refinery emissions that are inevitable to an extent beyond absolute control. Perhaps Delaware environmentalists became somewhat emboldened by DNREC's fine of PBF's refinery for its emission violations. And surely their criticism of the refinery's new rail hub was not over, especially in the wake of the July 6, 2013, fiery and fatal derailment of a runaway train carrying seventy-two tank carloads of North American crude in Quebec near the Maine border that killed about fifty people. "If it can happen there, it can happen here," many northern Delawareans must have been thinking.[52]

It was unlikely that environmental groups would remain silent in response to state decisions that refinery operations did not contravene the CZA. One option was for challengers to appeal such decisions to the courts. But Christine Whitehead, a retired attorney and civic leader, cautioned that Audubon and Sierra faced huge expenses in appealing such decisions. "It would be a huge fight, and I'm not sure in the end that they would win," Whitehead said. "It seems to me that the necessity for jobs in this state is so great that people in charge are willing to take almost any risk to provide those jobs." Another option was to convince state legislators to revamp that law to insert provisions that would forbid PBF's rail and barge operations, a difficult scenario to comprehend at best.[53] Local businessman Michael Oates asserted that the state legislature ought to review the CZA to deal with the fact that its administrative regulations have never been completely defined and developed, and have therefore been ambiguous with respect especially to the refinery's permit issues.[54]

Harry Themal, longtime Wilmington newspaper columnist, asserted that the Sierra and Audubon groups' legal actions "could result in a shutdown of the PBF refinery in Delaware City," and thus constituted a dangerous and unwarranted assault on Delaware industry "at a time when jobs are desperately needed." He continued:

> Their actions must remind us of the 18th-century Luddites in England who fought against industrialization. . . . .
> The state, environmental lobbyists and Delaware City residents should certainly be keeping a close watch on the refinery. But it is wrong to threaten

its lifeline, the crude shipped from Canadian shale oil fields. Would it be better if there were a pipeline? . . .

As the United States relies ever more on domestic oil production, and I include Canada in "domestic," these groups are attacking an important pillar in reducing the need for importing foreign products.[55]

Meanwhile, PBF made known in 2014 that Delaware crude shipments by rail could continue to mushroom to 210,000 barrels per day, and that the company planned to use 5,900 safer rail cars for crude service by the end of 2015.[56] While on October 31, 2014, during a briefing for investors, PBF officials acknowledged that they had indeed shelved their billion-dollar expansion, in its place, they sought a permit for a new $100 million hydrogen plant to support ultra-low-sulfur fuel production, with a start-up goal of November 2016.[57]

In a larger context, the battle over the Delaware City refinery was a classic case of conflicting political goals. One side argued that the refinery was protecting and creating jobs, while the other side proclaimed that the refinery caused damages to Delaware residents' health and to the environment. The role of government was to mediate between these two sides.[58]

NOTES

Portions of this chapter were previously published as Bergstrom-Lynch, Cara A. "How Children Rearrange the Closet: Disclosure Practices of Gay, Lesbian, and Bisexual Prospective Parents." *Journal of GLBT Family Studies* 8, no. 2 (2012): 173-95. Printed by permission of Taylor and Francis.

1. John A. Munroe, *History of Delaware* (Newark: University of Delaware Press, 3rd ed., 1993), 231.

2. See Andrew D. Zimmerman, Frank R. Selby, and William J. Cohen, *Life in a Refinery Town: The History and Impact of the Getty Oil Company in Delaware City, Delaware* (Newark: William J. Cohen and Associates, 1983), 125, 126. See also Bill Frank, "Questions about a Refinery's Effect," Wilmington *News Journal*, February 1, 1983, and Frank, "What Was Getty's Effect on Town?" ibid., February 2, 1983.

3. Between 1987 and 1997, Delaware's state government received more than 3,700 complaints about Star refinery odors, according to Dennis Thompson Jr., "Population Growth Adds to Star's Woes," Wilmington *News Journal*, January 14, 1997, A1, A8.

4. Merritt Wallick, "Report: Star Plant Unsafe," Wilmington *News Journal*, October 19, 1990, A1, A4; and Merritt Wallick, "State Labels Refinery 'Imminent Hazard,'" ibid., October 17, 1990, A1, A8.

5. See these articles by Molly Murray in the Wilmington *News Journal*: "Star Refinery Sued over Odors," March 11, 1995, A1; and "For $175,000, State Drops Suit against Star," March 29, 1996, B3.

6. *Investigation Report: Refinery Incident, Motiva Enterprises LLC, Delaware City Refinery, July 17, 2001* (Washington, DC: U.S. Chemical Safety and Hazard Investigation Board, Report No. 2001-05-I-DE, October 2002).

7. U.S. Department of Justice News Release, "Motiva Enterprises Settles Federal-State Lawsuit Resulting from Explosion at Delaware City Refinery," September 20, 2005, www.justice.gov/opa/pr/2005/September/05_enrd-488.html (accessed February 28, 2013).

8. Simon Condliffe, *Economic Impact of Motiva Enterprises Delaware City Refinery* (Newark: CADSR, University of Delaware, October 2002), 2.

9. Ibid., 11.

10. "Motiva Settles 20 Year Delaware Refinery Water Pollution Case," *Environment News Service*, October 8, 2007, www.ens-newswire.com/ens/oct2007/2007-10-08-094.asp (accessed February 21, 2013).

11. Premcor News Release, "Premcor to Acquire Motiva Delaware City Refining Complex," January 14, 2004, www.sec.gov/Archives/edgar/data/20762/000119312504005466/dex991.htm (accessed March 4, 2013).

12. Jeff Montgomery, "State Approves Upgrade for Premcor," Wilmington *News Journal*, December 1, 2004, B1.

13. Joe Carroll, "Valero to Buy Premcor for $6.9 Bln in Cash, Stock," *Bloomberg News*, April 25, 2005.

14. Jeff Montgomery, "Delaware City Refinery Closing: Valero Can't Find Buyer for Plant; DNREC to Supervise Shutdown," Wilmington *News Journal*, November 21, 2009.

15. Duff & Phelps Corporation, "Refining Industry Analysis," *Standard and Poor's Industry Surveys—Oil and Gas: Production and Marketing*, March 29, 2012, 151.

16. See, for example, Daniel Shea, "HOVENSA's Closure is Part of Larger Trend in Industry," *Virgin Islands Daily News*, January 23, 2012, virginislandsdailynews.com/news/hovensa-s-closure-is-part-of-larger-trend-in-industry (accessed January 24, 2012).

17. "Sale Finalized for Delaware City Refinery," *WHYY News and Information*, June 1, 2011, whyy.org/cms/news/regional-news/delaware/2010/06/01/sale-finalized (accessed March 4, 2013).

18. "Fisker Automotive and the Delaware City Refinery Company Secure Grant and Loan Recommendations," *Delaware Business Weekly Round Up*, April 23, 2010, www.delawarebusinessblog.com/?=1066 (accessed January 2, 2012).

19. PBF Press Release, "PBF Celebrates Successful Restart of Its Delaware City Refinery," October 7, 2011, www.blackstone.com/cps/rde/xchg/bxcom/hs/news_pressrelease_6937.htm (accessed January 2, 2012).

20. Address by Herman Seedorf, "Refinery Upstart Challenges," Quarterly Luncheon, Port of Wilmington Maritime Society, Chase Center, Wilmington, October 11, 2012.

21. PBF Press Release, "PBF Announces Major Project at the Delaware City Refinery," December 21, 2011, http://finance.yahoo.com/news/pbf-announces-major-project-delaware-175300640.html (accessed January 2, 2012).

22. Jeff Montgomery, "$1B Refinery Addition Proposed," Wilmington *News Journal*, December 22, 2011, A1, A11.

23. Aaron Nathans, "PBF Energy to Go Public in Sign of Industry's Recovery from 2008 Crash," Wilmington *News Journal*, December 4, 2012, A1, A6.

24. See Matthew Daly, Associated Press, "Boehner: No Reason to Block Keystone Oil Pipeline," Wilmington *News Journal*, March 3, 2013, A9; Coral Davenport, "Senate Fails to Override Obama's Keystone Pipeline Veto," *New York Times*, March 4, 2015, A1; and Kurtis Lee, "Keystone XL Oil Pipeline: What You Need to Know about the Dispute," *Los Angeles Times*, March 6, 2015.

25. See these articles by Jeff Montgomery and Melissa Nann Burke in the Wilmington *News Journal*: "New Crude-by-Rail Yard to Be Expanded," February 5, 2013, A1, A10; "As Rail Plans Grow, So Does Backlash," February 10, 2013, A1, A8; and "Delaware Joins National Debate," February 10, 2013, A1, A9.

26. Jeff Montgomery and Melissa Nann Burke, "Boom Year for PBF," Wilmington *News Journal*, February 22, 2013, A8, A9.

27. Jeff Montgomery, "Refinery Moving Ahead on Plan," Wilmington *News Journal*, June 7, 2012, A1, A8.

28. Jeff Montgomery, "DNREC Reviewing New Delaware City Pollution Study," Wilmington *News Journal*, May 24, 2012, B1, B2.

29. Jeff Montgomery, "PBF Will Meet with Del. City Residents," Wilmington *News Journal*, January 4, 2012, B1.

30. Jeff Montgomery, "Sierra Club Cautions on Faster Refinery Review," Wilmington *News Journal*, June 13, 2012, B1, B3.

31. Amy Roe, "Fish Impacts by Delaware City Refinery, July 9 Forum," emailed notice to Sierra Club Delaware Chapter members, July 3, 2012.

32. Delaware Chapter, Sierra Club, "Delaware City Refinery," delaware.sierraclub.org/content/delaware-city-refinery-0 (accessed February 21, 2013).

33. Jeff Montgomery, "Breakdown Draws Attention," Wilmington *News Journal*, January 27, 2013, B1, B8.

34. Randall Chase, "Delaware City Refinery Manager Not Ruling Out Future Expansion," Wilmington *News Journal*, October 12, 2012, B3.

35. Jeff Montgomery and Melissa Nann Burke, "Oil Tank Gripes Fire Up Meeting," Wilmington *News Journal*, February 28, 2013, A1, A5.

36. Ibid.

37. Michael Marx, Sierra Club Beyond Oil Campaign Director, "When Delaware's Sky Is on Fire," email to Sierra Club members, May 24, 2013.

38. Jeff Montgomery, "PBF Ramping It Up, Plans a Rail Terminal Handling 180K Barrels," Wilmington *News Journal*, May 3, 2013, A12, A13.

39. See, for example, Jeff Montgomery, "PBF to Boost Oil-by-Rail," Wilmington *News Journal*, November 1, 2013, B1, B2; Jeff Montgomery, "Delaware Crude Shipments Could Mushroom," ibid., August 2, 2014, A1, A9; Jose Dominguez, "Refinery Committed to Improving Rail Safety," ibid., March 3, 2014, A12; Melissa Nann Burke and Jeff Montgomery, "Rail Safety, With More Rail Traffic on Horizon, Residents Work on Plans," ibid., March 10, 2014, A1 A9; and Jeff Montgomery, "State Will Assess Oil Train Crash Readiness," ibid., March 27, 2014, A2.

40. Jeff Montgomery, "Del. City Refinery Faces Big Dogfight, Hearing to Consider Air Quality Permit Renewal," Wilmington News *Journal*, June 4, 2013, A1, A5.

41. See Jeff Montgomery and Robin Brown, "Fired Up over Refinery," Wilmington *News Journal*, June 5, 2013, A1, A2: and Global Community Monitor, "Delaware City Refinery Rail, Barge Permits Under Fire," June 11, 2013, www.governor.org/delaware-city-refinery-rail-barge-pemits-under-fire/ (accessed February 21, 2013).

42. See these articles by Jeff Montgomery in the Wilmington *News Journal*: "DNREC Refinery Rulings Fought," Wilmington *News Journal*, June 12, 2013, A1, A7; and "Markell's Moves Fuel Suspicion, Administration Seeks Outside Legal Guidance to Defend Decisions," ibid., June 16, 2013, A1, A10.

43. Jeff Montgomery, "Legal Fight Set for Refinery: Sierra, Audubon File New Challenge," Wilmington *News Journal*, June 15, 2013, A1, A2.

44. Jeff Montgomery, "Rail Deliveries of Crude Threatened," Wilmington *News Journal*, June 26, 2013, A1, A2.

45. Jeff Montgomery, "Loud Message Sent to PBF on Refinery Trains," Wilmington *News Journal*, June 7, 2013, A1, A5.

46. Joan Verplank, "Never Forget, Jobs Are at Stake in Refinery Dispute," Wilmington *News Journal*, June 25, 2013, A9.

47. William Moyer, "Refinery's Impact on Environment Must Be Considered," Wilmington *News Journal*, July 4, 2013, A10.

48. Harry Gravell, "Dishonest Tactics Being Used to Smear Refinery," Wilmington *News Journal*, July 11, 2013, A10.

49. Jeff Montgomery, "Key Hearing Begins Today," Wilmington *News Journal*, July 16, 2013, A1, A5.

50. See Jeff Montgomery, "Refinery Can Claim Victory in Round 1," Wilmington *News Journal*, July 17, 2013, A1, A5; and Jeff Montgomery, "Coastal Ruling Limits Dissent," ibid., August 17, 2013, A1, A2.

51. Jeff Montgomery, "Refinery Must Pay $529,000 for Pollution," Wilmington *News Journal*, July 25, 2013, A1, A2.

52. Jonathan Fahey, Associated Press, "Deadly Derailment Won't Stop Oil on Trains: Delaware City Refinery Part of Growing Trend," Wilmington *News Journal*, July 21, 2013, A17. See also Jeff Montgomery, "Safety on Rail Industry Leaders' Agenda: DC Meeting Centers on Quebec Derailment," ibid., August 27, 2013, A1, A2; and Nicole Gaudiano, "Coons Joins Senate Push for Oil-by-Rail Safety Fund," ibid., August 10, 2014, A5.

53. Jeff Montgomery, "Aging Coastal Law Seen as Out of Step: Rival Groups Weigh Opening Can of Worms for Updates," Wilmington *News Journal*, July 22, 2013, A1, A2.

54. Michael Oates, "Time to Revise the 1971 Coastal Zone Act," Wilmington *News Journal*, October 15, 2013, A10.

55. Harry F. Themal, "Assaults Unwarranted on Present, Future Delaware Industry," Wilmington *News Journal*, July 28, 2013, A12.

56. See these articles by Jeff Montgomery in the Wilmington *News Journal*: "Delaware Crude Shipments Could Mushroom," August 2, 2014, A1, A9; and "PBF Lines Up $250 Million Rail Car Buy," March 28, 2014, A2.

57. See Editorial, "Refinery Announcement Points to Long-Term Gain," Wilmington *News Journal*, December 22, 2011, A14; Jeff Montgomery, "Refinery Profitable, Considering New Venture," ibid., October 31, 2014, A1; and Jeff Montgomery, "Delaware City Refinery Seeks Project Permit," ibid., January 11, 2015, A13.

58. See, for example, Jeff Montgomery, "Refinery Hearing Attracts Hundreds," Wilmington *News Journal*, March 25, 2015, A1, A5.

Chapter Seven

A Potpourri of Grants

As noted in chapter 1, AstraZeneca in April 1999 chose to locate its North American headquarters in Delaware. The state offered AstraZeneca a land purchase of $10.7 million plus a state grant of $8 million, for a total incentive package of $18.7 million, not including a planned investment of $70 million in road construction and other improvements around the AstraZeneca site. This package was quickly followed in 2000 by Delaware's much smaller grant of $200,000 to AstroPower, Inc., a burgeoning solar cell production company that nevertheless became bankrupt in 2004.[1]

Both grants were justified by Democrat Governor Tom Carper's administration (1993–2001) as deals bolstering jobs in the First State. The zenith of Delaware's job-creating incentive deals, however, was yet to come, marked chiefly by the succeeding administrations of Democrats Ruth Ann Minner (2001–2009) and Jack Markell (2009–present).

The fact that our preceding chapters focus preponderantly on the more recent administration of Governor Markell should not obscure the significant job incentives created by preceding administrations. However, primarily because of involved companies' reluctance to have so-called "proprietary" information disclosed, it is difficult at best to discover details of incentive deals in such a less-than-transparent, business-friendly state.[2] Fortunately, from an unpublished report covering the 1997–2008 period,[3] we are able to construct the following table:

Only the Riverfront Development Corporation (RDC) was established as a state government corporation, later to be partially funded by state appropriations. All other twelve entities listed were nongovernmental recipients of state grants. AstraZeneca is discussed in chapter 1, whereas the RDC and AAA Mid-Atlantic are discussed in chapter 3. Of the remaining ten recip-

Table 7.1. Largest State Funded Businesses 1997–2008

Invista	$15,676,000
Fraunhofer	$14,300,500
AstraZeneca	$8,000,000
DuPont	$6,420,000
AAA Mid-Atlantic	$6,000,000
Bank One Delaware	$4,200,000
Riverfront Development Corp	$4,150,000
Playtex	$4,014,600
St. Francis Hospital	$4,000,000
CDNC Realty	$3,500,000
Allen Family Foods	$3,500,000
W.L. Gore	$3,000,000
Hercules	$2,795,000

ients listed above, seven invite our interest in this chapter: Invista, Fraunhofer, DuPont, Bank One Delaware, Playtex, Allen Family Foods, and Hercules.

INVISTA

Foremost among the largest Delaware state grants during the years 1997–2008 is the $14 million Delaware Strategic Fund grant awarded to Invista on September 27, 2004, then the largest strategic fund incentive package ever offered by state economic development officials. When DuPont Company sought to end its textile and fibers business (formerly known as DuPont Nylon), it sold its renamed DuPont Textiles and Interiors assets for $4.2 billion on April 30, 2004, to Koch Industries, Inc., a sprawling, private Kansas-based conglomerate of 60,000 employees around the world. Koch Industries was run by entrepreneurial multibillionaire industrialists Charles and David Koch. Their company owned many subsidiaries including Invista, which was assigned operation of DuPont's former Seaford plant. Regardless of the great wealth accrued by Koch Industries, Invista requested—and was granted in the spring of 2008 by Delaware's Council on Development Finance—a "competitive grant" of $1.676 million to offset capital infrastructure expenditures at the Seaford plant. Thus, the total of awards Invista received from the state was $15.676 million.

When announcing its initial $14 million grant in September 2004, state officials had said they were offering Invista the grant in order to retain 350 high-paying jobs, including jobs of former DuPont employees. To qualify for the grant, the officials stated that Invista had to keep the jobs in Delaware for six years, and their salaries had to be kept at a minimum of $90,000. Governor Ruth Ann Minner boasted at the time, "We saved 350 jobs keeping Invista in the First State, and I think that is worth our investment in time and resources."

In less than four years, however, after Koch Industries' company Invista became the recipient of the initial $14 million grant, Invista announced plans in October 2008 to lay off four hundred of the five hundred workers at its Seaford plant.[4] The loss of 80 percent of Invista's employees was to devastate Seaford's economy, as this excerpt of a March 2012 news story in the Wilmington *News Journal* implied:

> State Rep. Daniel B. Short, R-Seaford, a former mayor of the city, recalls the day when DuPont employed 4,600 people manufacturing nylon at a bustling plant. Seaford was known as the "nylon capital of the world." "The old site used to have 4,500 cars in its parking lot," Short said of the plant, which was sold to Invista as DuPont exited the fiber business. "Now you drive by and see 100 cars. That is a lot of empty parking spots."[5]

Companies that accept Delaware state grants seldom comply with imposed conditions—a fact that has evoked criticism by, among others, Delaware's conservative Caesar Rodney Institute, as follows:

> Are the awards simply bribes? Delaware is in competition with other states to retain and attract jobs, and that frequently requires the state to ante up.
> The job data maintained by DEDO [Delaware Economic Development Office], however, is what is promised at the time of the deal and is not subsequently adjusted. . . . There is no evidence that either DEDO or any other state agency follows up after grants are awarded to see if the terms of the original agreement are complied with (e.g., the promised number of jobs created or retained).[6]

FRAUNHOFER

Even before AstraZeneca chose Wilmington in April 1999 as the site for its North American headquarters, Delaware's New Castle County—as discussed in chapter 1—was on its way to becoming a regional biotechnology center. DuPont and other Delaware companies had already committed to the life sciences, and UD—a partner in creating The Biotechnology Institute—was hiring faculty to research and teach in related high-tech areas.

Second only to Invista, the enterprise awarded the most state funding during the 1997–2008 period was the so-called Center for Molecular Biotechnology (CMB). The center was a subsidiary of Fraunhofer USA, a branch of one of the world's largest research firms, Germany-based Fraunhofer Gesellschaft, which had more than eighty research units in 2013, comprising more than twenty thousand staff of mostly scientists and engineers. Shortly after the beginning of the administration of Governor Ruth Ann Minner (2001–2009), CMB was founded in July 2001 at the Delaware Technology Park, site of the Delaware Biotechnology Institute in Newark. As a partner of UD, CMB was the first established research center among six Fraunhofer USA research centers that became affiliated with major American research universities. The five other Fraunhofer USA research centers were affiliated, respectively, with Boston University, the University of Maryland, Michigan State University, the University of Michigan, and the Massachusetts Institute of Technology. Each Fraunhofer USA center was also partnered with a German Fraunhofer research institute. Accordingly, CMB was partnered with the Fraunhofer Institute for Molecular Biology in Aachen, Germany.[7]

From its beginning with only one employee, CMB numbered over one hundred employees in 2011 dedicated to finding new methods for creating vaccines. With funding from the state's Delaware Economic Development Office (DEDO) and UD, a new partnership between DEDO, UD, and CMB developed. From 2002 to 2007 alone, during the Minner Administration, CMB received a total of $14.3 million in grants from DEDO. Financial support of CMB, among other sizable grants it received during 2008–2010, also consisted of $4 million from the Department of Defense and about $20 million in other federal and private grants to help fund CMB's research and development (R&D).[8]

The relationship between CMB, UD, and DEDO became stronger in mid-July 2011 with the announcement of a new partnership agreement projecting a $32 million investment over six years to share between them. The agreement called for the state to provide $9 million for CMB—comprised of $6 million from the state's annual Bond Bill and $3 million from the state's Strategic Fund. In addition, UD pledged to provide $9 million of in-kind services in terms of access to UD facilities, staff, and high-tech research instruments. Fraunhofer promised to match this total of $18 million provided by the state and UD. For the state, the bottom line would be the creation of more jobs, a 5 percent equity stake in the Fraunhofer's U.S. operation, and a share in royalties should the company's research take off in case of vaccine commercialization. It remained to be seen whether the state would actually profit from such an agreement, or whether the German-based company would claim all profits. Should the latter happen, the state could get nothing. Regardless of this unpredictable question of commercial gain, however, DEDO Director Alan Levin said, "It's either going to be nothing, or it's going to be huge. It could be a game changer." Bond Bill co-chairman and State Senator Robert Venables added: "It's been one of the best investments I think we've made."[9]

DUPONT

As everybody in Delaware knew, the DuPont Company had long been the state's most eminent company in terms of wealth, prestige, influence, and employment. Moreover, the company surely retained its eminence after the rise and demise of Maryland Bank National Association (MBNA). For a few short years, MBNA had surpassed DuPont as the state's largest private employer only to lose its lofty position upon its purchase by Bank of America in January 2006.

The DuPont Capital Management Corporation (DCM), a subsidiary of the DuPont Company, was established in 1993 as a global investment firm to oversee assets held by its parent company. On April 22, 2004, DCM announced the appointment of a longtime veteran of the investment industry, Valerie J. Sill, as President and CEO. One year later—on May 23, 2005— Delaware's state government awarded DCM two Delaware Strategic Fund grants: one of $1.02 million as a "retention" grant for seventy-two employees; and the other of $400,000 listed as a "performance" grant for one unnamed employee (leaving to conjecture for whom it was designated). The total granted that day to DCM was $1.42 million. The announcement included this statement, among others: "Currently, DCM manages over $24 billion in U.S. and foreign pension assets for the DuPont Company and external clients."[10]

Also on the same day of May 23, 2005, the DuPont Experimental Station—the DuPont Company's largest R&D center—received another Delaware Strategic Fund grant of $5 million authorized by the General Assembly's Bond Bill. Accordingly, the DuPont Company, one of the world's most respected and oldest corporations, was awarded on that one day a grand total from the Delaware Strategic Fund of $6.42 million, as there was also road improvement money for the entrance to the experiment station written into the bond bill.

Thus, the DuPont Company, as well as Invista, illustrated that the wealth of a company has no necessary relationship with its possible candidacy for receiving substantial taxpayer money. Indeed, on January 27, 2012, the Wilmington *News Journal* published a letter to the editor by Edmund Dohnert of Wilmington, who questioned still another state grant to DuPont. That letter in its entirety follows:

> The state Council on Development has awarded the DuPont Co. a $920,000 grant to develop a prototype manufacturing center in Newark that will supposedly create 35 full-time jobs. I am totally baffled why DuPont, with revenues of $33 billion, $40 billion in assets, and a CEO whose annual compensation is over $11 million, would need a grant paid for by Delaware taxpayers to carry out what for a company its size is a small research and development project.

There is no reason why this shouldn't be funded totally from DuPont's considerable R&D budget. [11]

BANK ONE DELAWARE

Bank One Corporation was Chicago's largest financial institution and one of its largest employers when it sought to persuade the Illinois General Assembly to exempt it from certain consumer regulations as part of its cost-saving plan. However, Bank One's bid was unsuccessful, having been opposed by other banks and activists. Delaware Governor Ruth Ann Minner traveled to Chicago in 2002 to make a personal pitch to Jamie Dimon, Bank One's chairman and CEO. According to Minner, "Jamie Dimon has given me his commitment to maintain the bank's present long-term employment goals for Delaware." The upshot was Bank One's decision to move its $300 million planned computer operations to new facilities near its credit card operation in Wilmington, where it already employed about 2,500 employees.

Delaware put together a package of incentives including a Strategic Fund "special" grant of $4.2 million to buy about one-third of a 152-acre site Bank One owned near Wilmington, the state's sixth largest grant to a business entity during the 1997–2008 period. The state also agreed to help the bank to sell the rest of that site. Finally, the state's Bond Bill ordered road improvements for Bank One costing $20 million to $25 million. The city of Wilmington, moreover, agreed to sell a nineteen-acre site it owned outside the city limits to Bank One for $2.4 million for the bank to build its second data center.

DEDO Director Judy Mc Kinney-Cherry commented that the state's package of incentives was designed to retain Bank One's existing workforce in Delaware. She cited Bank One's own substantial investment and added, "We believe they will not move once they do this." A few years later, Bank One Delaware became a subsidiary of JPMorgan Chase, helping to make the latter one of the world's largest banks. [12]

PLAYTEX

Playtex Products, Inc. announced on December 8, 2005, that it had entered into "a partnership" agreement with the state of Delaware to continue its operations in Delaware where it employed approximately seven hundred "associates." The company had administrative and manufacturing facilities in Dover since 1937, where it became a leading manufacturer and distributor of diversified feminine and infant care products, including Playtex tampons, diapers, and infant feeding products. DEDO's stated purpose for awarding two grants to Playtex of a total of $4,014,600 were for the "retention of employees," capital expenditures, and R&D costs. For its part, the company agreed to maintain a minimum employment level of 630 full-time "associates" in Dover through at least the five-year grant period.

On the occasion of the company's announcement, Playtex President and Chief Executive Officer Neal P. DeFoe stated:

> We have formed an important partnership with the State of Delaware which will help us become more competitive in the global market and still remain in Dover. We are delighted with this outcome and have a great team of associates at Playtex. We are pleased with the State's commitment to business development and employment in Delaware, and their willingness to partner with Playtex. This is especially important given the requirements of employers to remain competitive on a global level. We want to thank the leadership of Delaware including Governor Minner and the Delaware Economic Development Office for their continued support of Playtex. [13]

Playtex continued to remain one of Dover's important firms thereafter.

ALLEN FAMILY FOODS

Although agriculture had been declining in Delaware for some time, broiler chicken production, combined with the growing of corn and soybeans to feed chickens, continued to clearly dominate Delaware agriculture. Chicken production had constituted 80 to 90 percent of the state's total agriculture output at the beginning of the twenty-first century. And Sussex County had long been one of the nation's leading chicken-producing counties. Within that county, Allen Family Foods—located in the town of Harbeson—contracted with more than two hundred farmers to grow chickens. But Allen Family Foods began to decline in its fortunes as the twenty-first century was under way.

On December 15, 2003, DEDO awarded Allen two Strategic Fund grants. One award of $500,000 was a "performance" grant with the condition that the company employ at least 946 employees, with October 20, 2012, designated as the "ending date of the recapture period." The other award of $2 million was a so-called CapEx (i.e., Capital Expenditure) grant also with the ending date of October 20, 2012. A third Strategic Fund grant of $1 million was awarded to Allen eleven months later, on November 22, 2004, for "training," with the ending date of December 31, 2009. Obviously, both DEDO and the company hoped that these infusions totaling $3.5 million (the eleventh largest state-funded business during 1997–2008) would assure lasting prosperity for Allen Family Foods. But this did not happen.

At its peak in early 2011, the ninety-two-year-old family-owned company employed more than 1,300 at its Harbeson plant. But hundreds of jobs were lost soon thereafter through attrition as fortunes faltered. On June 9, 2011, Allen filed for bankruptcy, thus acknowledging that it could not survive the Great Recession. The company attributed its downfall to the surging price of corn used as corn feed, plus its own operational mistakes, and, as reported by the Wilmington *News Journal*: "a move by the ailing Wilmington Trust bank that restricted the company's cash flow by slashing its line of credit by nearly 90 percent during the recent credit crunch—from $20 million to $2.5 million in August 2010. Allen defaulted on more than $500,000 in Wilmington Trust loans in March 2011, and had some checks bounce as the company collapsed into bankruptcy."[14]

At a July 2011 hearing, a federal bankruptcy judge in Wilmington approved a deal whereby the assets of Allen Family Foods would be sold to South Korea's largest poultry producer, the Harim Group. Montaire, a Mills-boro, Delaware-based poultry-producing company, had bid $30 million to acquire most of Allen's assets and to assume its debt obligations. However, Harim outbid Montaire by paying about $48 million to buy almost all of Allen's assets, as well as pledging to keep Allen's Harbeson plant running. Although Harim could not save Allen's night shift of two to three hundred workers, about five hundred workers would keep their jobs. Harim changed the name of the company to Allen Harim Foods.

Fast-food fried chicken franchises in South Korea had greatly increased the demand for chicken in Asia. Harim Group Chairman Hong Kuk Kim announced, "Through our knowledge of Asian consumer preferences, we plan to expand product offerings to include premium, value-added products that can be sold throughout the United States and Asia."[15] Delaware Governor Jack Markell and cabinet secretaries enthusiastically welcomed Harim Chairman Kim and his team to Delaware. In his press release of August 4, 2011, Markell said:

> We're very pleased to welcome Chairman Kim and his team to Delaware. We're especially pleased that they are planning to maintain the operations at Harbeson. I brought together senior officials from four cabinet agencies [including DEDO Director Alan Levin] to show Chairman Kim and Harim's executives that Delaware is different. We care about every job and work to create the conditions that will help make businesses successful. We know that Harim has many choices ahead and we want to make sure that Delaware is always the right choice.[16]

In March 2013, Governor Markell made the case for his administration's economic development strategy before a meeting of the Delaware State Chamber of Commerce. Noting that he had earlier in that day visited Harim's poultry processing plant in Harbeson, Markell asserted that work by the state, Sussex County government, and others "saved hundreds of jobs at the plant."[17] But as we have noted, the state's DEDO grants were to Allen

Family Foods in 2003, and none were awarded to Harim after it took over Allen.

If it appeared that Governor Markell's administration was giving an impression at the time that it had something to do with attracting Harim to Delaware, that appeared not to be what had happened. On the contrary, all of Governor Markell's relations with Harim appeared to have happened *after* the Korean company acquired the Allen plant. Indeed, Harim had attempted to enter Delaware's chicken business prior to Allen filing for bankruptcy on June 9, 2011. Earlier that year, according to the Wilmington *News Journal*, Harim was outbid in its attempt to acquire Georgetown-based Townsends Inc.[18]

However, Governor Markell and Secretary of Agriculture Ed Kee did make a trip to South Korea in December 2012 to visit Harim's facilities there. In April 2013, Harim announced its plan to add approximately seven hundred jobs in Delaware by purchasing the former Vlasic pickle plant in Millsboro of Sussex County, thus establishing a second poultry plant about three miles from its Allen Harim plant. Harim's Millsboro plant would be the sixth poultry plant in the state, and would strengthen Sussex County's ranking as the number one broiler production county in the nation. Harim publicly acknowledged that Markell's visit to Harim's headquarters in South Korea helped induce Harim to "cement" its Delaware relationship. Attracting Harim to Delaware was accomplished without any state financial incentives. But DEDO did offer to support the training of Harim employees in the future.[19]

A March 2013 review of Allen Harim's Millsboro site found elevated levels of hazardous chemicals and lead in groundwater, whereupon Allen Harim signed a so-called brownfields agreement that gave developers resources to put old industrial sites back into use. The agreement called for the Delaware Department of Natural Resources and Environmental Control (DNREC) to reimburse the company up to $225,000 for cleanup of their site. Nevertheless, nearby residents complained that plans to clean up the site were inadequate to allay their concerns over pollutants. It remains to be seen whether vocal opposition to Allen Harim's Millsboro plant will impair its operation. At issue is whether environmental effects from the plant will have a disproportionate impact on nearby communities.[20]

HERCULES

As we have noted in the Introduction, Al Giacco was president, chairman of the board, and CEO of Hercules Inc., all wrapped into one. Accordingly, he could more or less do what he wanted with the company. Moreover, he had a risk-taking and assertive personality. So when he threatened in 1979 to move

Hercules out of the state, as we recounted, or at least out of Wilmington, Delaware, notables reacted. Various destinations mentioned were Texas, nearby Chadds Ford in Pennsylvania, or suburban New Castle County. We also noted that Governor Pete du Pont (1977–1985) and his staff exerted important influence in convincing Hercules to remain in Wilmington. Ostensibly, Giacco's main complaint was about high state income tax rates, and Governor du Pont was instrumental in inducing the General Assembly in 1979 to reduce the top personal income tax from 19.8 to 13.5 percent. As also noted in the Introduction, according to the authors of one study, it was possible that Giacco was never really interested in moving. [21]

By passing the reduced tax rate, the state government had already helped Hercules to stay within Delaware. But the city of Wilmington could not afford to lose Hercules' 1,500 employees, nor could the city's reputation be tarnished by losing such a major corporation. How could the money-strapped city keep Hercules in town? Money alone was not adequate. So the mayor's office framed a full-page ad imploring Hercules to stay, containing signatures of all the city's major employers. Alternative sites for a new building for Hercules were considered. The former Brown Vocational School on the bank of the Brandywine River was selected. The city then created a new downtown development plan called "River to River" featuring a forty-two-story Hercules headquarters tower to be the tallest building in Wilmington. At this juncture, the city had to find the money, so it applied to the Federal Department of Housing and Urban Affairs (HUD) for an Urban Development Action Grant (UDAG). Meanwhile, Democratic Mayor William T. McLaughlin endorsed Democrat President Jimmy Carter for re-election.

Realtor Kevin McGonegal wrote what happened next, in his essay entitled "The Hercules Deal," as follows:

> Months of difficult negotiations ensued—with the state of Delaware to provide half of the development site along with road and parking improvements; with the DuPont Company to sell the other half of the development site. . . ; with the Federal Government's Economic Development Administration [EDA in the Department of Commerce] to finance a new parking garage; with HUD regarding elements of the UDAG application. . . .
>
> Wilmington created a new economic development entity called the Brandywine Gateway Corporation [BGC] to oversee the development and handle the financing. The BGC board was composed of three city and three state representatives to assure full involvement of State government. The DuPont Company agreed to sell their part of the project land for $3.9 million while the State agreed to demolish the former Vo-Tech School and construct a park between the new building and the Brandywine River, along with significant road and access improvements to the area. The EDA awarded a $1.5 million grant for a new parking garage to be built by the Wilmington Parking Authority. Hercules committed to a 25-year lease for the new building to be built and

owned by the developer, Integrated Resources, and to make good faith efforts
to hire economically disadvantaged city residents for any jobs created.

. . . The whole package was enough to convince HUD to award a $16
million UDAG to the City of Wilmington for the project. This financed the
land acquisition from DuPont and a major part of the construction
differential. [22]

In retrospect, it appeared that Giacco was able to accrue everything he
wanted for Hercules without spending any company money. Not disclosed
was the amount of money contributed by the state government to cement the
deal. The Pete Du Pont administration had yet to establish a central state
agency to handle such business incentives. DEDO was created in 1980 soon
after the Hercules deal was assured. But DEDO was to contribute taxpayers'
money several years later to Hercules, well after Al Giacco retired in 1987
from running Hercules to take the helm of Himont Inc., a joint venture in
polypropylene between Hercules and Italy's Montedison. [23]

On August 3, 1998, Hercules purchased Betz-Dearborn, Inc., a specialty
chemicals company. DEDO records reveal that it awarded on November 23,
1999, a Strategic Fund grant of $495,000 to Hercules for the relocation of
1,200 employees. A second DEDO grant to Hercules derived from Hercules'
announcement that it had decided to close its research facility in Jacksonville, Florida. Jacksonville's offer to retain the facility could not compete
with DEDO's incentives to relocate the facility and employees to Wilmington. [24] Those incentives comprised two DEDO awards to Hercules dated
August 22, 2005. The first was a DEDO award of $300,000 for a capital
expenditure grant, and the second was a Strategic Fund grant of $2 million
for the relocation of 360 employees.

The total of DEDO awards to Hercules—the lowest among our list of the
twelve largest state of Delaware–funded businesses during the 1997–2008
period—amounted to $2.795 million. Hercules was sold in 2008 to Ashland
Inc. of Covington, Kentucky, for $3.3 billion. [25] In the end, DEDO funding of
Hercules did not keep the company in Delaware.

FUNDING OF BIG BANKS, 2009–2013

Jack Markell began his tenure as Delaware's governor in January 2009 when
the Great Recession was already gripping the nation and the state. Governor
Markell was quick to appoint Republican Alan Levin as director of DEDO,
and to signal to all that his administration's highest priority was to grow
business and create jobs in Delaware. The result was significant acceleration
of the pace and extent of using state money as a job-creation incentive. Given
that the preceding rise and decline of the Financial Center Development Act
(FCDA) induced the credit card bonanza in the state, Markell administration

officials considered big banks as comprising fertile ground for job creation efforts. A recovery, of sorts, of the credit card industry appeared under way in 2011, which enhanced efforts to attract, keep, and increase bank jobs in Delaware.[26]

Even before 2011, state officials had turned their attention to Delaware's financial activities sector, which comprised about 11 percent of the state's workforce. In 2010, with the help of $19.9 million in Delaware Strategic Fund incentives, lender of student loans Sallie Mae moved its headquarters from Reston, Virginia, to near Newark, where it employed 1,200. In July 2011, an advisory panel approved a DEDO grant of $7.4 million to credit card issuer Discover Bank, not to create new jobs in Delaware but rather to keep its nine hundred employees in the state.[27]

A few days later, that same panel approved a grant of up to $3 million to giant Citigroup to establish a new credit card office in downtown Wilmington. New York–based Citi Cards had been in Delaware since 1982, lured to the state by the FCDA. In 2011, it had 2,200 employees working at three locations in the state, when—with a grant from DEDO—it acted to move its statewide base of operations to downtown Wilmington. DEDO awarded Citi a $3 million Strategic Fund grant contingent upon Citi adding about two hundred jobs.[28]

In October 2011, it appeared that the card unit of behemoth Bank of America (BofA) was destined for drastic job cuts among the thirty thousand worldwide layoffs in BofA's initial planned restructuring. The bank employed about seven thousand in Delaware, and its Delaware-based Global Card Services had been suffering declining profits, making it an ongoing target for staff reductions after the company had purchased the card unit from MBNA in 2006. However, after registering an overall $7.3 billion loss in the third quarter of 2010, a positive third quarter in 2011 at the bank's Wilmington-based credit card unit helped BofA realize a $6.23 billion turnaround profit for the same period.[29]

Rather than cutting Delaware jobs, then, BofA announced in October 2012 that it would add five hundred new jobs to its Delaware-based credit card business over the ensuing three years, solidifying its rank as Delaware's second largest employer. Local journalist Eric Ruth reported these laudatory comments:

> Bank of America officials said the jobs are being added here because of several factors.
> "No. 1 is the people of Delaware," which includes a talented and financially savvy workforce, said Susan Faulkner, who heads Bank of America's deposits and card products divisions. "The second is the community, and the community partnership we have. . . . In Delaware, it is unmatched."
> "The third key reason is the relationship with the state . . . with our community leaders and our elected officials," she said, adding that the state

has shown it appreciates the importance of creating an accommodating environment.

"Delaware is unique," she said. "Delaware is special."

"Gov. Markell has always encouraged us to grow in Delaware," Bank of America Co-Chief Operating Officer David Darnell said in a statement. . . .

In September, the bank's chief executive disclosed that tens of thousands of workers would be laid off during the next two to three years as the firm resizes its business and attempts to steady its performance.

To see growth in such circumstances is remarkable, officials said. "We know it's because we have such a wonderful financial services workforce here in the state," Markell said. [30]

Moreover, BofA planned in 2012 to invest even more than credit card jobs in Delaware by creating a major data processing center employing sixty to seventy full-time workers, and spending $310 million to build and outfit the center. Bank officials requested $10 million at a meeting of the state's infrastructure committee, warning that the center could be built in another state, and that the $10 million would help pay for part of a new fiber-optic cable to connect to its new data center. DEDO Director Levin, chair of the committee, recommended giving BofA an initial infrastructure grant of around $7 million for the cable project plus $1.5 million in Strategic Fund money for BofA's data center project. [31]

Just two months after BofA decided to add five hundred jobs to its credit card operation in Delaware, JPMorgan Chase & Company (JPM) announced on April 14, 2012, that it planned to add 1,200 new jobs across several lines of its Delaware businesses. Similar to the experience of BofA, JPM had likewise posted a smaller profit prior to responding to a growing rebound in Delaware's financial sector. [32] JPM's job creation was funded with the help of a $10 million state job development grant from the Delaware Strategic Fund. DEDO announced that the grant carried provisions whereby JPM had committed not only to create new jobs with an average salary of $76,000, but also to maintain the positions for three years in order to receive the funding. "This is an example of Delaware continuing its commitment to the financial industry," DEDO director Levin said. "We have a very strong financial services workforce. That industry has changed where a lot of people have lost their jobs. We have them here and they are trained and ready to go and the banks know that." [33]

Five weeks later, JPM suffered a $2 billion loss from untimely international trades on credit derivatives, prompting Levin to inquire as to whether JPM's job commitment to Delaware would thereby be affected. "They were very emphatic they are still moving forward," said Levin. "Nothing has changed, because the commitment hasn't changed." In late March 2015, it was disclosed that JPM had acquired and started demolition of a major building of AstraZeneca's Fairfax complex, and that JPM by then employed more than 7,500 employees in Delaware.[34]

CONCLUSION

According to the dictionary, *potpourri* means "an incongruous combination." And *incongruous* is defined as "inconsistent" or "lacking in harmony." We contend these terms could appropriately describe Delaware's state grants to businesses as a whole. It is true that some grants were awarded to help create or retain jobs, but many grants did not produce these intended results. Moreover, many job-related grants appeared to have been awarded to large and wealthy companies that did not need taxpayers' money. And some grants were made to companies that were not financially capable of succeeding. There appeared to have been no consistent rationale that adequately described the grant-awarding process in its entirety, except to note that the process was not transparent, that secrecy abounded, and that leaders of almost any big or small business entity could be optimistic about successfully applying for state funding in Delaware.

A potpourri of state grants to diverse recipients, aside from those already described in this book, is illustrated by the following brief itemizations from various issues of the Wilmington *News Journal*:

> The biopharmaceutical firm, Incyte Corporation, which launched its first drug in 2011 announced in November 2013 its plan to move from its rental space at DuPont Experimental Station to the much larger nearby former John Wannamaker building. To stay in Delaware with its 372 employees, amidst fierce competition from other states, the biotech firm was being supported by an $11 million package of Delaware state government grants, of which a $10,070,505 Strategic Fund performance grant was contingent upon Incyte adding 191 employees by the end of 2016.[35]

> Amazon.com, an online book selling company, was reported in October 2012 to have received $7.5 million in state grants, including about $2 million tied to "hiring benchmarks" and up to $4 million from the state's New Jobs Infrastructure Fund. One year later, Amazon employees in Delaware numbered more than 1,600.[36]

> Computer Aid, Inc., an information services company, was reported in October 2011 to have received approval by a DEDO panel of a $500,000 Strategic Fund grant to add 250 workers.[37]

> Natural Dairy Products Corporation, an organic milk products company, was reported in May 2013 to have received DEDO's approval of grants of $140,169 for "job creation" and $134,831 for "capital expenditures."[38]

The Kent County Regional Sports Complex reported in July 2012 it would receive $3.25 million from the state's New Jobs Infrastructure Fund to help it construct a complex of sports fields.[39]

Hawker Beechcraft, Inc., a Kansas-based company, was reported in April 2012 to have received a Strategic Fund grant of $750,000 "to come to the state."[40]

All Metal Fabricators reported in May 2013 that it was awarded a Strategic Fund grant of $78,818 "to offset a multi-million-dollar investment recently completed."[41]

Advanced Materials Technology, which supports the life sciences, reported in May 2013 that it was awarded a Strategic Fund grant of $60,000 "to offset expansion of manufacturing, hire new employees and move its research and development operations to a larger facility to provide room for growth."[42]

A Strategic Fund grant package of more than $1 million was reported on January 3, 2014 for the creation of 235 new jobs by Indiana-based Springfield Financial Services should that company locate a call center in New Castle.[43]

All of these examples are evidence that companies understand the economic development strategies of the state. Indeed, firms exist that specialize in extracting the maximum in grants and other benefits for business entities. For all the attempts to create or retain jobs, however, it is not clear that such efforts guarantee long-term success. The key business factors considered when determining where to locate are a good labor force, reasonable wages, good quality of life, reasonable and reliable tax rates, moderately priced utilities, and a nonvolatile political climate. Were Delaware to be considered by companies as a poor place to locate their business, no amount of enticement would lead to success in attracting and keeping businesses, and creating jobs, in the long run.

NOTES

1. For troubles encountered by AstroPower, see Michelle Darnell, "Cash-charged Astro-Power Weighs Plant Location," Wilmington *News Journal*, October 14, 1999, A1; "AstroPower: Decline of a Solar Photovoltaic Star Remains an Untold Tragedy," *Gunther Portfolio*, August 14, 2006, guntherportfolio.blogspot.com/2006/08/astropower-decline-of-solar.html (accessed April 12, 2013); and "Former CEO and CFO of AstroPower, Inc. Settle Fraud Charges," *Securities Law Prof Blog*, March 10, 2009, lawprofessors.typepad.com/securities/2009/03/former-ceo-and.html (accessed April 12, 2013).
2. For example, before adjourning its meeting of June 27, 2011, at Public Hearing 373, Delaware's Council on Development Finance, according to its minutes, convened "into executive session to discuss confidential and privileged commercial and financial information" as permitted by the state's Freedom of Information law (*Delaware Code*, Title 29, Chapter 100, Section 10004 (b)).
3. Delaware Economic Development Office, *Detailed Strategic Fund Report (1997–2008)*, unpublished data, provided by DEDO.

4. Randall Chase, "Layoffs at Invista Come after Huge Incentive Package," *Manufacturing Net*, October 16, 2008, www.manufacturing.net/news/2008/10/layoffs-at-invista-come-after-huge-incentive- (accessed April 18, 2013).

5. Cori Anne Natoli, "Seal of Approval for Seaford," Wilmington *News Journal*, March 18, 2012.

6. John E. Stapleford, "Is the Strategic Fund Strategic?" *Caesar Rodney Institute Blog*, May 17, 2011, http://criblog.wordpress.com/2011/05/17/is-the-strategic-fund-strategic/ (accessed April 18, 2013).

7. See Fraunhofer USA, *2011 Annual Report* (Plymouth, MI: Fraunhofer USA, Inc., 2012), esp. 2, 24–27.

8. Fraunhofer USA, "News Briefs," *Center for Molecular Biotechnology*, January 11, 2008–July 14, 2011, www.fraunhofer-cmb.org/news.htm (accessed April 9, 2013).

9. Wade Malcolm, "State Gambles on Alliance," Wilmington *News Journal*, July 15, 2011, B1, B2.

10. "DuPont Capital Management Names Valerie J. Sill as President and CEO," *Business Wire*, April 22, 2004, www.businesswire.com/news/home/20040422005186/en/DuPont-Capital-Management (accessed May 16, 2013). See also "DCM/ DuPont Capital Management Company History," dupontcapital.com/our-company/company-history (accessed May 16, 2013).

11. Edmund Dohnert, "DuPont Doesn't Need a Grant for R&D Project," Wilmington *News Journal*, January 27, 2012, A14. See also minutes of the Council on Development Finance's Public Hearing 379 of January 23, 2012, approving this grant, at inde.delaware.gov/dedo.../2012/January23_2012_CDF_Meeting.pdf (accessed July 22, 2015).

12. Thomas A. Corfman, "Bank One Delivers 2nd Blow to Chicago, Delaware Wins Data Center Bid," *Chicago Tribune*, February 2, 2003. ; and Chapter 7 of Formerly Senate Bill No. 17, An Act Amending the Fiscal Year Bond and Capital Improvements Act and Amending the Laws of Delaware, delcode.delaware.gov/sessionlaws/ga142/chp007.shtml (accessed June 11, 2013).

13. "Playtex Announces Partnership with Delaware Economic Development Office to Remain in State," *The Free Library*, December 9, 2005.

14. Jonathan Starkey, "Division of South Korean Company Wins Bid for Allen," Wilmington *News Journal*, July 27, 2011, A1, A5.

15. "Korean Firm Buys 92-Year-Old Delaware Poultry Producer," *USA Today*, July 28, 2011.

16. News Release, "Governor Markell Welcomes Chairman Kim and the Harim Group to Delaware," Governor's *News Archives*, August 4, 2011, governor.delaware.gov/news/2011/1108august/20110804-harim_group.shtml (accessed May 24, 2013).

17. Doug Rainey, "Markell Defends Economic Development Strategy," *Delaware Business Daily*, March 21, 2013, delawarebusinessdaily.com/2013/03/markell-defends-economic-development-strategy/ (accessed May 24, 2013).

18. See Starkey, "Division of South Korean Company Wins Bid for Allen," A5.

19. Cori Anne Natoli and Doug Denison, "Pickle Plant Will Switch to Chicken: Allen Harim to Buy Millsboro Facility, Hire 700 Workers," Wilmington *News Journal*, April 2, 2013, A1, A2.

20. See, for example, Leigh Giangreco, "Chicken Plant's Impact Scored," Wilmington *News Journal*, November 22, 2013, B1, B3; and Jeff Montgomery, "Allen-Harim Opponents Appeal County Approval," ibid., December 5, 2013, B1, B2.

21. See William Boyer and Edward Ratledge, *Pivotal Policies in Delaware: From Desegregation to Deregulation* (Newark: University of Delaware Press, 2014), chapter 7; and Timothy Barnekov, Robin Boyle, and Daniel Rich, *Privatism and Urban Policy in Britain and the United States* (New York: Oxford University Press, 1989), 86.

22. Kevin McGonegal, "Wilmington: How We Got Here and Where We're Going—Part VI: The Hercules Deal," *Town Square Delaware*, September 20, 2012, townsquaredelaware.com/2012/09/20/wilmington-how-we-got-here-and-where-were (accessed May 28, 2013).

23. Claudia N. Deutsch, "Finally, Al Giacco Retires—Maybe," *New York Times*, March 29, 1987.

24. Joe Light, "Incentives Played Part in Hercules' Move to Delaware," *The Florida Times Union*, December 10, 2005.

25. See Maureen Milford, "Buyout Closes Curtain on Hercules," Wilmington *News Journal*, July 12, 2008, A1; and Reid Champagne, "Recalling Hercules," *Delaware Today*, December 2008.

26. For the credit card bonanza in Delaware, see chapter 8, "Credit Card Banking," in William Boyer and Edward Ratledge, *Pivotal Policies in Delaware* (Newark: University of Delaware Press, 2014). See also Christine Hauser, "Recovery Seen in Rising Use of Credit Cards," *New York Times*, May 14, 2011, B1, B2; Eileen AJ Connelly, "Card Law Working Well, Says New Study," Wilmington *News Journal*, May 11, 2011, A5; Connelly, "Credit Card Defaults Continue to Drop," ibid., May 18, 2011, A7, A10; and Eric Ruth, "Credit Card Banks Rebound," ibid., July 20, 2011, A1, A7.

27. See Wade Malcolm, "Sallie Mae at 40," Wilmington *News Journal*, May 14, 2013, A7, A9; Jonathan Starkey, "Del. Gives $16M to Financial Companies," ibid., August 28, 2011, C1, C4; and Starkey, "Proposed Discover Grant Adds to Discomfort over Transparency," ibid., August 12, 2011, A1, A5.

28. See Jonathan Starkey, "City, State Promise Citigroup Millions to Move to Wilmington," Wilmington *News Journal*, July 15, 2011, A1, A10; Starkey, "State Awards Citi $3M in Grants," ibid., July 26, 2011, A6, A7; and Eric Ruth, "Citi Cards Calls Wilmington Home," ibid., February 11, 2012, A6, A7.

29. See Eric Ruth, "Card Unit Could Be Targeted for Layoffs," Wilmington *News Journal*, October 13, 2011, A1, A2; and Ruth, "With Boost from Card Unit, BofA Posts Profit," ibid., October 19, 2011, A10.

30. Eric Ruth, "Bank of America May Hire 500 in Delaware," Wilmington *News Journal*, February 17, 2012, A1, A2. See also Wade Malcolm, "Right Kills Make Financial Services a Land of Plenty," ibid., December 8, 2013, A1, A8.

31. Doug Denison and Eric Ruth, "BofA Moves Plan Forward," Wilmington *News Journal*, October 18, 2012, A1, A8.

32. Eric Ruth, "Chase Posts Smaller Profit," Wilmington *News Journal*, July 15, 2011, A8, A9.

33. Cori Anne Natoli, "Chase to Add 1,200 Well-paid Positions," Wilmington *News Journal*, April 14, 2012, A1, A2.

34. Cori Anne Natoli, "JPMorgan Chase: Still Expanding in Delaware," Wilmington *News Journal*, May 22, 2012, A8. See also Jonathan Starkey, "JPMorgan Chase Offered $1.5M Grant," ibid., March 8, 2014, A1, A12; Starkey, "$1.5M Grant to Help JPMorgan Chase Create 500 Del. Jobs," ibid., March 25, 2014, A1, A4; and Jeff Mordock, "JPMorgan Clears Out Old AstraZeneca Site," ibid., March 29, 2015, E1, E5.

35. Wade Malcolm and Cori Anne Natoli, "Incyte Signs 15-Year Lease," Wilmington *News Journal*, November 16, 2013, A1, A2.

36. See Aaron Nathans, "Amazon's Middletown Fulfillment Center Open," Wilmington *News Journal*, October 21, 2012, E1; and Robin Brown, "Amazon Workforce Hits 1,600 in a Year," Wilmington *News Journal*, October 11, 2013, A8.

37. Jonathan Starkey, "Panel OKs $500,000 Grant to Help IT Firm Add 250 Jobs," Wilmington *News Journal*, October 27, 2011, A1.

38. Wade Malcolm, "Organic Dairy Company Heads to Newark," Wilmington *News Journal*, May 25, 2013, A6, A7.

39. Doug Denison, "Complex Wins Funding," Wilmington *News Journal*, July 18, 2012, B1, B2.

40. Eric Ruth, "Del. Aircraft Facility Expected to Take Off," Wilmington *News Journal*, April 22, 2012, E1, E3.

41. Cori Anne Natoli, "DEDO Grants Boost Growth at 2 Firms," Wilmington *News Journal*, May 9, 2013, A8.

42. Ibid.

43. Cori Anne Natoli, "Del. Offers Grant to Springleaf," Wilmington *News Journal*, January 3, 2014, A8.

Chapter Eight

Growing Business by Other Means

The purpose of this chapter is to explore various means of growing businesses and jobs, other than awarding Delaware taxpayers' money as incentives to companies.

As we have noted, it is difficult to shed much more light on the Delaware Economic Development Office's (DEDO's) funding of businesses to augment the numbers of jobs in the state because of the lack of transparency that permeates the process. The *New York Times*, in recognition that there was no nationwide accounting of business incentives, spent months investigating business incentives awarded by hundreds of cities, counties, and states to companies. The *Times* used a variety of sources for information from over one hundred records requests, numerous government reports, and organizations such as Investment Consulting Associates and Good Jobs First, a non-profit policy center that focuses on economic development. The newspaper put together an extensive database accessible beginning in December 2012 and found that the nation's local governments gave up $80.4 billion in incentives "in the most recent year available" comprising 156,573 grants.

The database, accessible for each state via the Internet, revealed that Delaware's state and local governments spent at least $43.1 million per year on incentive and subsidies programs, roughly $48 per capita yearly—or one cent per dollar of the state's budget—during the 1999–2011 period. Included was $21.7 million per year labeled the state government's "cash grant, loan or loan guarantee," of which $20 million was contributed from the Delaware Strategic Fund. Important for this chapter is the fact that the *Times* database also showed that of the total $43.1 million of Delaware's state and local governments' incentives per year, nearly 48 percent, comprising $20.5 million, was labeled the state government's "corporate income tax credit, rebate or reduction."[1] Accordingly, almost half of all Delaware's state and local business incentives were attributed to the state government's corporate income tax incentives. Given that fact, they are included among what the Delaware state Department of Finance characterizes as "tax preferences."

TAX PREFERENCES

Delaware law defines "tax preference" as meaning "any law of the United States or of the State of Delaware which exempts, in whole or in part, certain persons, income, goods, services or property from the impact of established taxes, including . . . tax deductions, tax exclusions, tax credits, tax deferrals, and tax exemptions."[2] The law requires that the Delaware state Division of Revenue issue a biennial report that estimates the fiscal impact of existing tax preferences, assessing them quantitatively and qualitatively. The division's 2011 report includes this qualifying statement:

> Many tax preferences are based on the argument that they will promote economic development by encouraging businesses to locate in Delaware or to invest in existing Delaware enterprises. Tax preferences can increase tax revenues if they attract investments that enlarge the economy. Whether preferences do enhance economic growth is up to question. On the downside, tax preferences may actually become growth impediments if they cause other, nonpreferred activities to pay higher taxes. Higher rates impede economic growth because they reduce the after-tax return available on investments.[3]

Each corporation that conducts business in Delaware is required to file a corporate income tax return unless specifically exempted by law.[4] The corporate income tax rate is 8.7 percent of taxable income. It appears that the most pertinent job-related Delaware tax preferences involve: (1) investment holding companies that manage intangibles; (2) debtor corporations that claim deductions of interest income from affiliated companies; (3) firms that claim tax credits for the creation of jobs; and (4) firms that claim tax credits for qualified research and development. The Division of Revenue's 2011 report is distinguished by the clarity of its language describing each of these complex tax preferences.

(1) *Companies Managing Intangibles.* Investment holding companies, the activities of which are confined to intangibles, are exempt from the corporate income tax under the Investment Company Act of 1940.[5] According to the Division of Revenue:

> This provision is designed to spur economic development in the State. The tax preference is intended to strengthen the State's reputation as a major financial center, and to signal to the financial community that Delaware is a progressive state in terms of liberalizing its financial regulatory environment. . . . On

July 1, 1990, this provision was extended to include corporations that invest
the funds of a mutual fund.

Eligible firms file only information returns, establishing their eligibility for
the exemption and, therefore, do not have to file a corporate income tax return.
This makes an accurate assessment of the revenue impact of this provision
little more than guesswork. As investment holding companies are established
in Delaware primarily because of this tax exemption, it is likely that, given the
inherent mobility of intangible assets, many of them would leave the State if
the exemption were repealed or narrowed significantly. However, no data exist
by which the Division of Revenue could make its own estimate of the revenue
loss generated by this exemption. [6]

The "estimated revenue loss" of this tax preference was "unknown," according to the Division of Revenue.

(2) *Deduction of Interest.* Delaware law permits corporations (creditors)
to deduct the amount of income from interest (including discounts) earned on
the inter-corporate transactions (such as loans, advances, or similar contracts)
of affiliated companies. To qualify for interest deductions, creditor corporations are subject to taxation and the debtor corporation must not claim deductions in determining their net incomes for purposes of the Delaware corporate
income tax. [7] According to the Division of Revenue:

> The corporate income tax deduction for interest from affiliated corporations
> allows related companies to shift interest income and related expenses among
> members of a group that is eligible to file a federal consolidated return. . . . By
> creating a tax advantage for the management of inherently mobile intangible
> assets, such as inter-company obligations, Delaware enhances its reputation as
> a financial center and may also produce a secondary effect in the form of
> relatively small employment gains for Delaware's financial and legal communities. Because the case with which intangible assets could be moved from
> Delaware is so great, it is clear that a tax incentive's impact on the decision to
> locate such assets in Delaware is critical.
>
> In fact, many argue that a business's decision to "locate" intangible assets
> in Delaware occurs solely due to the tax incentive. Unlike tangible business
> assets (e.g., a production or research facility), the location of intangible assets
> is not dependent upon the quality of public infrastructures, access to markets, a
> well-trained pool of labor, or quality of life considerations. In the event of its
> repeal, the vast majority of the intangible assets covered under this provision
> would leave the State drastically reducing any revenue loss estimate produced
> on a static basis. . . .
>
> Affiliated finance companies (AFCs) present a special case under this tax
> preference. By purchasing receivables from their affiliate or "core business" (a
> large retailer, for example), the AFC acts as a creditor for its affiliate. The
> affiliate (retailer) usually has a very small apportionment percentage because
> sales in Delaware make up only a small part of its market. The AFC, however,
> usually has a very high apportionment percentage (frequently 100 percent).
> Therefore, the interest on a large loan from an AFC to the core business is

often sufficient, when deducted from the AFC's net income, to totally eliminate its tax liability. The AFC's primary function is to enhance the financial
position of the core business; correspondingly, large loans are not uncommon.
It is evident that this preference is the reason behind the establishment of
AFCs in Delaware. The fact that so many AFCs were established in Delaware
in response to this provision suggests that its elimination would cause many
AFCs to move to other states. [8]

The "estimated revenue loss" of this tax preference was stated by the Division of Revenue as "likely to be negligible" because such estimates "are
confounded by unknown market responses to a change in this tax law. Although the elimination of this provision could cause a temporary, short-term
increase in revenues, firms likely would move these operations out of the
State as quickly as possible, erasing any long-term revenue gain."[9]

  (3) *Tax Credits for Creation of Jobs and Qualified Investments.* Any
corporate taxpayer engaged in stated qualified activities that invests
$200,000 or more in an enterprise and that employs five or more employees
may, if eligible as noted, receive credits of $500 for each $100,000 invested,
not to exceed 50 percent of their tax liability in a given year. Unused credits
may be carried forward, and the "sunset" provision for this program has been
eliminated.[10] This provision was later expanded to allow employers engaged
in certain "commercial or retail activity," defined as noted, to receive an
additional credit of $250 (tacked on to the original $500) for each additional
full-time employee, for each $100,000 of investment in qualified facilities
located in "targeted areas."[11] The Division of Revenue assessed these tax
preferences as follows:

> The first goal of these credits is to promote job creation and investment in
> Delaware by giving employers incentives to hire additional full-time employ-
> ees or to expand business activities. . . .
>   These credits may indeed serve as a useful promotional tool for State
> development officials. But there is an equally strong probability that most
> firms are simply "rewarded" with a bonus for actions that they would have
> taken without the existence of a credit, rather than "earning" a credit for
> actions that would not have occurred without them.[12]

The "estimated revenue loss" for these tax credits was $7.6 million for fiscal
year 2011 and $4.0 million to $8.0 million for fiscal year 2012, according to
the Division of Revenue.

  (4) *Tax Credits for Research and Development.* This preference permits a
tax credit for Delaware companies conducting qualified research within Delaware. The cap on such credits is $5 million per year. Although unused
credits may not be claimed retroactively, they may be carried forward up to
fifteen years, meaning it is possible for the revenue loss to end up exceeding
$5 million during any given year.[13] According to the Division of Revenue:

The purpose of this preference is to enhance Delaware's reputation as a home for research intensive firms (e.g., pharmaceutical and biotechnology firms). Like all business tax incentives, it is difficult to isolate that portion which actually results in "new" economic activity from the part which merely serves as a bonus to firms that would have engaged in the desired activity in the absence of the incentive. Because the Research and Development Credit is used by many firms that already had significant research and development activity in Delaware prior to its enactment, it is likely that a large portion of the provision's costs does nothing to add to the level of research and development conducted in Delaware. On the other hand, the Research and Development Credits may be considered an unavoidable cost of doing business for states, like Delaware, that hope to compete successfully in the area of high-tech economic development.[14]

The Division of Revenue's "estimated revenue loss" for this corporate tax preference was $7.7 million for fiscal year 2011, and $4.0 million to $8.0 million for fiscal year 2012.

The basic or "bottom-line" issue that remains is whether Delaware corporate tax preferences are effective in attracting and retaining firms that add significant numbers of jobs in the state. A statement of the Division of Revenue, excerpted from its 2012 *Tax Preference Report*, appears to raise doubt, as follows:

> In general . . . the impact of taxes on business location decisions is often of secondary importance to other elements of a State's business climate. Access to markets, labor skill and supply, and infrastructure quality are typically more important considerations in a business's location decision. It is often unclear whether tax credits are a critical element, without which a firm would have chosen to locate elsewhere, or if they merely serve as a bonus to firms that would have chosen a particular state regardless of the credit. The size of the incentives suggests that they are unlikely to have a significant impact on businesses' location decisions. Despite this, proponents argue that such credits must be offered for businesses to even consider Delaware as a potential location. Even if the credits are not the deciding factor in the location decision, they may be of enough importance to retain. They may even be considered a cost of doing business for State development efforts.[15]

Although corporate tax preferences or incentives may indeed have minimal impact on business location decisions, and hence on their creation of jobs, they nevertheless are frequently included in packages offered by Delaware's state and local governments to attract businesses. Perhaps reducing unnecessary state regulations on businesses may also have some indirect impact in convincing company executives that Delaware is a business-friendly state. Governor Jack Markell's initiative in this direction is germane.

REMOVING REGULATORY HURDLES

During Jack Markell's successful campaigns for state treasurer and governor, he emphasized the efficacy of his experience as a business executive. His tenure as governor, beginning in 2009, was marked chiefly by the saliency of his business- and employment-friendly public posture and a suspicious eye toward government regulation of business. With regard to government regulation, Governor Markell resorted to an extraordinary initiative to strengthen Delaware's ranking as "one of the best states in the country to conduct business." On June 14, 2012, he signed Executive Order 36, which, according to his press release, "launches a statewide effort that brings citizens, businesses and state agencies together to identify and remove regulatory hurdles." The press release also stated that Governor Markell "visited over 750 businesses in Delaware since his swearing-in."

Executive Order 36 required executive branch agencies to closely review their regulations that had been in existence for at least three years. Each agency was required to hold at least one public hearing in each county, and also accept written submissions from citizens who believed certain regulations were no longer working. At the conclusion of the "public input period," each agency was required to evaluate the proposals and recommendations it received, and decide which regulations to change, keep, or eliminate in accordance with procedures required by the state's Administrative Procedure Act. The executive order provided that within one year, the governor's office would submit a report to the General Assembly setting forth which regulations were to be eliminated or modified as a result of this process.[16]

At the end of the year-long review undertaken by twelve executive branch agencies, Governor Markell submitted a seventy-page report from his office, dated June 27, 2013, to the General Assembly detailing results with respect to a total of 385 regulations subjected to review required by his Executive Order 36. Simultaneously, his office issued a press release summarizing highlights of the report. Of the 385 regulations reviewed, eighty-three were amended and sixty-one were deleted after thirty-nine public hearings—thirteen in each of the three counties—were conducted during the process. For example, the Department of Transportation amended a regulation to allow flexibility in low-density population areas in enforcing requirements that sidewalks be installed in new developments. The Department of Labor reduced the number of unemployment insurance regulations from forty-five to twenty-one, while updating the remaining regulations to reflect statutory and technological changes. The Economic Development Office amended or deleted nine of ten regulations examined, including the elimination of four regulations related to tourism programs no longer in operation.

It may be a stretch to connect this process to the creation of more jobs in Delaware. However, the initiative could help government officials to characterize deregulation as still another feature that makes Delaware a "business-friendly" state. Although most of the resulting changes related to small businesses, Governor Markell claimed in his press release: "As a result of the changes . . . , we are making it easier to do business in Delaware, making government more efficient, and making agency rules simpler to use and understand." He added that the process would be continued: "EO 36 calls for another full review process no more than three years after the submission of today's report to the General Assembly."[17]

STATE-FUNDED TRIPS ABROAD

Another indirect influence on company executives abroad to consider Delaware as a favorable location for their business is meeting with state officials who travel with their business-friendly message. As noted in the last chapter, Governor Jack Markell and State Agriculture Secretary Ed Kee took a government-funded trip to Japan, and also to South Korea where they visited Harim's poultry processing plant. In late January 2013, Governor Markell traveled to Switzerland to attend the World Economic Forum's annual meeting—a trip paid by the National Governors Association, then chaired by Markell. In February 2013, Markell was about to embark to India to speak to Internet business leaders when these various trips evoked this response by Delaware Republican Party Chairman John Sigler: "While the citizens of Delaware fight through a bad economy and try to make ends meet under an even heavier tax burden, our Governor is jetting around the world. The people of Delaware deserve better than this 'do as I say, not as I do' attitude from the Governor." Markell's office immediately retorted:

> The Governor's trips to Korea and India are about jobs for Delawareans. Mr. Sigler should explain to the hundreds of employees of Harim in Sussex County—workers who almost lost their jobs—why he thinks the Governor should not have gone to Korea to show Harim leaders what a great workforce and poultry industry we have in Delaware. . . . Or Mr. Sigler should explain to Delaware's current and future technology workers why the Governor should not pitch Delaware to 1,500 representatives of the Indian IT industry, which has a growing number of employees in the U.S. Economic development in the modern world doesn't occur sitting at a desk. You have to work for it and that's what the Governor is doing.[18]

In July 2013, Governor Markell traveled to Israel with DEDO Director Alan Levin, in recognition of the fact that thousands of Israeli businesses were incorporated in Delaware, and that corporate taxes funded more than a third of Delaware's annual budget. It was reported that the trips to Israel, Korea, and India each cost $60,000. Some critics questioned what Delaware was receiving for the cost of such travel, pointing to Delaware's slow economic growth and an unemployment rate of more than 7 percent. Republican State Senator Greg Lavelle suggested that Governor Markell's trips abroad were tied to his search for political gain. "As some have suggested," Lavelle said, "the governor needs to be sensitive to the fact that he shouldn't be building his national political resume with international travel paid for by Delaware taxpayers." Governor Markell rejected Lavelle's contention as "absolutely false." Stating that he visits Delaware businesses all the time, Markell said: "I'm always looking for new opportunities. I do the same thing with businesses that are based in other countries."[19]

Without mentioning Governor Markell's trips overseas, one local small business manager asserted in an op-ed column that Delaware's economic growth depended on international trade, as follows:

> What Delaware has been able to accomplish in the global marketplace is impressive. . . . Delaware is competitive in attracting investors and exporting products. I cannot overemphasize the important role our elected officials play in helping our Delaware businesses in the global marketplace. When we travel to visit with current and potential distributors, they consistently express that they are impressed by three things: the quality of our U.S.-made products, that we meet with them face-to-face, and the fact that our elected officials have visited their country and support our efforts.
>
> . . . Here's how this works.
>
> We, as a state, invest the resources to send government and business leaders to strategic markets around the world to promote Delaware manufacturers. This leads to Delaware businesses growing, creating new jobs, or at the very least being able to sustain them and not have to lay off employees. . . .[20]

In addition to courting businesses out of state and abroad, that the state government resorts to extraordinary measures to save jobs of businesses already existing in Delaware is another factor that may influence company executives elsewhere to consider Delaware as a business-friendly location. State action in 2013 to help Delaware's faltering casinos offers a case in point.

SAVING CASINO JOBS?

Among the most popular tourist destinations in Delaware in the 1990s were Dover Downs racetrack in Kent County, the Harrington harness racetrack also in Kent County, and the Delaware Park racetrack in New Castle County. With the introduction of slot machines in racetrack casinos in the mid-1990s, gambling profits soon became a significant source of state income, regardless of the fact that Delaware's Constitution expressly forbade "slot machines."[21] Delaware voters had resoundingly rejected a 1976 initiative to allow slot machine gambling. A 1989 bill to allow slot machines had been vetoed by

Republican Governor Mike Castle, and a similar 1993 bill was also vetoed by Democratic Governor Tom Carper.[22] But state legislators continued to defy the constitutional prohibition. The General Assembly passed a July 1994 enactment, which became law, without Carper's signature, that permitted slot machines but made no mention of them specifically by virtue of referring to them as so-called video lottery machines, defined as machines "in which bills, coins, or tokens are deposited in order to play a game of chance."[23]

By the end of 1996, slot machines were thriving in the state's three casinos at Dover Downs, Harrington, and Delaware Park. Over $2 billion had been put into slot machines during their first year, yielding $27 million in revenue as the state's 25 percent share in their first eight months of operation.[24] The state's share was lowest among the states that operated slots at the time, compared to, for example, West Virginia (30 percent), Rhode Island (46 percent), South Dakota (50 percent), and Oregon (58 percent). It was only a matter of time before the heyday of Delaware's casinos would wane as the Great Recession and competition from Pennsylvania, Maryland, and New Jersey casinos gained traction. In short, Delaware casinos could not match nearby bigger states in attracting customers, especially now that with Internet gambling, people could remain at home to gamble.

Moreover, Delaware's share on slots had grown to 43.5 percent as of 2013, thus shrinking its casinos' take even more.[25] By mid-October 2013, Delaware Park was forecasting a 17 percent drop in revenues in 2013, Harrington expected to lose about 4 percent, and Dover Downs' revenue from slot machines had fallen more than 20 percent since 2007. Whereas the state's revenue from gambling had funded more than 6 percent of the state's operating budget in 2012, its tax collections from gambling were predicted to fall to $227 million in the 2013 budget year—resulting in the lowest total since 2004. These dire projections led Dr. James Butkiewicz, head of the University of Delaware's Department of Economics, to conclude, "Gambling is just never going to recover" in Delaware. "You don't go from a monopoly to competition and make the same rate of return."[26]

In June 2013, Delaware's casinos faced the prospect of reducing their estimated combined workforce by three thousand jobs. Casino operators asked the state to reduce slot machine taxes from 43.5 percent to 37 percent and to bail out the state's casino industry. Governor Jack Markell responded by suggesting a plan to provide a one-time allocation of $8 million, from higher-than-expected overall tax revenue, to be split among the three casinos, hopefully to hold the line on jobs. Delaware lawmakers supported Markell's plan, which was promptly made part of the end-of-session bond bill that passed without debate.[27] The casino operators nevertheless complained that $8 million was not enough to avoid job cuts. An editorial in the state's leading newspaper proposed that "Delaware should start getting out of the gambling business. It is too dependent on what was once the easy money of a state-controlled monopoly."[28]

On October 31, 2013, Delaware became the first state to launch what state officials called a "full suite" of Internet gambling to revive at least a modicum of gambling profits and revenue from the three Delaware casinos. Anybody registered and physically in Delaware would be able to play slots, poker, blackjack, and roulette for money via the Internet. This online gambling innovation was intended to attract young adults—ages twenty-five to thirty-five—who normally did not frequent the casinos where the average gambler's age was in the late fifties.[29]

Internet gambling in Delaware would be the latest addition to so-called legalized gambling in Delaware, restricted to slot machines when it began in 1995. Only Nevada offered online gambling at the time, but restricted it to poker only. Subsequently, Delaware and Nevada officials began considering the possibility of allowing both states to play poker online with each other. The federal government had shut down the three largest online poker companies in 2011, making it illegal to process payments for Internet poker.[30]

In any event, the future of Delaware casinos by 2013 remained certainly bleak. They illustrated that if businesses do not remain profitable, they may fail or at least shed jobs.

CHRISTIANA MALL AND BARLEY MILL PLAZA

Those who engage in real estate development often do so to set the stage for attracting profit-making business tenants that in turn create sustainable jobs. This process is beset with formidable challenges. Establishment of Delaware's Christiana Mall area, for instance, was successful, whereas long-time real estate development efforts to establish the state's so-called Barley Mill Plaza complex remained uncertain well into 2014. Both developments illustrate the critical importance of developers' efforts to create businesses and jobs in a small state with limited resources.

Christiana Mall, near Newark, is by far the largest shopping mall in Delaware. It is located near an exit off Interstate 95 close to the center of the Boston/Washington megalopolis. This super-regional, mid-range-to-upscale shopping mall contained more than 130 shops in 2010, employing many full- and part-time employees, in a sales area of 1,090,000 square feet. Because Delaware did not have a sales tax, Christiana Mall became a very popular destination for out-of-state shoppers—mainly from Virginia, Maryland, Pennsylvania, New Jersey, and New York—seeking to save money.[31]

In 2013, it was revealed that Delaware officials had approved nearly two million square feet to be used for new commercial space in the vicinity of Christiana Mall, roughly equivalent to the size of two more Christiana Malls.

This would mean the creation of many more construction jobs, followed by many more commercial jobs, and would attract many more shoppers, and vehicles, while bringing about both the construction of more roadways and of course much more traffic congestion. Larry Tarabicos, attorney for two of the included mall expansion projects, commented, "This area has been targeted for 40 years to be the retail hub of New Castle County." The gigantic commercial expansion in the area featured developer Frank Acierno's effort, dating from the 1990s, to build a massive 915,000-square-foot retail project adjacent to the Christiana Mall. Tenants of the expanded area had yet to be announced. Residents of nearby Christiana Village apartment complex, already worried mostly about traffic congestion, were not powerful enough effectively to challenge the expansion.[32]

The contrast of Christiana Mall's development with a protracted attempt to establish the Barley Mill Plaza shopping mall also in New Castle County, nearly half the size of the expanding Christiana Mall, was mind-boggling to say the least. The land-use development effort of Barley Mill was beset with a labyrinth of complex issues stretching over seven years, from 2007 through 2013, involving powerful adversaries, state and local politics, intense community conflict, intricate legal battles, and dramatic twists and turns. At stake was the prospective creation of many businesses and jobs in a small state struggling with well over thirty thousand jobless Delawareans.

The effort to develop Barley Mill began in 2007 when Stoltz Real Estate Partners bought the plaza, a half-vacant DuPont Company office park of ninety-two acres at the intersection of Delaware Route 141 and Lancaster Pike in New Castle County, by paying $94 million, or nearly $1 million per acre. In 2008, Stoltz announced a 2.8-million-square-foot, mixed land-use plan for the property that would have been as large as Pennsylvania's massive King of Prussia Mall. The Stoltz plan called for 700,000 square feet of commercial space, including a 200,000-square-foot hotel, another 700,000 square feet of residential space, including a nine-story residential tower, plus 1.4 million square feet of office space. The plan evoked strenuous opposition from nearby upscale Greenville homeowners, at the long-protected gateway of Northern New Castle County's elite "chateau country," who immediately mobilized to form a protest group known as Citizens for Responsible Growth (CRG). New Castle County residents had long harbored suspicions that developers seldom failed to obtain what they wanted from the New Castle County government, regardless that its "most important function is to control development through land-use control, especially zoning."[33]

CRG was determined to thwart the Stoltz plan. In September 2010, a truce of sorts was reached when County Executive Chris Coons helped craft a compromise agreement between CRG and Stoltz. The new Stoltz plan eliminated the residential component and reduced the commercial and office space, thus decreasing the total plan from 2.85 million square feet to 1.65

million square feet. The agreement was hailed by some as a model of cooperation, and CRG agreed to help Stoltz influence the County Council to approve the compromise. In October 2011, the County Council rezoned the remaining property from office to commercial use by a seven to six vote, thus approving the compromise plan. Not all CRG members supported the revised plan, though. A splinter group of CRG was formed known as Save Our County (SOC). In December 2011, SOC brought a lawsuit against Stoltz and the county to reverse its rezoning of Barley Mill. Accordingly, the county government and Stoltz joined forces through 2012 to defend against SOC's lawsuit.[34] At this juncture, it is instructive to make reference to a four-page article of March 31, 2013, by investigative reporters of the Wilmington *News Journal*, headlined "Influence, Access Taint Land-use Decisions: After Five Years, Barley Mill Project Still Awaits Traffic Study." The article began in part as follows:

> Proposed in 2008 as the largest commercial and residential development in state history, Barley Mill escaped scrutiny that could have required millions more in needed traffic improvements thanks to a powerful lobbyist and a politically connected lawyer who benefited from the state's dysfunctional planning process, the investigation found.
>
> Residents and community leaders who oppose the project have long argued that taxpayers were left in the dark and short-changed by an unfair process that favored the developer. They appear to be right. Evidence from state meetings and correspondence shows the Stoltz Real Estate Partners project was managed from the beginning to sidestep a rigorous traffic study. "The land-use system in New Castle County, including DelDOT's role in it, is horribly broken," said New Castle County Councilman Bob Weiner. "Access and influence is the key—and in the case of Barley Mill Plaza, Stoltz had it."[35]

The "powerful lobbyist" hired by Stoltz was identified in the article as Roger Roy, a former state representative who was the legislature's longtime Bond Bill Committee chairman with much influence over Delaware transportation matters. The "politically-connected lawyer" for Stoltz was longtime development lawyer Pam Scott, married to former County Council President Paul Clark, who later became county executive while the project was being debated. Roy and Scott worked behind the scenes, according to the article, to influence Delaware's Department of Transportation (DelDOT) to opt for requiring a more flexible "traffic operational analysis" rather than a rigorous and comprehensive "traffic impact study" (TIS) that, some argued, "would have forced Stoltz to spend more on traffic improvements or scale back the Barley Mill project."[36]

County Executive Chris Coons became U.S. senator in November 2010, and Tom Gordon took office as county executive in November 2012, after making his opposition to the Barley Mill project the central theme in his campaign against intervening incumbent Paul Clark. Concerning the weakened traffic study, County Executive Gordon said, "I think it was a flawed process. . . . You can now see by the evidence that it was not a fair process for the public." Once in office, Gordon immediately sided with Save Our County, although he was still technically a defendant in the case brought by SOC, thus adding a unique twist in the Barley Mill saga.[37]

Meanwhile, an editorial in the Wilmington *News Journal* called on Del-DOT to "clean up its act" and to "restore credibility" by simply imposing the recommendations of the larger impact study. "The developer would have to pay to bring critical intersections up to capacity," said the editorial, "Otherwise, the cost of fixing any overloaded roads would fall on the taxpayers and the people traveling the roads."[38]

The focus of the Barley Mill saga next turned to SOC's court case against Stoltz. In a daylong hearing in April 2013 before the Chancery Court over the rezoning of Barley Mill, Vice Chancellor Sam Glasscock III repeatedly questioned whether New Castle County Council members were misinformed about their ability to consider the key traffic impact issue at the time of their rezoning vote.[39] In June, Vice Chancellor Glasscock ruled that the rezoning was invalid because the County Council had erred by not considering the traffic issue before the rezoning vote. Greenville resident Sandra Anderson, a founder of SOC, said she was "absolutely ecstatic" about the decision, explaining that "five housewives sitting around a kitchen table started this thing, and to now know we've gotten this far, is very gratifying." County Executive Tom Gordon commented, "To not have traffic impact data for the largest development in the history of New Castle County is just appalling. We ought to go back to the beginning, start over again, and do it correctly without any political interference." Gordon added that it was wrong for Pam Scott to legally represent Stoltz during her husband Paul Clark's tenure as County Council president and then as county executive.[40]

Another chapter in the seemingly unending Barley Mill saga was written when Stoltz attorneys appealed to Delaware's Supreme Court to reverse Vice Chancellor Glasscock's ruling invalidating the County Council's rezoning vote. They contended that state law did not require the council to consider traffic data prior to votes to rezone properties.[41]

Meanwhile, in January 2014, a 101-page report on state campaign finance practices was released by special prosecutor E. Norman Veasey, former chief justice of the Delaware Supreme Court. Among the findings in the report was the revelation that Governor Jack Markell's campaign committee received more than $20,000 from about a dozen business entities affiliated with Stoltz, some of which Veasey said were improper. The inference was made by many that such money bought access and influence connected to the decision not to require a traffic impact study prior to rezoning the Barley Mill real estate development. For example, SOC leader Tom Dawson commented that the conclusion from Veasey's report "just further erodes our faith in the democratic process. Every step in the Barley Mill process has an odor about it."[42]

In late March 2014, the Stoltz Barley Mill redevelopment project was put on hold, if not in limbo, by virtue of the Delaware Supreme Court's unanimous decision upholding Vice Chancellor Glasscock's ruling that struck down the 2011 rezoning that would have allowed Stoltz's investment to proceed.[43]

In August 2014, Odyssey Charter School, which sought to expand to a full K–12 school, filed plans to create a campus of more than thirty-five acres—or more than one-third of Stoltz's original 2.8-million-square-foot development plan—at the Barley Mill Plaza site. This was welcome news to nearby residents who had successfully protested Stoltz's plans to use the site for commercial and residential use, including high-rise condominiums and a shopping center. Odyssey Charter enlisted the Delaware Economic Development Office to help the school obtain bond financing for its new campus.[44]

WORKFORCE DEVELOPMENT

Another dimension of growing business and jobs in Delaware by means other than Strategic Fund awards relates to the obvious reliance of business on an educated and well-trained workforce.

A 2000 study concluded that after the state's launch in 1992 of the public school education reform initiative known as New Directions, "education reform in Delaware was business-driven." According to that study, "Education reform in Delaware has been driven by a community partnership of business, government, and education leaders. Business has been more engaged in public education than in other public policy areas."[45]

Thereafter, corporate leaders continued to show that they can influence educational reform in Delaware to develop a workforce vital for their businesses. Accordingly, Rodel Inc., a specialty chemicals company founded in 1969 and headquartered in Newark, Delaware, created the Rodel Foundations—of Delaware in 1999 and of Arizona in 1973—to improve public education in the two states.[46]

In 2006, the Rodel Foundation of Delaware helped develop a coalition of business, education, government, and civic leaders, which launched the "Vision 2015" plan designed to "provide a world-class education to all public school students in Delaware," according to its website. The challenge in Delaware was formidable, as illustrated by a 2010 Georgetown University report linking projected jobs and education requirements through 2018 among the states and the District of Columbia. The report's summary with respect to Delaware was the following:

Between 2008 and 2018, new jobs in Delaware requiring postsecondary education and training will grow by 26,000 while jobs for high school graduates and dropouts will grow by 14,000.

Between 2008 and 2018, Delaware will create 144,000 job vacancies both from new jobs and from job openings due to retirement.

83,000 of these job vacancies will be for those with postsecondary credentials, 46,000 for high school graduates and 14,000 for high school dropouts.

Delaware ranks 30th in terms of its 2018 jobs that will require a Bachelor's degree, and is 27th in jobs for high school dropouts.

59 percent of all jobs in Delaware (300,000 jobs) will require some postsecondary training beyond high school in 2018. . . . This is 4 percentage points below the national average of 63 percent. Delaware ranks 35th in postsecondary education intensity for 2018.[47]

Regardless of Delaware's below-average national ranking, Vision 2015's progress helped lead to Delaware's first-place selection in federal competition among the states. U.S. Secretary of Education Arne Duncan announced in March 2010 that Delaware was the first-place winner of "Race to the Top"—the federal government's largest competitive grants program to improve public education. The $119 million four-year grant was an enormous recognition for Delaware, placing the First State at the forefront of national education reform.[48]

One should note that the connection of workforce development with business in the state involves all levels of public education—from elementary grades through PhD programs of the University of Delaware (UD). It was announced in October 2013 by one of the world's largest banks that JPMorgan Chase (JPMC) planned to give UD $17 million to help create a new PhD program in financial analytics. The program would improve and maintain computer infrastructure that would allow financial institutions to more effectively process trades, manage risk, and improve their operations. According to Bruce Weber, dean of UD's Lerner College of Business and Economics, "What industry is telling us is that they need thought leaders that can help make better use of their computer resources."[49] UD's provost, Domenico Grasso, elaborated:

Today's ubiquitous networks and e-commerce growth have created an explosion of data and opportunities for innovation. The financial services industry is particularly reliant on technology and the management of data. A number of UD faculty members are already exploring research and educational opportunities in this evolving field.

A new PhD program was conceptualized in conjunction with JPMorgan Chase, who helped us define critical needs and knowledge gaps of the financial industry in general. The joint program between the Lerner College of Business and Economics and the College of Engineering brings together top-flight faculty. . . . As a world leader in financial services, JPMC provides insights into the challenges and future of the industry.

> . . . We are fortunate that a corporation of JPMC's stature has elected to
> partner with UD in developing the new knowledge and tools necessary for
> success in the big-data-rich economy of the twenty-first century. With gener-
> ous financial support from JPMC, UD is structuring the first PhD program in
> Financial Services Analytics.[50]

The University of Delaware was not the only higher educational institution in the state engaged in workforce development for business. Other such
institutions included Delaware State University, Wesley College, Widener
University School of Law, Wilmington University, and Delaware Technical
and Community College. An August 2013 editorial commented:

> More American employers need to start thinking more broadly about the qual-
> ity of our future workers as other countries take the lead in recognizing the
> value of cultivating young people's appetite for good paying jobs in their
> industries.
> Delaware Technical and Community College and Wilmington University
> have invested in similar programs, often at the request of employers worried
> they won't be able to remain competitive locally or globally. . . .
> The White House and the nation's prominent Business Roundtable should
> push for more of these initiatives because they address what the United States
> currently lacks among the global community—a reputation for a workforce
> prepared for the innovation and challenges of the coming future.[51]

Among a number of Delaware state government agencies engaged in
nonacademic workforce development, DEDO, the Department of Labor's
Division of Employment & Training (DET), and the Department of Education were prominent. DEDO aimed to coordinate and fund employment and
customized training activities for new and existing employers to achieve their
company goals, and to improve the employability of individuals to meet the
needs of Delaware employers. DET aimed to provide services to enable
employers and job seekers to make informed employment and training
choices. The Department of Education developed a so-called Soft Skills Es-
sentials curriculum comprised of customized lessons whereby employed
state residents could download modules individually or in a training class-
room, customized for their specific job training needs.

There is general agreement among those concerned with job losses and
gains, both globally and locally, that the changing world economy driven by
new technology requires worker education and training that emphasize basic
math and science, or what is known as STEM education. The term "STEM"
is an abbreviation that stands for science, technology, engineering, and math.
To close gaps in needed skills, careers centered on STEM education run the
gamut of all educational levels—elementary, secondary, vocational schools,
community colleges, four-year and post-graduate colleges and universities,
and so-called in-service or workforce training. Even jobs that are not specifi-

cally scientific or engineering-related still increasingly require basic skills in those areas. For example, at a Delaware job conference, panelist Governor Markell stated: "More and more there has to be a focus on what I call 'Just in time training,' where training is more over a period of weeks, as opposed to a period of years. . . . It's by far the number one thing I hear from employers. We always hear about workforce training."[52]

According to a Georgetown University study, as discussed above, a total of 59 percent of jobs in Delaware by 2018 will require a degree from a two-year or four-year higher educational institution. But according to 2011 Census data, only about 30 percent of working-age Delawareans possessed such degrees—a 22 percent gap that Delaware needed to close. Its pace in growing its pool of college graduates was much too slow. Moreover, according to another 2013 report, Delaware had an amazing 3.8 STEM jobs available for every unemployed person qualified to do science-based work, almost twice the national average. The report also stated that less than 10 percent of college degrees were being awarded in STEM fields statewide.

At UD in 2013, only about one-third of degrees earned by male students were in STEM fields, whereas only about 12 percent of women graduates had chosen STEM majors. Female and low-income students and students of color were greatly underrepresented in STEM fields.[53] In 2013, sixty-four students in Delaware took the Advanced Placement (AP) computer science exam. Of those sixty-four, only nine were girls, two were blacks, and one was Latino. These data suggest that when one considers the importance of STEM education and the growing of a skilled workforce, one must also consider the issue of equity.[54]

After all is said in support of STEM education, one wonders whether that is enough. What about communication skills? According to Professor James Butkiewicz, chairman of UD's Economics Department, "The one clear path to improving opportunities for everyone is increased emphasis on education, especially mathematics, science, computer literacy and other technical skills, as well as reading comprehension, beginning in the earliest elementary grades."[55]

CONCLUSION

We believe that this chapter has revealed a broad spectrum of strategies for promoting business growth, and hopefully increasing the flow of jobs for Delaware residents. We have been left with the impression, however, that there has not been a thoughtful and well-developed plan to ensure success.

It has appeared elementary to us that statistics can often be found to bolster both optimistic and pessimistic portrayals of reality. The case of past unemployment statistics in Delaware offers an example. It was reported in

June 2012 that Delaware's unemployment rate for the preceding month of April was 6.8 percent, compared to the much higher national rate of 8.1 percent, and that Delaware had 1,900 fewer unemployed people in June 2012 than it did in November 2011. Governor Markell attributed these favorable statistics partly to his approach to business.[56]

On the other hand, in October 2012, the Third District of the Philadelphia Federal Reserve noted the following:

> During the Great Recession, employment levels in the nation and in many states plummeted from a peak in January 2008 to a trough in February 2010. As of September 2012, the United States had recovered 48 percent of the jobs lost from the peak to the trough; the three-state region had recovered 43 percent. However, performance varied significantly within the Third District. Delaware had a 25 percent recapture rate; New Jersey had a 24 percent rate; and Pennsylvania was the leader with a 65 percent recovery rate.[57]

Unanswered by the Fed was why Delaware and New Jersey lagged so far behind Pennsylvania in job recovery in 2012. Delaware finally recovered two years later from the plummeted 2008 peak of the Great Recession.

The impact of the state's slow-growing revenue structure appeared to be in question. While individually the state's tax preferences and grants generally were small, collectively they were significant. The lack of coordination that derived from the state's piecemeal approach may not have yielded the type of outcomes anticipated or desired. Perhaps simplifying the approach by reducing preferences and grants, while lowering the overall business tax rates might have been more effective. For example, Delaware's corporate tax rate was raised from 7.2 percent to 8.7 percent in 1977 when the top rate of the personal income tax was raised from 18 percent to a whopping 19.8 percent rate. In 2014, the top rate of the personal income tax was 6.6 percent. Businesses, of course, expect to be taxed, but high and unstable rates comprise a significant factor in their decisions to locate or to expand.

Another problem area revealed in this chapter deals with relations between state and local governments and how they operate. Land-use decisions are largely left to local governments. Yet, in Delaware, DelDOT and the Department of Natural Resources and Environmental Control (DNREC) especially have regulatory power relating to certain transportation and environmental impact activities. These state agencies can effectively veto or force the action of a developer that may measurably change the cost of a development project. And as our discussion of the Barley Mill case illustrates, DelDOT chose not to impose a traffic impact study prior to New Castle County's rezoning decision.

We should also note that, in some other cases discussed in this chapter, businesses evinced significant interest in property taxes generated by local governments and school districts. It is fundamental that the local tax base has an important impact on the views of different groups toward any economic development. The problem remains that the property tax has been the most poorly administered of all taxes in Delaware, mainly because the three counties have not reassessed their respective properties for decades. Besides the importance of local property taxes, mention should be made of two significant tax initiatives to attract businesses and jobs to Delaware. A new law and tax incentive to attract the formation of captive insurance companies went into effect as of July 12, 2005.[58] Moreover, the alternative bank franchise tax—effective January 1, 2007—encouraged major banks to locate in Delaware, adding many associated jobs.[59]

Workforce development appears promising, since it is central to the issue of making Delaware attractive to businesses. However, understanding the development of skills for the future is difficult, and is achievable only with an educational system capable of reacting to new requirements as needed. It is unclear that current workforce development programs are that flexible. Recent efforts to increase the quality of the vocational-technical schools and to refocus on those not bound for college with more relevant skills, and identification of individual passions in specific areas are not addressed by the current curriculum. These are national issues but are also very apparent in Delaware.

NOTES

1. Louise Story and Tiff Fehr, "Explore Government Subsidies—Interactive Feature—NYTimes.com," *New York Times*, December 1, 2012. See also articles by Louise Story, e.g.: "The Empty Promise of Tax Incentives," *New York Times*, December 2, 2012, A1, A30, A31; and "Lines Blur as Texas Gives Industries a Bonanza," ibid., December 3, 2012, A1, A18, A19.
2. See Title 29, Section 8305(6), *Delaware Code*.
3. Division of Revenue, *Tax Preference Report* (Dover: Department of Finance, 2011 Edition), 7.
4. See Title 30, Chapters 19 and 64, *Delaware Code*.
5. Title 30, Chapter 19, Section 1902(b)(8), *Delaware Code*.
6. Division of Revenue, *Tax Preference Report*, 2-2, 2-3.
7. Title 30, Chapter 19, Section 1903(a)(2), *Delaware Code*.
8. Division of Revenue, *Tax Preference Report*, 2-4, 2-5.
9. Ibid., 2-3, 2-5.
10. Title 30, Chapter 20, Subchapter II, Sections 2010, 2011, *Delaware Code*.
11. See Title 30, Chapter 20, Subsection III, Sections 2020–2023, *Delaware Code*.
12. Division of Revenue, *Tax Preference Report*, 2-9, 2-11.
13. Title 30, Chapter 20, Sections 2070–2075, *Delaware Code*.
14. Division of Revenue, *Tax Preference Report*, 2-15, 2-16.
15. Division of Revenue, *Tax Preference Report*, 2-10.
16. Governor's Office News Release, "Executive Order Launches Regulatory Reform and Review," *Executive Order 36*, June 14, 2012, www.newsdelaware.gov/2012/06/14/executive - order-launches-regulatory-reform-and-review (accessed June 15, 2012).
17. Governor's Office News Release, "Governor Markell Executive Oder Reduces Burden of Regulations on Delawareans," June 27, 2013, www.news.delaware.gov/2013/06/27/govern-or-markell-executive-order-reduces-burden-of regulations-on-delawareans (accessed June 28, 2013). See also Office of Governor Jack Markell, *Executive Order No. 36: Report to the*

General Assembly (June 27, 2013), at governor.delaware.gov/orders/eo36report.pdf (accessed June 28, 2013); Doug Denison, "State Cuts Down on Regulations," Wilmington *News Journal*, June 28, 2013, B3; and Editorial, "Good Regulation Work Should Bring Even More," ibid., June 28, 2013, A14.

18. Jonathan Starkey, "Republicans Target Markell's Overseas Trips," Wilmington *News Journal*, February 5, 2013.

19. Jonathan Starkey, "Markell's Israel Trip Cost State More Than $60K," Wilmington *News Journal*, September 1, 2013, A1, A21. See also Starkey, "Markell Winds Down Israel Trip," ibid., July 11, 2013, B3.

20. Steven C. Miles, General Manager, Analtech, Inc., "International Trade Is Key to Delaware Growth," Wilmington *News Journal*, September 6, 2013, A12.

21. See *Delaware Constitution* of 1897, Article 2, Section 17 (as amended), which expressly prohibits "slot machines."

22. See Nancy Kesler, "Opening Culminates 20-Year Push for Machines," Wilmington *News Journal*, December 29, 1995, A18.

23. See Chapter 446, 69 *Del. Laws*, July 16, 1994; Title 29, Section 4803(g), *Delaware Code Annotated.*

24. See Jane Brooks, "Delaware's Gamble Strikes Gold," Wilmington *News Journal*, December 29, 1996, A1, A14; and J. L. Miller, "In Slots Rivalry, All 3 Venues Are Winners," ibid., September 11, 1996, A1.

25. Wade Malcolm, "Casino Competition Hits Delaware in the Wallet," Wilmington *News Journal*, June 20, 2013.

26. Jonathan Starkey, "UD Professor: Casinos Won't Recover," Wilmington *News Journal*, October 13, 2013, B3.

27. See Doug Denison, "Markell Casino Plan Has Support," Wilmington *News Journal*, June 19, 2013, B1; and Doug Denison and Jonathan Starkey, "Panel Finalizes Casino Plan," ibid., June 21, 2013, A1. For subsequent proposals to increase aid to Delaware casinos, see Jonathan Starkey, "Focus Turns to Casinos: Markell, Lawmakers Again Eye Tax Relief," ibid., December 5, 2013, B1, B2; and Jon Offredo, "Panel Backs $30M in Casino Aid: Opponents Worry Breaks Will Strain State Budget Too Much," ibid., March 12, 2014, A3.

28. Editorial, "Delaware Should Get Out of the Gaming Business," Wilmington *News Journal*, July 18, 2013, A10. See also these subsequent Wilmington *News Journal* editorials: "Delaware Should Get Out of the Casino Business," October 10, 2013, A11; "Why Is Gambling Money Better Than Making Things?" November 26, 2013, A10; and "Time for a Tough Talk on Del. Gambling," March 16, 2014, A37.

29. Cris Barrish, "State Ups Ante with Its Online Gambling Sites," Wilmington *News Journal*, October 31, 2013, A1, A7.

30. Cris Barrish, "Del., Nevada Talk Poker Deal," Wilmington *New Journal*, November 16, 2013, B3. Delaware and Nevada signed an agreement in January 2015 to commence online poker, see www.poker-king-articles.php?article=1853 (accessed July 23, 2015).

31. See Evelyn Nieves, "Tax Phobia Fills a Mall in Delaware," *New York Times*, December 11, 1996.

32. Melissa Nann Burke, "New Shops, New Roads: Projected Retail Expansion Near Christiana Demands More Access," Wilmington *News Journal*, April 4, 2013, A1, A2.

33. See William W. Boyer, *Governing Delaware: Policy Problems in the First State* (Newark: University of Delaware Press, 2000), 92.

34. Maureen Milford and Adam Taylor, "Debacle or Compromise, Court Considers Fate of Barley Mill Project in Case Expected to Impact Development across Delaware," Wilmington *News Journal*, April 1, 2013, A1, A6, A7.

35. Maureen Milford and Adam Taylor, "Influence, Access Taint Land-use Decisions: After Five Years, Barley Mill Project Still Awaits Traffic Study," Wilmington *News Journal*, March 31, 2013, A1, A14, A15, A16.

36. Ibid., A16.

37. Ibid., A14.

38. Editorial, "DelDOT Should Clean Up Its Act, Restore Credibility," Wilmington *News Journal*, March 31, 2013, A20.

39. Maureen Milford and Adam Taylor, "Hearing's Focus Turns to Traffic, Council Misinformed before 2011 Vote?" Wilmington *News Journal*, April 23, 2013, A1, A5.

40. Maureen Milford and Adam Taylor, "Citizens Score Win at Barley Mill," Wilmington *News Journal*, June 11, 2013, A1, A5.

41. Adam Taylor, "Did Judge Misread Weiner's Comment? Stoltz Appeals Brief Claims Glasscock Erred," Wilmington *News Journal*, September 25, 2013, A1, A5.

42. Maureen Milford, "Mistrust Validated by Report: 'Pay to Play' a Real Fear for Residents," Wilmington *News Journal*, January 12, 2014, A1, A8, A9.

43. See Maureen Milford, "High Court Blocks Barley Mill Project," Wilmington *News Journal*, March 26, 2014, A1, A10; and Editorial, "Justices Made Right Call for Barley Mill," ibid., March 27, 2014, A9.

44. Matthew Albright, "Odyssey Eyes Barley Mill Site for New K-12 Campus," Wilmington *News Journal*, August 6, 2014, A1, A7.

45. See "Chapter 12: Public Education," in Boyer, *Governing Delaware*, 195–206, esp. 197, 205.

46. See the website of the Rodel Foundations at www.rodel.com/.

47. Georgetown University Center on Education and the Workforce, *Help Wanted: Projections of Jobs and Education Requirements through 2018* (Washington, DC: Georgetown University, June 2010), 25. Compare Delaware's rank of thirty-fifth with neighboring states: Maryland ranked ninth; New Jersey sixteenth; and Pennsylvania thirty-ninth.

48. For Delaware's Vision 2015 conference held in 2013, and spearheaded by the nonprofit Rodel Foundation, see e.g., Matthew Albright, "School Leaders See Some Progress," Wilmington *News Journal*, October 10, 2013, B1, B2.

49. Matthew Albright, "PhD Plans Elicit Unease, JP Morgan to Give UD $17M to Help Start New Program," Wilmington *News Journal*, October 8, 2013, A1, A10.

50. Email from Provost Domenico Grasso to University of Delaware Faculty, "Proposed Ph.D. Program in Financial Services Analytics," October 10, 2013.

51. Editorial, "Start Training Next Generation of Workers," Wilmington *News Journal*, August 21, 2013, A13.

52. Jeff Montgomery and Jonathan Starkey, "Revolutionizing the Workforce: Panelists Stress Need for Better Training," Wilmington *News Journal*, December 13, 2013, A1, A2.

53. Matthew Albright, "Jobs There, But Skills Haven't Kept Up the Pace: As Landscape Changes, More Education Needed," Wilmington *News Journal*, December 9, 2013, A1, A10, A11.

54. EdSurge, "Three States Had No Girls Take AP CS Exam," January 8, 2014, www.edsurge.com/.../2014-12-08-three-states-had-no-girls-take-ap-cs-exam (accessed January 13, 2014).

55. James Butkiewicz, "Job Loss and Income Inequality Are Global Problems," Wilmington *News Journal*, December 16, 2013, A10.

56. Sonali Kohli, "Markell: Uncertainty Keeps Job Creation in Check," Wilmington *News Journal*, June 15, 2012, A12.

57. Eric Ruth, "Philly Fed: Delaware Lags Badly in Job Recovery," Wilmington *News Journal*, October 24, 2012, A12.

58. See Captive Insurance Statutes (75 Delaware Laws c 150; HB218). Captive insurance companies are created or bought by a parent company with the express intent of insuring risks incurred by the parent company.

59. See 75 Delaware Laws c 223; SB249. This statute provided an alternative to the current bank franchise tax consisting of a three-factor apportioned income tax and a location benefit tax.

Chapter Nine

Politics of Economic Development

After World War II, Delaware's economy boomed. General Motors and Chrysler automobile assembly plants opened and employed thousands of blue-collar Delawareans. DuPont continued to thrive. But in the late 1970s, the economy began to falter to the extent that incoming Governor Pete du Pont (1977–1985) characterized Delaware's state government as "bankrupt." Though that remark was slightly off the mark, the economy needed a dramatic boost. Fortunately, New York banks convinced the state to enact the so-called Financial Center Development Act (FCDA) in 1981. The new law ushered in the heyday of credit card banking, employing thousands more Delawareans.[1] Big banks became paramount in Delaware's economy. The hefty financial services sector, plus the pharmaceutical industry, continued to characterize Delaware's economy until the onset of the "Great Recession" of 2007–2008. Financial hardship in Delaware ensued as economic decline and massive unemployment began to grip the nation and much of the world. This was the setting, then, for the permeation of the politics of job creation in Delaware.

2013 RECESSION IN DELAWARE

Portents of economic trouble in the state began as early as 1989 when Delaware's homegrown behemoth, the DuPont Corporation, began to cut 40,000 employees worldwide. The company dropped its total employment numbers 27 percent to about 100,000, including 15,000 in Delaware—a number that fell further to about 8,200 in 2005. When MBNA, Delaware's largest employer and the nation's leading credit card issuer, was taken over by huge Bank of America in 2006, a total of 3,100 more Delaware jobs were lost.

Directly related to the Great Recession was the calamitous 2008–2009 closing of the auto assembly plants of Chrysler and General Motors in New Castle County. At their peak, they employed a combined total of about 10,500 workers, not including the sizable number of jobs that were then lost by other companies servicing those plants. Fisker Automotive was one of many companies to receive direct taxpayer cash grants wielded by the Markell administration to lure companies and jobs to Delaware. But, as we have noted, Fisker's plans to open the former General Motors Boxwood plant to build luxury cars went awry, leaving Fisker well on its way toward bankruptcy in 2013 and the former General Motors plant empty. Meanwhile, AstraZeneca reduced its employment from a high of 5,300 in 2005 to about 2,300 in 2013.

In March of 2013, Delaware's economic situation appeared serious enough to prompt the state's business leaders to sponsor a summit to brainstorm economic development. David M. Wolfenden, president of the business group's Committee of 100, commented that Delaware was at a disadvantage to recover from the recession, compared with other states. "Economic data supports the idea that the states across the country that are either doing well or have signs of doing well had something to pull them out of this economic downturn," he said. "States at the top of the list all have one thing in common, oil or gas or energy. Delaware does not have that. I would go one step further and say that today, Delaware doesn't necessarily have anything that can pull us out."[2] There was little question that Delaware, being a small state in terms of land, population, and resources, in comparison with larger, populous, and wealthy states, found it tough sledding competing with most other states to keep and attract business and jobs. Delaware's challenges also included higher electricity rates than most states, higher wages than some states, a strong union presence, and workers lacking skills some businesses needed. As our previous chapters attest, Governor Markell's two-pronged strategy to create and/or keep jobs was assisting companies with state funds, and making Delaware a more attractive place to do business, focusing on education and training programs to produce better-skilled workers. But was that enough? As of 2013, promised new jobs in the financial sector and the construction industry had yet to fully materialize. New jobs had yet to exceed lost jobs, and available jobs had not kept pace with the state's population growth. A March 2013 local editorial expressed in part Delaware's dilemma with this lament:

> Governors across the country are competing to bring companies with jobs to town and they are willing to pay a pretty penny to get them there. You can say it is the way of the world today, when big companies can go practically anywhere they like and hold no allegiance to any one town, county or state. Or you can say it is a form of extortion.

Even without cash incentives, businesses are looking for low-cost environments, which usually mean non-union, low-tax, low-regulation states like Texas. They also are looking for a highly skilled workforce, something which depends on the quality of the education system, a lot of good weather with mild temperatures and plentiful and low-cost energy. In other words, they want everything. And they want it cheap to boot.

So what are Delaware's options? Delaware can fit some of those requirements, but not all of them. While we want to create a job-friendly atmosphere, some requirements are impossible and some really aren't desirable.[3]

One knowledgeable Delaware economist added that the state would pay a price without a stronger recovery and more jobs. "You haven't made a dent, and you have a much larger group of the underemployed and 'left the labor force' people. Many of them will show up on the Medicaid rolls. Those numbers have slowed down a little, but they're still running close to a quarter of a million people," he said.[4] Needless to say, a quarter of a million people constituted about one-fourth of Delaware's total population.

MORE BAD NEWS

As the year 2013 continued, news about Delaware's unemployment rate became more ominous. While the nation's unemployment rate was trending downward, Delaware's unemployment rate was increasing. In August, Delaware's rate of 7.4 percent equaled the national average for the first time in decades.[5] Simply put, Delaware remained lagging behind most of the nation in job creation. The U.S. Bureau of Labor Statistics data showed that forty-three of the fifty states had done better than Delaware at recovering jobs lost during the recession.[6]

Then in September, a very negative report about Delaware's economy was released by a prestigious national economic and demographic research organization. Moody's Analytics, a subsidiary of Moody's Corporation, was established in 2007 to focus on economic research regarding risk, performance, and financial ratings so that users could identify investment opportunities.[7] On September 11, 2013, Moody's economic forecasting firm released a report stating that Delaware was the only state in the nation still at risk of falling back into an economic recession. This adverse report about Delaware's economy was based on the state's employment trends, housing starts, home prices, and industrial production—indicators the firm studied in all of the states to evaluate economic progress four years after the end of the recession. The report noted that Delaware's unemployment rate remained at 7.4 percent a year after the nation's job market had slowly improved. The report also noted the slowness of improvement of the state's housing market. In sum, the report emphasized that Delaware's economy remained essentially flat, having posted only 0.2 percent growth in the state's gross domestic product in 2012. Steven Cochrane, managing head of Moody's Analytics, said, "One thing about the Delaware economy is it's so small, it can be affected by shifts in a single industry or a couple of industries."[8]

The day after publicizing Moody's grim report, Governor Jack Markell's administration portrayed it as inaccurate by alleging that its methodology was wrong. And a Wilmington *News Journal* editorial also took exception to Moody's assessment. The newspaper noted, "Businesses in the state are creating jobs. More are in the planning stage." Accordingly, Governor Markell's administration disputed Moody's forecast "that Delaware is the only state in trouble." The editorial also noted, however, that in a different rating, *Governing Magazine* "recently listed Delaware as 47th in overall economic rankings."[9]

In less than a month after Moody's report, another prestigious national financial organization released its independent analysis pinpointing Delaware's weak economy. The Bloomberg Economic Evaluation of States ranked Delaware near the bottom in overall economic health, at forty-sixth among the fifty states and the District of Colombia, and last behind states within its region—namely Connecticut, Maryland, New Jersey, New York, Ohio, Pennsylvania, Virginia, and DC. Delaware also ranked last, according to Bloomberg, in personal income, tax revenue, employment, and stock performance. Bloomberg's online economic health timeline index showed that Delaware's economic health had steadily declined below the U.S. average since January 2011.[10] Seeming to corroborate Moody's and Bloomberg's assessments was the following Wilmington *News Journal* statement about housing in Delaware: "Home values have started gaining ground in Delaware, but at a much slower rate relative to the rest of the country. . . . Housing values in the First State rose 2 percent during September [2013], the fourth slowest growth rate of any state in the country, according to CoreLogic's Home Price Index. . . . Nationwide, the index reported an increase of 12 percent."[11] Also in September, regarding Delaware's own falling state revenue estimates, the Delaware Economic and Financial Advisory Council (DEFAC) had projected at least a $150 million budget deficit for the next year, unless the state government took corrective measures.[12]

To make matters worse, it was announced in mid-October 2013 that two more Delaware companies were planning to close. Georgia-Pacific planned to close its Color-Box packaging facility in Harrington in Kent County with ninety-five people losing their jobs. The facility made corrugated boxes such as juice and cereal boxes for grocery stores, as well as bulk packaging for supermarkets. The work performed at the factory, said a spokeswoman, would be moved to Indiana and Mississippi, nearer to where a majority of their customers were located. Four days later, Delaware's manufacturing sector sustained an even larger blow when Evraz Steel plant located in Claymont in New Castle County announced its plan to suspend operations. Company officials cited difficulties in the steel industry as the reason for stopping operations at the ninety-five-year-old plant. Workers to lose their jobs, whose average pay was $75,000, numbered 375, approximately two hundred of whom lived in Delaware. Steel manufacturing in Claymont on the 425-acre property employed as many as two thousand workers at its peak. Early in 2015, the property was finally acquired by a St. Louis development company with a reputation for converting shuttered manufacturing sites into new ventures. Thus, hope was revived among local residents, businesses owners, and community leaders that many jobs might be forthcoming.[13]

MARKELL ON THE HOT SEAT

As Delaware's economy seemingly worsened during 2013, whereby national monitoring authorities pegged Delaware as having one of the most sluggish economies among the states, Governor Jack Markell sought to defend his administration's strategy of growing business with state incentives to create jobs. To his credit, Markell reached out to Delawareans at multiple meetings defending his work to attract employers to build Delaware's economy. Having met with business leaders in Dover in March, he also reached out in June to both Republican and Democratic leaders during the legislative session to gauge support for possible new taxes to spend on road repair, state park maintenance, beach upgrades, and waterway improvements, all of which could provide jobs. But the legislative session was devoted to social issues rather than to capital infrastructure projects that could have boosted jobs and hence the economy.[14]

In late June 2013, a group of economic analysts of the Federal Reserve Bank of Philadelphia issued a mixed report about Delaware's economy that gained the attention of Delaware business and government leaders. The report acknowledged that key industries took a beating in the recession, taking a lasting toll on the state's attempt to revive the economy and labor market. Noting that between 1940 and 1998, Delaware's job growth frequently exceeded the rest of the country, job growth since the late 1990s lagged either behind or stayed about even with the rest of the country. Dragging down the state's economic progress were some persisting weaknesses, according to the analysts. For example, about 7.1 percent of Delaware mortgages were more than ninety days delinquent, compared with 6.4 percent nationwide. The report sought to reassure Delawareans, however, that—with the exception of auto manufacturing—Delaware's economy would recover. In a subsequent interview, Paul R. Flora, senior economic analyst with the Philadelphia Fed, cautioned, "You may not get the same dynamic growth you did in the past."[15]

In an August op-ed column of the Wilmington *News Journal*, House Minority Leader of the General Assembly, Republican Danny Short of Sussex County, took direct aim at Governor Markell and his supporters. He cited statistics showing job creation lagging behind the rest of the country, and that one of six Delaware residents was receiving food stamps. He asserted, "The administration of Gov. Jack Markell and the Democratic majority in the General Assembly have not given these problems the attention they warrant." He concluded that "our state's current economic development strategy has seemingly lost its way." He added:

> It feels like we are treading water, grabbing at the occasional piece of driftwood, but not decisively striking out in any particular direction with a sense of purpose.
> It is past time for us to develop a coordinated strategy that focuses on creating quality employment.
> Our state faces a potential budget shortfall in the next fiscal year, while unemployment remains uncomfortably high, and the local economy continues to sputter. An organized, coordinated effort to create jobs in our state holds the promise of remedying all three ills.[16]

One week later, Governor Markell, with his own op-ed column, responded to Representative Short. Markell had "three points to make in response." First, he cited various "successes" in creating jobs, including Allen Harim's chicken business in Millsboro, PBF's Delaware City refinery, Bloom Energy, Sallie Mae, thousands of jobs created by various Wilmington banks, and "scores of smaller companies." Second, he outlined a "multipronged strategy guided by what companies tell us they need—great schools, a skilled workforce, a good quality of life, a responsive government, an opportunity to connect with global customers and a reasonable cost of doing business." And third, "to build on our progress," he emphasized the need to promote economic development on multiple fronts, including "investing in infrastructure and tourism assets," and continuing "to promote entrepreneurship and make Delaware the Startup State." He concluded his op-ed response as follows:

> Legislation and Strategic Fund investments can both help create jobs. But often it is a day-to-day effort: the visits I make to businesses almost every week . . . or the weekly phone calls our economic development team and I make to companies looking for a new home. . . .
> I'm confident that CNBC got it right once again when it ranked Delaware best in the country for "Business Friendliness," and that Federal Reserve analysts were right when they recently concluded that Delaware is well positioned for decades of growth ahead.[17]

Unfortunately for Governor Markell and his economic development chief Alan Levin, their expressed optimism was not able to allay the mounting criticism occasioned by Fisker's demise, the release of adverse economic statistics, Bloom-induced surging surcharges, the Moody and Bloomberg reports, and the growing number of unemployed and poverty-stricken Delawareans, not to mention the near-record unemployment among those in the building trades. Amid challenging developments, Governor Markell met critics head-on by scheduling town hall–type meetings in each of the state's three counties—a somewhat remarkable if not risky political move.[18]

Governor Markell's bold action to confront critics in meetings throughout the state came off well enough, because his administration's effort to create jobs also aroused support from unemployed Delawareans. As a matter of fact, a Princeton University poll conducted in September 2013, which was commissioned by the University of Delaware's (UD's) Center for Political Communication, revealed that 39 percent of Delawareans polled said the state's most pressing issue was jobs or the economy, with only 11.7 percent identifying education, and 7.4 percent answering crime, as the most pressing issue. The poll also appeared to put to rest mounting criticism of Governor Markell. Indeed, whereas 64 percent of adult Delawareans who were polled had answered they had a favorable view of Attorney General Beau Biden, right behind Biden with 62 percent was Markell. According to the poll, Biden's and Markell's numbers were not statistically different. Moreover, those Delawareans polled represented a politically diverse sample in which 22 percent identified as Republican, 39.5 percent as Democrat, and 34.1 percent as independent.[19]

PERVASIVE POLITICS

Our foregoing analysis prompts us to reflect about the permeation of politics throughout the process of growing business and job creation in the small state of Delaware. It is elementary for most economists to define *politics* as "the allocation of resources." Similarly, political scientists generally accept Harold Laswell's definition embodied in his landmark 1936 book entitled *Politics: Who Gets What, When, How.* In essence, Laswell defined political science as the study of *power* in society, and *power* as the capacity to allocate resources. Hence, politics is the process of affecting the allocation of resources, or simply who gets what, when, and how, as Laswell put it.[20] In this sense, politics becomes ubiquitous, involving all principal actors and organizations in the process—variously the media, political parties, special interests, government and business leaders, and/or ordinary citizens and their organizations—depending on the situation.[21]

All of these principal actors and organizations politically interact in Delaware, mainly within the pages of the Wilmington *News Journal*. Because Delaware is such a small state, this unique newspaper provides a very significant vehicle for the public consumption of political news and opinion. Likewise, the *Newark Post* is sometimes particularly relevant for Newark residents just as the *Delaware State News* is for Dover residents and the *Cape Gazette* is for Lewes and Rehoboth residents. Local radio provides only minimal competition, and WHYY's public television station long ago had abandoned such a role.

Editorial page editor of the *News Journal* John Sweeney wrote a series of editorials throughout 2013–2014 about the political complexities of growing business and job creation in Delaware. For example, referring in October 2013 to the controversial proposed data center project on the former Chrysler plant site in Newark, Sweeney ruminated about the politics of the situation, saying in part as follows:

> I wonder if we are seeing a budding political split emerging, with environmentalists on one side and labor on the other. This will be a tough one if it happens. How will the Democratic Party straddle the split, since the party is presumably the home of both factions?
>
> Reality is intruding. Jobs are the obvious short-term and long-term challenge for Delaware. Right now no one has the answer, not the governor, not the legislators, not the environmentalists, and not the business leaders. I subscribe to the belief that governors don't really create jobs. The best they can do . . . is set the table. Business has to serve the dinner. . . .
>
> That Chrysler plant in Newark, as dirty and noisy as it once was, helped create the middle class in Delaware. How many kids of auto workers got to go to college on the good wages and benefits that Chrysler and General Motors paid?
>
> Where are those jobs now? They are gone. And for the most part, they are not coming back.
>
> That's why Markell grabbed at the Fisker proposal. That's why there is a deal with Bloom. Were they smart choices? Fisker's obviously wasn't—as hindsight tells us now. Will Bloom's be? That remains to be seen. [22]

Politicians of both political parties also resorted to the editorial pages of the Wilmington newspaper to express their opinions about jobs. And in doing so, they sometimes even used op-ed columns to express infighting within their own party. For example, Governor Markell took to task one of his own Democratic party members who opposed the proposed data center in Newark, namely State Representative John Kowalko of Newark. "This is not a partisan issue when any elected official, including one in my own party, seems to forget that creating good jobs is Job One," Markell stated. "That's why it matters when Rep. John Kowalko suggests that some of his constituents opposed to the data center want jobs, just not these jobs near their neighborhood. But if we want to avoid turning more farms into industrial tracts," he added, "it is sites like this where 7 million vehicles were built, that need to continue to be economic catalysts in our communities."[23] Markell's "vindictive" comment evoked a letter to the editor claiming that the governor had "thrown John Kowalko under the bus for daring to do the job he was elected to do, . . . represent his constituents."[24]

The Wilmington newspaper reported comments by Republican politicians that also betrayed stark differences among them about job creation. Republican State Senator Gregory F. Lavelle, in his September 2013 op-ed piece, questioned Governor Markell's basic strategy as "simply not creating the job environment we need." He added, "the Strategic Fund can't be the biggest tool in the box given competing needs and the fact that there's simply not enough money to buy every job. Rather than literally being able to point to each job 'created' by government with the use of tax dollars, wouldn't a return to the old normal of systemic job creation be the ultimate goal we all agree on and strive for?"[25] In October, after latching onto the Moody and Bloomberg reports, Republican Gary Simpson, state senate minority leader, said, "These are not opinions, these are facts. And the fact is we have a sluggish, underperforming economy. And for the governor and his administration to simply dismiss these reports . . . is misguided and doesn't help Delawareans."[26]

In November, all fourteen Republican state representatives and six of the eight Republican state senators jointly signed on to a collective op-ed column fully supporting the proposed data center complex in Newark for providing "a unique opportunity to capture numerous benefits for countless Delawareans." Among the benefits they cited would be the employment of as many as five thousand construction workers over a three-year period, followed by an estimated 290 full-time employees at an average annual salary of $46,500. Accordingly, the proposed Newark data center can be said to have had the overwhelming bipartisan support of Delaware's General Assembly.[27]

Besides news stories and op-ed columns in Wilmington's newspaper, a growing number of citizens joined the political fray by penning letters to the editor variously supporting the pursuit of more jobs or defending the environment. Those choosing the environment were often critical of Governor Markell. For example, a letter from David Carter, conservation chair of the Delaware Audubon Society and former Department of Natural Resources and Environmental Control (DNREC) employee, said in part the following:

> Gov. Markell's op-ed on jobs clearly demonstrated his solution to the "jobs crises" is more propaganda, not public policy or government accountability. . . .
>
>   A large part of our solution to "jobs" rests with better accountability of government officials that have forgotten they take a constitutional oath to

uphold . . . laws. Short-sighted reactionary government that grants special privileges will not solve the problem. We hope the governor will back off his deceptive propaganda campaign, and face the reality that we need a more thoughtful long-term approach to job creation that also protects our residents and environment.[28]

DIVISIVE POLITICS IN NEWARK

In April 2013, the *Newark Post* revealed that a Pennsylvania company—The Data Centers, LLC, based in West Chester—could be joining Bloom Energy as a second company to move to UD's 272-acre former Chrysler site.

The aim of the new company was to build a huge "off-grid" 900,000-square-foot data center complete with its own power-generating facility. City of Newark officials had been in talks with the company for more than six months, according to the *Newark Post*.[29] Within a week, on May 3, the newspaper confirmed that DEDO had given provisional approval of a $7.5 million infrastructure grant, most of which would fund "12 miles of new high-pressure natural gas transmission pipelines from a pumping station in Parkesburg, Pa., plus nine miles of a much larger pipeline from a pumping station in Hockessin."[30]

More details became known, such as that The Data Centers (TDC) planned to lease forty-three acres from the university, about 16 percent of UD Science, Technology and Advanced Research (STAR) Campus. "We liked a lot about the site," company CEO Gene Kern said. "It had the space we need. We picked it for its location near the university. We were looking for research areas, and researchers use high-performance computing for their data." The total cost of the project was estimated to become $1.1 billion, supporting thousands of temporary construction jobs, and creating 290 full-time jobs plus fifty part-time jobs.

Because the natural gas would operate a turbine generating power system, the facility itself would draw no electricity from the grid. TDC considered that the power supplied by the grid would be too expensive to make its business profitable. From Bloom's experience, TDC officials knew that the high cost of electricity from the grid in Delaware was largely a result of decisions that had been made by Delaware's Public Service Commission and the Delmarva Power Company. Indeed, TDC intended that the electric power generated by its turbines would exceed that needed by the facility, enabling the company to sell its additional electric power to the grid while also being available to the city of Newark at lower cost for all of its electricity customers. The company also projected it would pay an estimated total of $20 million combined in property taxes per year to the city of Newark, New Castle County, and the Christina School District. DEDO Director Alan Levin said, "It's a big technological advance for the state. It's something that will not only aid the Star campus, but the Newark region. It will allow for greater growth."[31]

All seemed positive about the new data center until the good news was tarnished by concerns that emerged two months later. In late July 2013, State Representative from Newark, Democrat John Kowalko, questioned whether the data center's power-generating turbines would cause noise pollution and adversely affect Newark's quality of life. "We're talking 248 megawatts," Kowalko said. "What we're . . . allowing to happen here, is plopping a major power-generation facility in the middle of 30,000 residents." Amy Roe, who lived within a mile of the site and collected related emails and documents from the city, questioned whether the power generation would be "incidental and subordinate" to the data center's purpose. "To characterize this power plant as a minor consequence . . . is a gross misrepresentation of the facts," Roe said. "There is nothing subordinate about the power plant. . . . [T]he data center is subordinate to the power plant."[32]

Readers of the last chapter will recall Amy Roe's vehement opposition to the Delaware City refinery in her capacity as conservation chair of the Delaware chapter of the Sierra Club. About the data center project, Roe said she was speaking as a citizen and not in her Sierra Club role. Nevertheless, it was not long before the Sierra Club's chapter became fully engaged in organizing "NoNewarkPowerPlant.org"—a major Sierra Club–supported citizens' protest movement that stretched through the fall of 2013. In response to residents' concerns about excessive noise pollution at a Newark meeting of an estimated four hundred people, company officials stated that they planned to enclose the gas-fired turbines and engines in a building and to put dampers on the turbines to reduce their sound. They also planned to include a berm and landscaping to further reduce the sound to carry. TDC officials also voiced assurances that water usage and the emission of toxic air would not be excessive. Regarding the latter, the facility would produce about two thousand tons per day of carbon dioxide, at least 45 percent of which would be recaptured. Although an estimated eighty tons of nitrous oxide per year also would be generated, the company said the turbines would produce less nitrous oxide per unit of heat than conventional technology generates. But many residents remained unconvinced, and planned to demonstrate and organize protests. Meanwhile, the project had the support of local labor union leaders, business advocates, and state government officials, who emphasized the jobs and tax revenues that would be brought to the area.[33]

Regardless of multiple meetings at which company officials sought to alleviate citizen concerns—at Newark's City Council chambers, UD, and other venues—citizen protests did not diminish. Indeed, a petition of more than 1,200 signatures against TDC's power plant was presented to the Newark City Council in mid-October of 2013, a remarkable phenomenon given the fact that Newark's total population was only about 30,000. Indomitable leader of the protest, Amy Roe, announced her candidacy to become mayor of Newark.[34]

Governor Markell's posture appeared to be that it is the responsibility of the representatives of the people of Delaware's state government—legislators, administrators, and judges—to regulate business, not opposing groups with different values, whether they are businesses, labor unions, or other special interest groups. Accordingly, he noted that the state government's primary function would be to monitor TDC's emissions. He commented in this respect that Delawareans could expect a cleaner operation than existed when Chrysler was building cars at the site: "People are wringing their hands about the need for more jobs. I agree. It's important we deal with the facts. The facts are good jobs, much less pollution than existed there before."[35]

The month of November 2013 in the small city of Newark became replete with unprecedented political divisiveness, splitting the community over the competing issues of jobs and the environment—as if these two subjects were mutually exclusive. UD President Patrick T. Harker's vision of the STAR Campus was expressed in an interview, benign enough, as that of a campus where innovation and inspiration would be propelled by interaction between private industry and the university's faculty and students, as follows:

> First, when it comes to the education of our citizens, the litmus test for anybody who goes on STAR is they have to be open to the faculty research, and in particular student internships.
>
> What we are trying to do is create places and experiences where students can learn by doing. Not just knowledge transfer from my head to your head, but really learning by doing.
>
> Of course, the second part of that is our land grant mission. We are trying to use that campus to get technology out the door, to make a difference and to create jobs for this economy. I mean that is also part of our mission, which is different than a private university.[36]

Meanwhile, CEO Gene Kern of TDC sought to alleviate the rising political tempest over the proposed data center and its massive power plant, which would generate 279 megawatts of electricity. In a full-page "open letter" to the *Newark Post*, Kern wrote in part:

> For weeks now, there has been a widening gap between the truth about the data center project . . . and the misinformation generated by opponents. I'm writing to you to set the record straight.
>
> The project known as Wolf Technology Center 1, will be a large-scale data management and storage facility offering its customers 100 percent reliability due to a self-contained "energy hub" employing a Combined Heat and Power (CHP) design. Reliability is essential because when power to a data center fails, everything shuts down. That means we are no longer able to service the need of our customers and irreplaceable data is lost.

Some opponents charge that the energy hub will pollute the air. Wolf 1 will operate under the strict supervision of the USEPA and . . . DNREC. Recently, we submitted our air permit application to DNREC. Data supporting the application show that emissions from Wolf 1 will be well within government standards that protect human health and the environment and much, much lower than the site's previous occupant.

Opponents . . . refer to it as "a power plant." Their goal is to frighten people by purposely evoking images of contaminant-belching smokestacks. Nothing could be farther from the truth. . . . This will not be a public utility. The energy hub will exist primarily to serve Wolf 1's operations. The architectural and engineering designs of the energy hub will bear no resemblance to a conventional "power plant."

Wolf 1 will be quiet and we are working on models to prove just that. All of its turbines will be enclosed in acoustically shielded buildings to mitigate noise and comply with the City of Newark's strict noise ordinance. Most of the steam it produces will be reused to create cooling and electricity for the data center and much of the CO_2 generated will be captured and sold to industry.

Wolf 1 will help jumpstart the area's economic engine. Construction will take about 2.5 years and employ about 5,000 union workers during its course. Purchasing materials and supplies locally will be a priority and local retailers and service providers will benefit.

Once Wolf 1 is completed, some 290 good-paying fulltime and 50 part time jobs will be created. And that doesn't include the 300–500 employees of customers who will manage the data and equipment stored with us. The availability of a skilled and well-educated workforce is one of the factors that attracted us to Delaware in the first place! Groundbreaking is still months away, but we have already received hundreds of resumes from local residents seeking those jobs!

Finally, we have repeatedly heard that the project was developed in secret through some sort of conspiracy. Not true in any sense. People with business experience know that companies routinely ask third parties, including government agencies, to agree to protect proprietary information shared in the course of doing business. These "secrecy agreements," also known as "non-disclosure agreements" are absolutely necessary to protect intellectual property, the life-blood of high-tech businesses like ours. There's no conspiracy here—just prudent, common business practices.[37]

Gene Kern's "open letter" appeared to have little effect on opponents of TDC's electric power generating plans. Charges of pollution still abounded. Complaints of a secret deal persisted. Confusion over whether Newark's zoning ordinance permitted TDC's power plant became an issue. And DNREC refused to process TDC's application for an air permit until that issue was resolved.[38]

While many Newark residents were taking diametrically opposite sides between those opposing the proposed power plant for environmental reasons and those supporting the TDC project because of the new jobs it promised, raw politics began to take over Newark as never before. The reason for this was the city's upcoming mayoral race, the first such race to be contested since 2007.

THE RACE FOR MAYOR OF NEWARK

Vance A. Funk III was Newark's very popular mayor, having been elected in 2004, easily reelected in 2007, and running unopposed in 2010 and 2013. After nine years as mayor, Funk abruptly resigned on September 30, 2013, citing health problems. Two weeks later, he was named "Mayor of Main Street" by the so-called Downtown Newark Partnership for his many contributions to and cooperation on community projects.[39]

In a special election scheduled for November 26 to choose Funk's successor, seven candidates—three women and four men—were registered. With less than a week to go before the election, the latest available campaign reports through November 18, 2013, showed that only the three female candidates had raised significant money, namely Polly Sierer, who raised nearly $15,000, followed by Amy Roe with about $8,900, and Rebecca Powers with about $5,700. Former mayor Funk, who endorsed Sierer, predicted that these three women would split a majority of the votes. It soon became apparent that the planned data center with its power plant on UD's STAR Campus was likely to be a polarizing issue.[40]

With regard to the power plant, the three female candidates had distinguishable postures. Though not specifically supporting the power plant project, Polly Sierer appeared to have the backing of labor and to support the creation of more jobs, stating: "For Newark to be a thriving, vibrant community, we need to create opportunities for jobs and attract quality businesses." Well-known environmental activist Amy Roe (see chapter 7), on the other hand, unambiguously was the leader of the so-called Residents Against the Power Plant, and had the endorsement of Newark's State Representative John Kowalko. Rebecca Powers seemed to be somewhat in the middle; while questioning the STAR Campus as "an appropriate site for a large power plant," she promised to "work with all stakeholders," and had the endorsement of three state senators and former city councilman Ezra Temko. Accordingly, in terms of the power plant issue, of the three candidates who had raised the most money, Polly Sierer appeared to be the most pro-labor candidate, Amy Roe the most pro-environment candidate, with Rebecca Powers straddling a middle position.[41]

Two significant developments occurred on late Monday—the day before the special election. One was a rally of three to four hundred union workers outside the STAR Campus in support of the data center and its power plant, whose jobs they touted as being needed to aid Delaware's laggard construction industry. They hoisted bright green signs reading "We Support the Data

Center" for passing motorists to see.[42] Possibly the more important development, however, was the last-minute release of documents showing that a political action committee supporting Polly Sierer—"Polly's Plan" PAC—was funded by Delaware Jobs Now, a leading group supporting the data center project. The group was the PAC's sole donor, providing $45,000 used in part to create and distribute pamphlets in Newark including a photo of Sierer with former mayor Funk and a claim that "Polly's Plan" would bring thousands of jobs to Newark. According to the documents, Delaware Jobs Now was in care of the group "Delawareans for Environmental and Economic Development," which characterized itself as "a unique coalition of Delaware labor and business leaders" who believed that "economic growth and environmental protection are not mutually exclusive." Among this parent group's founding board members was Andrew Lubin, a UD officer responsible for the development of the STAR Campus. Sierer disavowed "the actions of whomever is behind this. . . . Let me be clear. This is from an outside group and was done without my knowledge, approval, or involvement."[43]

Polly Sierer won the special election for mayor, garnering 41 percent of the vote with 1,506 votes, followed by Amy Roe with 1,391 votes, or 38 percent, and Rebecca Powers with 487 votes. It might never be known definitively whether Sierer's victory was attributable to the preceding day's developments. Councilman Mark Morehead, finishing a distant fourth with only 148 votes, but still the front-runner among the four male candidates, concluded that the influence of the "Polly's Plan" PAC was bad for Newark and for Sierer's victory. "She doesn't know what would have happened without the outside influence," Morehead said. "Now, our elections are for sale. That's not how it's supposed to run."[44] As for Sierer, she said she was still waiting until "more facts come out" to make a decision on the data center. "I still need to keep an open mind," she said.

While TDC struggled to gain public trust, it faced a number of hurdles to surmount before it could finalize its plans and break ground, namely resolving the zoning issue and acquiring air quality and building permits. As the year 2013 was ending, CEO Gene Kern voiced his increasing frustration, as follows:

> Everybody wants all our details. Everybody wants us to prove everything we say in advance—far in advance of it ever happening. We have to prove what we are doing for the city of Newark, and the state of Delaware to bring a billion-dollar job to the state. We have to jump through every kind of hoop imaginable and possible. . . .
>
> The larger problem is that some in Newark don't understand the project, or the boost it will bring to the city. They can accept the fact that when large-scale business comes into the area, there's an economic benefit for residents. Or they can say no to business, and that's the way it is. I don't know which way the city of Newark is going to go long term.[45]

Meanwhile, some opponents of TDC's power plant took a NIMBY ("not-in-my-back-yard") approach, by organizing a quasi-organization known as NRAPP—Newark Residents Against the Power Plant. One NRAPP activity was to post signs on a number of lawns throughout Newark proclaiming their opposition.

CONCLUSION

From our foregoing analysis, we contend that it is easy to understand why politicians make announcements of aggressive economic projects that promise increased job opportunities. Notables chime in to applaud such prospects. The media, especially the press, promote bestowing the accolades that prematurely assume all that is promised will come to fruition. Politicians seek to benefit early from such pronouncements, but results if any of economic strategies are not made known until much later, often perhaps after an election cycle. Unfortunately, small planned and coordinated efforts do not enjoy such press coverage or political acclaim and are not given much weight in the economic development process. Big projects that are debt-financed by the state, however, are favored by political allocators since they enjoy the benefits of investment upfront, while the costs are felt in the future.

Logic ordains that those who live near industrial sites must contend with low property values. Indeed, opponents of the Data Center's proposed billion-dollar power plant at UD's STAR Campus in Newark contended that environmental pollution from the power plant would lower their property values. Proponents of TDC's power plant, including Governor Markell, claimed that TDC's power plant would cause less environmental pollution than that which was caused by its predecessor, Chrysler's auto assembly plant. TDC's real estate attorney Richard Forsten wrote: "It is difficult to believe that houses which back up to rail lines and a railroad switching yard can claim their property values will be reduced by a cogeneration facility that almost no one will be able to see, and which will be better for air quality than if the data center were powered by the grid."[46]

It was difficult at best to determine who was right, when construction of the Data Center's complex would not begin until months if not years into the future. Moreover, questions relating to property values of nearby residences could surely remain unanswered even beyond then, such as: How might such property values during the tenure of Chrysler be compared with those of the yet-to-be constructed data center? Have the property values of neighbors' houses increased since Chrysler left, and if so, how much?

In the end, the costs and benefits had to be balanced while giving weight to residents who lived in Newark, and by ensuring a careful regulatory analysis and enforcement of state statutes. On July 10, 2014, UD terminated its lease with TDC, thus ending the controversial plan to build the data center and its 279-megawatt power plant on the university's STAR campus. UD President Patrick Harker stated: "We have carefully examined The Data Centers' plans, and have determined that they are not a good fit for the STAR Campus."[47]

While rumors abounded thereafter that TDC officials were looking elsewhere to build its data center, including in nearby Maryland's Cecil County, it was revealed that Newark's city government had spent more than $577,000 on legal and consulting fees alone relating to TDC's proposal to build its data center at UD's former Chrysler site.[48]

If politics is really about the allocation of resources, politics will then always be prevalent in economic development. The release of the former Delaware Supreme Court Justice E. Norman Veasey's report on campaign financing in Delaware identified certain developers and other business operators as supplying dollars to politicians in violation of opaque campaign finance laws.[49] Supporting those who have the power to allocate resources makes sense to those who expect to benefit from their contributions. Veasey recommended ways for making the campaign financing process more transparent and less attractive to those who play that game. Still, politics and economic development are kindred and interdependent.

The interaction between politics and economic development is pervasive, complex, and less than transparent, as our preceding chapters attest. The more that is hidden, the greater the likelihood of a misallocation of resources and the assumption of levels of risk that are inconsistent with the proper role of government. Hopefully, once a bright light is shone on these issues, the resources provided by the taxpayers will be used more wisely. Lubricating the squeaking wheel, or resorting to the use of blue smoke and mirrors, are strategies that should play a very small part in economic development.

NOTES

1. See chapter 8, "Credit Card Banking," in Boyer and Ratledge, *Pivotal Policies in Delaware: From Desegregation to Deregulation* (Newark: University of Delaware Press, 2014).
2. Jonathan Starkey and Jeff Montgomery, "Growth in Jobs Remains Sluggish," Wilmington *News Journal*, March 24, 2013, A1, A2.
3. Editorial, "Home-grown Jobs Offer State Best Hope," Wilmington *News Journal*, March 24, 2013, A21.
4. See Starkey and Montgomery, "Growth in Jobs Remains Sluggish," A2, where UD economist Edward Ratledge is quoted. For noting that Delaware's unemployment rate fell to 6 percent in 2014, see Aaron Nathans, "Unemployment Rate Dips to 6.1 Percent," Wilmington *News Journal*, March 8, 2014, A5.
5. Wade Malcolm, "Mixed Report," Wilmington *News Journal*, August 17, 2013, A6.
6. See Editorial, "State Needs Coordinated Strategy for Job Creation," Wilmington *News Journal*, August 7, 2013, A10. Note, however, that the federal government's September 2013 release of unemployment data for Delaware showed a seasonally adjusted rate of 7.0 percent, a

drop from 7.3 percent in August, according to Aaron Nathans, "Unemployment Drops," ibid., November 16, 2013, A6.

7. See Moody's Analytics, www.moodysanalytics.com (accessed September 12, 2013).

8. Jonathan Starkey and Wade Malcolm, "Moody's Sees Risk of Slump in Jobs Data," Wilmington *News Journal*, September 12, 2013, A1.

9. Editorial, "Forecasts or Not, the Jobs Challenge Is Still with Us," Wilmington *News Journal*, September 13, 2013, A10.

10. For Bloomberg's state-by-state online data, see www.bloomberg.com/visual-data/state-by-state/ (accessed November 1, 2013).

11. Wade Malcolm, "Slow Del. Housing Price Gain," Wilmington *News Journal*, November 6, 2013, A8.

12. Delaware Economic and Financial Advisory Council, "Minutes from September 16, 2013" (Dover: Delaware Department of Finance, September 16, 2013).

13. See Aaron Nathans, "Color-Box Closing; 95 Jobs Lost," Wilmington *News Journal*, October 11, 2013, A8; Aaron Nathans and William H. McMichael, "Evraz Shutting Down Claymont Steel Plant," ibid., October 15, 2013, A1, A6; and Xerxes Wilson, "In Claymont, Hope for a Revival, Plans to Redevelop Steel Mill Bringing Optimism to Residents," ibid., April 28, 2015, A1, A5.

14. See, for example, Jonathan Starkey and Jeff Montgomery, "Growth in Jobs Remains Sluggish, But Gov. Markell Sees Bright Spots," Wilmington *News Journal*, March 24, 2013, A1, A2; Jonathan Starkey and Melissa Nann Burke, "Tax, Fee Increases on Table: Markell Proposals Would Support Jobs," ibid., June 9, 2013, A1, A6; and Jonathan Starkey, "Session Marked by Social Debates: Inaction on Economic Issues Draws Criticism," ibid., June 30, 2013, A1, A18.

15. Wade Malcolm, "Fed: Del. Future Bright," Wilmington *News Journal*, June 26, 2013, A8. See also, "Federal Reserve Visits Delaware," *UDaily* (University of Delaware), July 8, 2013.

16. Danny Short, "State Needs Coordinated Strategy for Job Creation," Wilmington *News Journal*, August 7, 2013, A10.

17. Jack Markell, "Delaware Is Building on Its Economic Successes," Wilmington *News Journal*, August 14, 2013, A11.

18. See, for example, Jonathan Starkey, "Markell, Levin Defend Efforts to Create Jobs," Wilmington *News Journal*, September 25, 2013, A1, A2; and Jonathan Starkey, "Markell Back on Hot Seat, New Castle Stop Is Last of His Town Forums," ibid., October 10, 2013, B1, B2.

19. Jonathan Starkey, "Beau Biden Tops in Popularity Contest, UD Poll Concludes," Wilmington *News Journal*, October 27, 2013, B1, B4.

20. See Harold D. Laswell, *Politics: Who Gets What, When, How* (New York: P. Smith, 1950), originally published in 1936.

21. See, for example, William W. Boyer, *Bureaucracy on Trial, Policy Making by Government Agencies* (Indianapolis: Bobbs-Merrill, 1964), esp. chapter 2.

22. See, for example, John Sweeney, Editorials, "Jobs for Delawareans Still Remains the Biggest Story," Wilmington *News Journal*, October 13, 2013, A26; and "Delaware Should Keep Pushing for Jobs," ibid., November 30, 2014, A28. See also Jeff Montgomery, Jonathan Starkey, and Patrick Sweet, "WHERE ARE THE JOBS?" ibid., December 8, 2013, A1, A6, A7; and Alan Levin, "Delaware Entrepreneurs Drive Economy," ibid., October 5, 2014, E5.

23. Gov. Jack Markell, "Let's Create Jobs Here, Not Send Them Away," Wilmington *News Journal*, November 3, 2012, A29.

24. Steve Bear, "Markell Throws Kowalko 'Under the Bus,'" Wilmington *News Journal*, November 16, 2013, A8.

25. George F. Lavelle, "On Economy, Keeping Fingers Crossed and Eyes Wide," Wilmington *News Journal*, September 13, 2013. See also Lavelle's similar op-ed column, "State Must Attend to Job Fundamentals," ibid., December 9, 2011, A2.

26. Jonathan Starkey, "Markell Back on Hot Seat," Wilmington *New Journal*, October 10, 2013, B1, B2.

27. GOP Legislators, "Republicans Extend Support for Data Center Complex," Wilmington *News Journal*, November 5, 2013, A11.

28. David Carter, "Markell Policies Hinder Growth of Jobs," Wilmington *News Journal*, November 7, 2013, A11.

29. John Shannon, "Data Center May Create 300 Jobs: Company Interested in Chrysler Site," *Newark Post*, April 26, 2013, 1.

30. Al Kemp, "Data Center Grant Receives Initial OK," *Newark Post*, May 3, 2013, 1, 10.

31. Wade Malcolm, "Huge Data Center Eyes UD Site: Pa.-Based Firm Plans $1B Facility, 290 Jobs," Wilmington *News Journal*, May 17, 2013, A1, A7.

32. Melissa Nann Burke, "Newark Airs Concerns over Data Center: Facility Planned at Chrysler Site Focus of Talks," Wilmington *News Journal*, July 23, 2013, A1, B2.

33. See Melissa Nann Burke, "Newark Residents Rebuff Proposed Data Center," Wilmington *News Journal*, September 4, 2013, A1, A2; and Karie Simmons, "Questions Raised About Power Plant: Residents Pack Meeting on Proposed Data Center Project," *Newark Post*, September 6, 2013, A1, A11.

34. Karie Simmons, "1,200 Sign Petition against Power Plant," *Newark Post*, October 18, 2013, A1, A11.

35. Jonathan Starkey, "Markell Defends Computer Center," Wilmington *News Journal*, October 11, 2013, A1, A2.

36. William H. McMichael and Nichole Dobo, "Developer: 10-Story Tower Worth Taking Risk," Wilmington *News Journal*, November 10, 2013, A1, A6, A7.

37. "An Open Letter from Gene Kern, CEO of The Data Centers, LLC," *Newark Post*, November 1, 2013, 20.

38. See, for example, Melissa Nann Burke, "Newark Defers Zoning Decision on Power Plant Plan," Wilmington *News Journal*, November 4, 2013, A1, A7; Melissa Nann Burke, "State Declines to Issue Data Centers Permit," ibid., November 6, 2013, B3; and Karie Simmons, "TDC Request Ruled Incomplete," *Newark Post*, November 8, 2013, 1, 7.

39. Karie Simmons, "Downtown Newark Partnership Celebrates 15 Years," *Newark Post*, November 22, 2013, 2.

40. See Melissa Nann Burke, "Data Center Motivator at Polls," Wilmington *News Journal*, November 25, 2013, A1, A2; and Josh Shannon, "Voters Head to Polls Tuesday," *Newark Post*, November 22, 2013, 1, 9. Note that this issue of the *Newark Post* included eight pages of election coverage, including candidates' profiles.

41. See the three candidates' statements, respectively, "In Her Own Words," *Newark Post*, November 22, 2013, 5, 8.

42. Melissa Nann Burke, "Data Center Supporters Hold Rally," Wilmington *News Journal*, November 26, 2013, A1, A2.

43. Josh Shannon, "'Polly's Plan' PAC Funded by Group Supporting Data Center, Documents Show," *Newark Post*, November 25, 2013.

44. Melissa Nann Burke, "Sierer Wins Newark Mayoral Race," Wilmington *News Journal*, November 27, 2013, A1, A2.

45. Melissa Nann Burke and Jeff Montgomery, "Questions Remain for Data Center in Newark: Environmental, Zoning Hurdles May Slow STAR Campus Project," Wilmington *News Journal*, December 28, 2013.

46. Melissa Nann Burke, "EPA Says It Didn't Back Data Center," Wilmington *News Journal*, March 18, 2014, A1.

47. Josh Shannon and Karie Simmons, "UD Nixes TDC Project," *Newark Post*, July 18, 2014, 1, 10.

48. Melissa Nann Burke, "Newark Has Spent $577K in Battle over Data Center," Wilmington *News Journal*, September 10, 2014, A1, A7.

49. See E. Norman Veasey and Christine T. Di Guglielmo, December 28, 2013, "Report of Independent Counsel on Investigation of Violations of Delaware Campaign Finance and Related State Laws," accessible at attorneygeneral.delaware.gov/documents/Chief_Justice_Veasey_Report.pdf.

Chapter Ten

Lessons Learned

Throughout the nation, state and local governments have long encouraged their businesses to expand their operations, and sought to attract businesses elsewhere to locate within their borders. Their objective has been to increase economic development and thereby to increase employment. The priority of job creation reached its height after the onset of the Great Recession.

There are two basic strategies that governments have employed to this end. The first has been to improve the overall attractiveness of their jurisdiction as a place to operate a business. Examples of such efforts include improving the education and skill level of the workforce, providing adequate infrastructure, regulating with sensitivity to cost, offering a good quality of life for employers and employees alike including available and appropriate housing, and providing reasonably priced public utilities. The benefits of this strategy tend to be distributed broadly.

The second strategy has been to offer specific firms awards such as cash grants and loans, and—according to the situation—to provide favorable tax abatements and rates, enact legislation favorable to a business, make available free or low-cost worker training, donate a desirable work site, or reduce some specific cost of doing business (such as subsidizing energy). The benefits of this strategy tend to flow just to the particular business being wooed, rather than being broadly distributed among many businesses. All of these options and others have been illustrated in this book. It is this second strategy that has been employed primarily in modern Delaware to create jobs. Results have varied. What may we learn from this experience?

A major lesson is that so-called due diligence (adequate prior research) before employing this second strategy is required, which has not always been done. This does not mean that prompt action by government is inappropriate when an opportunity arises. The best example of this lesson was the creation of the Financial Center Development Act (FCDA), after due diligence during the administration of Governor du Pont. Because Delaware is a small state, it was able to react quickly to provide the type of environment to attract a particular segment of the banking industry without negatively impacting Delaware's local banks. The FCDA was a net gain for the state because the credit card industry was beginning to grow, and Delaware did not lose any tax benefits. Other states meanwhile were competing with Delaware using similar inducements. Indeed, South Dakota managed to land Citibank, while Delaware successfully courted other banks. The FCDA enjoyed longevity, enabling Delaware's banks to grow to nearly fifty thousand employees, and even to survive the Great Recession relatively intact, paying taxes and maintaining forty-five thousand employees within the entire financial sector. The FCDA, more than thirty years old, was still providing tangible benefits in 2015.

Another important lesson learned from Delaware's policy approach to job creation is the recognition of a truism that businesses are subject to changing market forces, some of which affect individual companies, while other forces affect entire industries. Due diligence again is required, and opinions of knowledgeable sector experts and analysts should be sought to preclude adversity. The biotechnology industry, for instance, appeared to be a natural fit for Delaware, in the sense that building a regional biotech/pharmaceutical cluster of firms in Delaware seemed within reach. Accordingly, when Astra and Zeneca merged to form AstraZeneca (AZ), Delaware moved with dispatch to capture the combined company's North American headquarters, research, and sales functions. On this occasion, the state employed the second strategy mentioned above by loading its offer with incentives. Delaware bought a site and donated it to AZ. The state also constructed a major road configuration to support the consequent increase in traffic volume near the headquarters, and funded worker training. The true cost of the venture approached $200 million. In less than fifteen years, the biotech cluster had dissipated with AZ's near demise in the lead. AZ employment in the state was cut by more than 50 percent, and the firm's buildings were scheduled for sale or demolition. Both the industry in general, and AZ specifically, were in trouble. Ironically, JPMorgan Chase stepped in to buy one of the major remaining AZ buildings. Still, the lifetime of the necessary investments far exceeded the roughly fifteen-year lifetime of AZ's major contributions to the Delaware economy. Further exploration of AZ's product pipeline and position in the industry might have reduced the investment Delaware made to one more consistent with AZ's likely fortunes in the future.

Venture capitalists, operating on the steep slope of investment, normally may put together portfolios of ten to twenty fledgling companies in order to discover one really successful winner. However, the state government of Delaware during the nadir of the Great Recession had the portfolio of only one fledgling firm, namely Fisker Automotive. Granted, the state was still reeling from the loss of thousands of jobs with the closing of its two auto plants by 2008. Moreover, Fisker came to Delaware armed with more than $500 million in federal loan guarantees, and with the support of Delaware's congressional delegation. The state invested in excess of $20 million of loans and grants in Fisker plus $8 million for utility costs at the site of the proposed Fisker plant. While the state probably assumed that the federal loans made the success of this firm likely, due diligence had not been performed. Analysts on Wall Street probably would have provided a more realistic assessment, since the market for expensive electric automobiles was still problematic at the height of the recession. As we know, by 2013, after a series of setbacks, Fisker filed for bankruptcy.

Governor Jack Markell and Delaware Economic Development Office (DEDO) Director Alan Levin certainly took a lot of heat over the Fisker debacle. For example, Fisker Automotive's impending demise evoked a salient comment from a director of the conservative Caesar Rodney Institute, namely that "the state apparently has no system in place for tracking the outcomes of the millions of dollars provided in grants and low interest loans from the Delaware Strategic Fund. Would anyone voluntarily put their money in a bank that disregards loan performance?"[1] It appeared that little or none of the taxpayers' money given to Fisker would ever be recovered by the state. New Castle County and its school districts were able to collect accrued property taxes owed by the company. However, the same could not be said about the state money spent on utilities to maintain the empty Boxwood auto plant in the vain hope that Fisker or its new owner could somehow overcome troubles to reopen the plant and produce cars there. As we noted in chapter 4, ownership of the Boxwood plant via Fisker's bankruptcy was purchased by Wanxiang, a Chinese company.[2]

Markell, of course, responded to critics by citing DEDO deals on his watch that created jobs, such as those for the Delaware City refinery and the Allen Harim chicken processing facility in Sussex County. He also claimed in his January 2014 State of the State address that Delaware's job growth had outpaced the national average.[3] As if to foil critics, DEDO had chosen January 1, 2014, to publicize its list of the largest job-creating deals finalized in 2013. All told, DEDO's 2013 list of these biggest deals allegedly would create 1,365 jobs.[4]

Regardless of the recitation of its job-creation successes, the Markell administration was unable to allay increasing criticism. Some critics appeared to agree that the basic strategy of paying businesses to create jobs should be abandoned, to be replaced by other pro-business measures. Illustrative were two mid-December 2013 op-ed columns calling for a better pro-business climate in Delaware, both mostly alike in substance but markedly differing in tone.

Two associate professors of economics at the University of Delaware—Stacie Beck and Eleanor Craig—wrote a co-authored op-ed newspaper column in December 2013 asserting: "With heightened global competition and rapid technical change, it is impossible to predict which companies will succeed. State policy should switch from choosing companies to subsidize, to creating a better business climate for all, including startups." Specifically, they explained:

> Delaware's trend to higher taxes should be reversed. Gross receipts taxes increased an average of 34 percent. The top income tax rate increased 17 percent and is the second highest in the Mid-Atlantic region. Delaware has the highest state corporate income tax.
>
> Delaware should reduce other business costs. It can end its push to green energy costs vis-a-vis nearby states. It can pass right-to-work laws to give employees the freedom to choose whether to join a union. States with right-to-work laws experience relatively more job and income growth. High minimum wages cause employers to add fewer jobs, translating into fewer opportunities for young people to move up into the middle class. . . .
>
> The quality of public schools is lower than surrounding states, including Virginia, which ranks comparatively in funding per student. Two-thirds of Delaware's public school eighth-graders aren't proficient in either reading or math and scores have stagnated. . . . Since the public schools have proven resistant to improvement, expand charter schools and provide tuition tax credits to help low- and middle-income families.
>
> . . . Delaware's significant advantages in location and its business-friendly legal system can be leveraged by implementing pro-growth policies. Currently, Delaware's growth potential, relative to the 50 states, is ranked among the lowest, including that by the U.S. Chamber of Commerce (47th), Moody's Analytics (50th), Bloomberg (46th) and CNBC (bottom half). States with better growth prospects, like Virginia and Texas, excel in public school performance and have low and decreasing tax rates, . . . and right-to-work laws.
>
> Pro-growth policies help everyone, most especially the low and middle class, through the job opportunities that are created.[5]

According to Fred Cullis of Wilmington, president of a manufacturer's representative agency, the main lesson learned from the failed Fisker investment was that the state's approach to economic development simply did not work. In his December 2013 hard-hitting op-ed column, Cullis called for replacing the "recruiting of unproven and exotic companies by offering them exorbitant subsidies" with "correcting the three largest objections to locating here that prospective companies cite—the gross receipts tax, our electric rates and our public education system. " He elaborated:

> Our gross receipts tax is a blind, barbaric and senseless revenue generator. It is a red flag that screams "our state is not business savvy or friendly" to prospective companies. . . . Only 11 states have a gross receipts tax. . . .

Similarly, Delaware's high electric rates keep good manufacturing companies and their jobs from locating in Delaware. Delaware's electric rates are 50 percent higher than the national average. . . . The Regional Greenhouse Gas initiative and the Bloom Energy subsidy have taken high rates and made them even higher. . . . Delaware needs to exit the RGGI and build lower-cost gas fired generation . . . to become competitive. . . .

The deplorable condition of the public education system in Delaware is an oft-cited reason prospective companies pass Delaware by. . . . A school voucher/choice system would . . . allow market forces to sort out the winning schools from those that do not succeed. . . .

Improving Delaware by addressing these issues not only helps us attract new businesses, it provides a fertile field where existing businesses can flourish and expand, thereby safeguarding existing jobs while adding new jobs at existing Delaware companies.[6]

It was apparent, then, that two competing paths to create jobs were proposed—one to continue paying specific businesses to create jobs, and the other to choose instead measures aimed at creating a better business climate.

Another lesson learned from Delaware's job creation policies is that it is problematic when government invests in companies that are in conflict with other goals. This is what happened with the state's investment to attract Bloom Energy to manufacture fuel cells in Newark. Bloom Energy had been searching for a site on the East Coast to expand its sale of Bloom boxes, which convert natural gas, a fossil fuel, into electricity. Bloom was provided with substantial subsidies in its home state of California, and it was unclear how subsidies would work on the East Coast. Meanwhile, Delaware had committed itself to searching for manufacturing jobs, while fervently in favor of carbon-free electricity. However, Delmarva Power would only support the project if the Bloom boxes counted as part of its renewable energy quota (Renewable Portfolio Standards [RPS]), as backed by Delaware law. Accordingly, the General Assembly forthwith changed that law by legislating that, in this case, natural gas was to be counted as a renewable energy whereby Delmarva Power could credit it as part of its RPS, thus stretching credulity by declaring a fossil fuel as a state-supported renewable energy. The next step, which also stretched credulity, was to guarantee that all electric power generated by the thirty-megawatt Bloom units would be fully paid for at the agreed price even though other sources of power were much cheaper. This meant that by the end of 2014, ratepayers were being gouged by shouldering over $34 million of non-bypassable electric costs.[7] This assured that electricity in Delaware became more expensive than electricity produced in the vast majority of other states in the nation. Such an unprecedented phenomenon in Delaware continued to be in direct conflict with a key factor for economic development, namely the availability of public utilities at a reasonable price. Meanwhile, Bloom Energy in Delaware lagged notoriously behind its promised schedule to produce jobs, doubtlessly because the lofty market for its product had failed to materialize.

Adverse results experienced by Delaware taxpayers with respect to the Fisker and Bloom investments did not detract from some successful investments by the state to create jobs. Results in fact have been mixed. For example, the Wilmington Riverfront turned its longtime shameful brownfields into commercial and residential success stories that emulated Baltimore's Inner Harbor development. The Wilmington waterfront venture is a classic case of a win-win investment proposition. The Riverfront Development Corporation (RDC) was established by the state in 1995 to lead the effort to create a safe and aesthetic environment for businesses, tourists, and Delawareans overall to have pleasurable access to this unique locale. Since its creation, the RDC's effort has cost the state and local government contributors a total of only $346,000 in 2011 dollars. As of 2012, the effort had returned in revenues (largely taxes) a total of $230,173, also in 2011 dollars. Forecasts in 2014 showed that taxpayers will be fully compensated by 2017, at which time they will have a clean vibrant waterfront, publically accessible and economically sustainable.[8] The latest investment in the riverfront as of 2014 was a new hotel connected to the Chase Center, which was developed without taxpayer subsidies.

It may be said that "politics"—which we define here as the allocation of resources—permeates all of public affairs, including the growing of business and jobs in Delaware. But sometimes, the mixing of politics and economic development can be poisonous, as we believe happened with respect to Delaware's port among other ventures discussed in this book. The Diamond State Port Corporation was created by the General Assembly in 1995, namely to assume both the assets and important liabilities of the city of Wilmington's port. The port had become an unsustainable financial burden that the city government could no longer afford, particularly in its last years when the port lost money. The overall cost of the state's takeover investment was initially $91 million. Subsequently, the state funneled an additional $177 million into the port. However, the port continued to lose money annually. As general economic conditions deteriorated during the Great Recession, the General Assembly and the governor became uneasy to say the least. Accordingly, the governor and DEDO attempted to find a company that could lease the port, bring in additional capital, and/or operate the facility in an efficient and profitable manner. After a likely partner firm was identified, and the process of negotiation ensued, the General Assembly intervened with legislation to require its approval of any such arrangement. Together with labor union recalcitrance, the single likely lessor company withdrew. By the end of 2014, the state had invested more than $300 million in the port without any sign of any incremental return to Delaware taxpayers, a stark comparison with the RDC, which was also created in 1995. From the day of the state's takeover of the port, the mixture of politics and economic development ordained that it would become highly unlikely that the port's status quo could be sustainable.

Ultimately, markets matter for economic development to be successful, and timing may mean everything to make a venture positive. The successive Getty/Star/Premcor/Valero-owned refinery in Delaware City had comprised a successful and very important cog in Delaware's economy for decades. But Valero became a victim of the bottom of the Great Recession in 2009 when it had to close the refinery. Fortunately, PBF Energy—a strong Swiss refinery—entered the picture and purchased the refinery with a supportive $20 million loan/grant from Delaware taxpayers via DEDO. Delaware's contribution was a mere pittance, compared with the fact that PBF subsequently spent nearly $500 million on the plant before it began operations. Key factors for PBF's remarkable success were that it was a knowledgeable private sector company that knew the market, and it correctly assessed that the recently generated abundance of crude oil recovered by fracking needed a reliable refinery's resources. PBF in 2014–2015 was refining hundreds of tanker-cars-worth of this oil daily. Although Delaware's financial contribution was comparatively small, the state government had to be willing to work with PBF, regardless of the environmental headaches the refinery continued to create over the decades.

On March 11, 2015, the Wilmington *News Journal's* front-page headline was "Del. Gives Millions in Corporate Incentives, State Lawmakers Seek Transparency at DEDO." The news story in part reported:

> Since mid-2009, Gov. Jack Markell's administration has committed $213 million to companies for jobs-related grants and loans through the Delaware Economic Development Office's Strategic Fund.
>
> Award recipients must report job creation to the state. But virtually no reports are available online, earning Delaware a dead-last rating from a group studying economic development transparency.

According to the news story, DEDO Director Alan Levin responded that Strategic Fund grants and loans were part of the reason why the state's jobless rate fell from a high of 8.4 percent to 5.4 percent in December 2014. "The results speak for themselves," he said. And, he explained, "the push for increased transparency is often a challenge when attracting prospects to the state, due to their privacy and confidentiality concerns."[9] Alan Levin also could have added that privacy and confidential concerns doubtlessly influenced state lawmakers to expressly exempt from Delaware's Freedom of Information Act "trade secrets and commercial or financial information . . . which is of a privileged or confidential nature."[10]

One may note that the very next day, the *News Journal* reported: "The Delaware Department of Labor's monthly review said the state's unemployment rate plunged to 5 percent in January, down from 6.1 percent during the same month last year. A separate study, conducted . . . by Gallup, ranked Delaware among the top ten states for job creation."[11] Delaware's Department of Labor reported in April 2015 that the state's unemployment rate fell further to 4.6 percent—the lowest level since June 2008.[12]

Without question, Delaware's post-recession plummeting unemployment and high ranking in job creation were significant gains celebrated by state leaders. But lest they continue to bask in self-congratulation, they should consider an April 2015 column in Britain's *The Economist*, headlined "The First State Comes Last, Living Standards Drop in America's Business Capital." This column stated in part the following:

> Wage growth in America has been measly for years, but since the recession one state has fared particularly badly: Delaware, an east coast tax haven. From 2009 to 2014, it was the only state in which hourly and weekly earnings dropped in cash terms.
>
> At first glance, this is puzzling. Unemployment in Delaware, at 4.8%, is well below the national average; many would expect such a tight labour market to result in rising wages. . . . A quarter of Delawareans work in finance or business services, a higher proportion than in any other state. Such vocations typically pay well. But dig deeper and problems appear. In recent years, Delaware business-services industry has not looked so hot. In company litigation, its courts have lost out to rivals, particularly federal ones. Excessive litigation encourages companies to move. And Wilmington, the largest city in the state, is losing its appeal as a place to do business because of its high crime rate. . . .
>
> All this has taken a toll. The number of full-blown public and private corporations registered in Delaware is 11 percent lower than it was in 2000. . . . Small wonder, then, that over the same period unemployment in Delaware's professional and business-services sector has dropped by a tenth. Wages in that industry have fallen for the past few years. They have also tumbled in the financial sector, which has struggled recently with low profits. Delaware's moneymen are earning 25% less per hour than they did before the financial crisis.
>
> Other parts of the economy are suffering, too. Delaware's manufacturing sector is one. Two car plants, which once employed 10,000 workers between them, have gone: Chrysler's in 2008 and General Motors' in 2009. Since the recession ended, manufacturing jobs (which typically pay well) have continued to wither in the state, despite a nationwide recovery. Delaware's industrial electricity prices, which are 25% higher than the American average, partly explain the lackluster performance. John Stapleford of the Caesar Rodney libertarian think-tank near Wilmington laments the absence of a "right-to-work" law (which would prevent workers from being forced to join a union as a condition of employment). Without one, says Stapleford, Delaware is an unattractive place to locate a factory: manufacturing jobs go elsewhere.[13]

Indeed, more than twenty thousand manufacturing jobs in Delaware had been lost since 1990—a devastating phenomenon in such a small state. Fifteen state Republican lawmakers in 2015 backed a "right-to-work" law,[14] after

Volvo Cars reportedly ignored top economic development officials to consider manufacturing in Delaware. But Governor Markell and the Democrat majority in the state legislature were expected to oppose such a law backed by the Republicans. Thus, another chapter in the politics of economic development and job creation was about to be written in the state.[15]

Ultimately, however, it seemed that, all too often, Delaware's Council on Development Finance, DEDO, and a succession of governors had allowed political and/or social engineering factors to influence their economic and fiduciary judgment. In retrospect, there have been significant successes and failures in growing business and creating jobs in Delaware over recent decades. The lessons are many. A small state's limited money and resources may not always reap rewards, but responsive and business-friendly state and local governments may greatly reduce that handicap. Delaware governments should continue to reach out to—and work with—the private sector, exercise due diligence early in the process of each investment venture to avoid the temptation of politically alluring but unsustainable ventures, and avoid projects with goals that conflict with other goals of the state government and its citizenry. Perhaps most importantly, Delaware leaders need to understand and correctly assess the markets involved in potential investments toward job creation, and the direction of those markets—factors that affect every successful financial enterprise.

NOTES

1. John E. Stapleford, "Lessons Learned from Fisker Motors," *Caesar Rodney Institute*, www.caesarrodney.org/index.cfm?ref=30200&ref2=316 (accessed August 16, 2012).

2. See, for example, Aaron Nathans, "Hybrid Could Exclude Plant from Bankruptcy Sale," Wilmington *News Journal*, January 9, 2014, A8.

3. Governor Jack A. Markell, *State of the State* address, January 23, 2014, governor. delaware.gov/speeches/2014StateOfTheState/. According to the federal Bureau of Labor Statistics, the total number of jobs in the state was 414,000 at the end of 2013, compared with 428,000 at the end of 2007 (www.bls.gov).

4. Aaron Nathans, "Ashland Tops Del. Jobs Deals," Wilmington *News Journal*, January 1, 2014, A8.

5. Stacie Beck and Eleanor Craig, "More Economic Growth Can Help the Middle Class," Wilmington *News Journal*, December 12, 2013.

6. Fred Cullis, "Lessons Learned From the Fisker Investment," Wilmington *News Journal*, December 13, 2013, A21.

7. Delaware Public Service Commission, *Appendices to 2012 Delaware Integrated Resource Plan*, Appendix 6, "Delmarva RPS Compliance Cost," Attachment D, p. 51.

8. See Daniel Brown, *The Fiscal Impact of the Wilmington Water Front* (Newark: Center for Applied Demography and Survey Research, University of Delaware, April 2012), Table 20, p. 53.

9. Jonathan Starkey and Melissa Nann Burke, "Del. Gives Millions in Corporate Incentives, State Lawmakers Seek Transparency at DEDO," Wilmington *News Journal*, March 11, 2015, A1, A7.

10. See Freedom of Information Act, Title 29, Chapter 100, Section 10002, Subsection (2), *Delaware Code*.

11. Jeff Murdock, "Unemployment Numbers Decline, Del. Ranked among Top 10 States for Job Creation," Wilmington *News Journal*, March 12, 2015, A7.

12. Jonathan Starkey, "Delaware Unemployment Rate Drops to 4.6 Percent," Wilmington *News Journal*, April 18, 2015, A5.

13. "The First State Comes Last, Living Standards Drop in America's Business Capital," *The Economist*, April 4, 2015, 29.

14. This law allows the employee to work without having to join a labor union and without having labor union dues automatically deducted from his or her pay. It is almost universally opposed by labor unions.

15. Jonathan Starkey, "Republicans Target Unions, They Say Proposal Will Help Revitalize Manufacturing," Wilmington *News Journal*, April 8, 2015, A1, A7.

Selected References

"An Act to Amend the Delaware Code to Increase the Renewable Energy Portfolio Standard" (Senate Bill 19 Amended by House Bill 1, Approved July 24, 2007).

"An Act to Amend Title 26 of the Delaware Code Relating to the Renewable Energy Portfolio Standards" (Senate Bill 119, Approved July 28, 2010).

Barnekov, Timothy, Robin Boyle, and Daniel Rich. *Privatism and Urban Policy in Britain and the United States.* New York: Oxford University Press, 1989.

Black, Lewis S. Jr. *Why Corporations Choose Delaware.* Dover: Delaware Department of State, 2007.

Boyer, William W. *Bureaucracy on Trial: Policy Making by Government Agencies.* Indianapolis: Bobbs-Merrill, 1964.

_____ . *Governing Delaware: Policy Problems in the First State.* Newark: University of Delaware Press, 2000.

Boyer, William W., and Edward C. Ratledge. *Delaware Politics and Government.* Lincoln: University of Nebraska Press, 2009.

_____ . *Pivotal Policies in Delaware: From Desegregation to Deregulation.* Newark: University of Delaware Press, 2014.

Brown, Daniel. *The Fiscal Impact of the Wilmington Riverfront.* Newark: Center for Applied Demography and Survey Research, University of Delaware, April 2012.

Bullock, Jeffrey W., Secretary of State of Delaware. *Delaware Division of Corporations 2010 Annual Report.* Dover: Delaware Department of State, April 5, 2011.

Champagne, Reid. "Recalling Hercules." *Delaware Today*, December 2008.

Cooper, Rachel. "AstraZeneca Is in Need of Radical Surgery after Chief Brennan Retires." *The Telegraph*, April 16, 2012.

Condliffe, Simon. *The Fiscal and Economic Impact of the Wilmington Riverfront.* Newark: Center for Applied Demography and Survey Research, University of Delaware, April 2007.

Content, Thomas. "Johnson Controls Bids on Battery-Maker A123's Assets." *Journal Sentinel*, October 16, 2012.

Cresap, McCormick, and Paget. *City of Wilmington, Delaware: Future Development of the Port Terminal* (Volume I, Economic and Administrative Considerations, October 1968).

Delaware Code.

Delaware Constitution of 1897.

Delaware Division of Revenue. *Tax Preference Report.* Dover: Department of Finance, 2011.

Delaware Economic and Financial Advisory Council (DEFAC). *2013 Delaware Fiscal Notebook.* Dover: Department of Finance, 2013, 60ff.

Delaware Regulations, Administrative Code. Title 1, 402: "Procedures Governing the Delaware Strategic Fund."

Dolan, Paul. *Government and Administration of Delaware.* New York: Thomas Y. Crowell, 1956.

Dolan, Paul, and James R. Soles. *Government of Delaware.* Newark: University of Delaware, 1976.

Feltner, Tom. "Capital One Application to Acquire ING Direct, CRA and Systemic Risk Concerns and Recommendations." *Woodstock Institute*, September 2011.

Forester and Company. *Delaware's Port of Wilmington, 75 Years of Personal Service.* Wilmington: Diamond State Port Corporation (1998).

Friend, Tad. "Elon Musk and Electric Cars." *The New Yorker*, August 2009.

Fraunhofer USA. *2011 Annual Report.* Plymouth, Michigan: Fraunhofer USA, Inc. Headquarters, 2012.

_____. "News Briefs." Center for Molecular Biotechnology

Giacco, Al. *Maverick Management: Strategies for Success.* Newark: University of Delaware Press, 2003.

Georgetown University Center on Education and the Workforce. *Help Wanted: Projections of Jobs and Education Requirements Through 2018.* Washington, DC: Georgetown University, June 2010.

Governor's Energy Advisory Council. *Delaware Energy Plan 2009–2014.* Dover: State of Delaware, March 26, 2009.

Grandy, Christopher. "The Economics of Multiple Governments: New Jersey Corporate Chartermongering, 1875–1929." *Business and Economic History*, Second Series 18 (1989): 19, 19.5.

Hoffecker, Carol E. *Democracy in Delaware: The Story of the First State's General Assembly.* Wilmington: Cedar Tree Books, 2004.

Investigation Report: Refinery Incident, Motiva Enterprises LLC., Delaware City Refinery, July 17, 2001. Washington DC: United States Chemical Safety and Hazard Investigation Board, Report No. 2001-05-I-DE, October 2002.

Kaouris, Demetrios G. "Is Delaware Still a Haven for Incorporation?" *Delaware Journal of Corporate Law* 20, no. 3 (1995).

Koehler, Bernard. Copy of "Fisker Automotive's Application to Delaware Economic Development Office." Dover, March 11, 2010.

Laswell, Harold D. *Politics: Who Gets What, When, How.* New York: P. Smith, 1950.

Levin, Alan B. Copy of "Memorandum to The Council on Development Finance" (Recommending Loan to Fisker Automotive). Dover: Delaware Economic Development Office, April 14, 2010.

McGonegal, Kevin. "Wilmington: How We Got Here and Where We're Going." *Town Square Delaware*, September 20, 2012.

Mangone, Gerard, ed. *Port of Wilmington: In the 21st Century.* Newark: Graduate College of Marine Studies, University of Delaware, January 1996.

Markell, Jack, Governor of Delaware. News Release. "Executive Order Launches Regulatory Reform and Review." Executive Order 36. Dover: Office of the Governor, June 14, 2012.

_____. News Release. "Governor Markell Executive Order Reduces Burden of Regulations on Delawareans." Dover: Office of the Governor, June 27, 2013; and Executive Order No. 36: Report to the General Assembly, June 27, 2013.

_____. Press Release. "Governor Markell Signs Landmark Clean Energy Jobs Package." Dover: Office of the Governor, July 28, 2010.

_____. *State of the State Address.* Dover: Office of the Governor, January 23, 2014.

Martin, Roger A. *Sherman W. Tribbitt, Governor of Delaware, 1973–1977.* Wilmington: Delaware Heritage Commission, Oral History Series, 1998.

Munroe, John A. *History of Delaware.* Newark: University of Delaware Press, 3rd edition, 1993.

Nagengast, Larry. *Pierre S. du Pont IV, Governor of Delaware, 1977–1985.* Oral History Series. Dover: Delaware Heritage Press, 2006.

Peterson, Russell, and Arthur Trabant. *A Vision for the Rivers: The Final Report of the Governor's Task Force on the Future of the Brandywine and Christina Rivers.* Dover: Department of Natural Resources and Environmental Control, October 11, 1994.

Pollicino, Joe. "Fisker Karma Owner Returns from Grocery Rub to Find Hybrid EV on Fire." *Engadget*, August 12, 2012.

Rubenstein, Harvey Bernard, Randy J. Holland, et al., eds. *The Delaware Constitution of 1897: The First One Hundred Years.* Wilmington: Delaware State Bar Association, 1997.

Stecker, Sarah. *Mapping the Route to Dollars: AAA Mid-Atlantic's Four-State Tour.* Trenton: New Jersey Policy Perspective, July 2006.

"The First State Comes Last, Living Standards Drop in America's Business Capital." *The Economist*, April 4, 2015, 29.

Thompson, Priscilla M., and Sally O'Byrne. *Images of America: Wilmington's Waterfront.* Charleston, SC: Arcadia Publishing, 1999.

Torchinsky, Jason. "Leaked Document Shows Fisker Has More Issues Than Fiery Cars." *Jalopnik*, August 22, 2012.

United States Department of Justice News Release, "Motiva Enterprises Settles Federal-State Lawsuit Resulting from Explosion at Delaware City Refinery." September 20, 2005.

Veasey, E. Norman. "I Have the Best Job in America." *Delaware Lawyer* 13, no. 4 (1995).

_____. "It Is Time to Give Credit." *Delaware Lawyer* 12, no. 4 (1994).

Zimmerman, Andrew D., Frank R. Selby, and William J. Cohen. *Life in a Refinery Town: The History and Impact of the Getty Oil Company in Delaware City, Delaware.* Newark: William J. Cohen and Associates, 1983.

Index

A123 Systems: demise of, 89–90; replacement of batteries by, 85; Wanxiang Group Corporation deal with, 89–90

AAA Mid-Atlantic, 66, 70, 73, 75, 76, 139, 140; Delaware incentives for, 71; Delaware officials and business leaders courted, 70; employee information regarding, 72; NJPP study of, 70, 71; Stecker on competition and secrecy in deal with, 71; Stecker on Delaware incentives for, 71; tax break information on, 72

Above Ground Storage Tank Act, 119

Allen Family Foods, 140, 184, 201; broiler chicken production of, 145; environmental effects of, 147; financial troubles of, 145–146; Harim Group purchase of, 146; Markell on Harim, 146–147; no state incentives for Harim, 147; Strategic Fund grants to, 145

Army Corps of Engineers, 43, 48

Article IX of the Constitution of 1897, stability in corporate law of, 2

AstraZeneca (AZ): acquiring smaller companies strategy of, 30–31; as acquisition target, 35; Astra prospective merger with Zeneca, 21–22; Brennan resignation from, 30–31; brought suit against FDA, 31; Chouhan on, 30; core objective of conspiracy, 28; Delaware confronting traffic congestion regarding, 25–27; Delaware incentive package for, 22, 23, 139; demolishing of buildings by, 34; elimination of jobs due to FDA, 28, 32; engaged in outsourcing, 28; felony conspiracy charge of, 27; generic competition litigation of, 31; key reasons for choosing Delaware, 23; lifting of traffic and deed restrictions for, 25; loss of patent protection, 29; Malik on, 30; MedImmune payoff for, 35; *News Journal* on location choice of, 23; no due diligence regarding, 200; Novartis forming new crop protection business with, 27; other job cuts by, 33–35; patent cliff of, 29, 33; Pennsylvania incentive package for, 22, 23; pharmaceutical manufacturing plant expansion of, 26–27; R & D pipeline faltering options in, 29; takeover rumors about, 28; three thousand manufacturing and distribution jobs lost at, 32

AZ. *See* AstraZeneca

Bank of America, 179; data processing center of, 151; grants to, 151; job cuts at, 150; Ruth on, 150–151; as second largest employer in Delaware, 150

Bank One Delaware, 140; incentive package for, 144; Minner pitch to Dimon regarding, 144

Barley Mill Plaza, 167, 174; court case in, 169; *News Journal* article on, 168; Odyssey Charter School use of, 170; SOC on rezoning of, 168; Stoltz Real Estate Partners mixed land-use plan for, 167; traffic impact study of, 168–169

Beck, Stacie, 202

Begatto, Michael, Markell blamed for Fisker's demise by, 92

"beggar-thy-neighbor" strategy, 17, 36

Biden, Beau, 131, 185

Biden, Joe, 80, 83

Biondi, Frank, 5, 8, 10

Bloomberg Economic Evaluation of States, 182

Bloom Energy, 184, 185, 203–204; additional agreements of, 106; "Bloom Boxes" locations of, 103; BPG arrangement with, 109; customers of, 108; Delmarva customers controversial aspect of arrangement with, 103–104; electric power for, 108; *Fortune* magazine on financials of, 110; hiring targets by, 112; Markell on, 99, 100, 105; natural gas use of, 101–102; New Jobs Infrastructure Fund to, 108; *News Journal* on increasing cost of surcharge by, 111–112; Nichols as citizen activist against, 109–110; no jobs or construction at, 109; O'Mara on clean energy future of, 102; PSC commissioners approval and apprehension of deal with, 106–107, 106–108; public controversy of, 104–106; renewable energy issue of, 101–103; rising costs of, 110–112; setbacks of, 108–110; state incentives for, 100; UD "no-cost ground lease" to, 107

BMO Capital Partners, 49, 51

Board of Harbor Commissioners, 42; development plan for Wilmington Marine Terminal by, 43

Boehner, John, 124

BP. *See* British Petroleum

BPG. *See* Buccini/Pollin Group

Brady, Jane, 119

Brandywine Civic Council, support of clover-leaf traffic interchange, 26

Brandywine River, 41, 63; General Assembly resolution on future of, 63

Brennan, David, 30–31, 33, 34

Bristol-Myers Squibb, Inc, 32

British Petroleum (BP), 51

Brown, Daniel T., 65–66

Buccini/Pollin Group (BPG), 73, 74; Bloom arrangement with, 109; RDC package of financial guarantees and land concessions to, for bank loan, 74

Building Delaware's Future Fund, 16; tax-related components of, 16

Bullock, Jeffrey, 55, 74; on incorporation services in Delaware, 3

Bureau of Labor Statistics, 207n3

Bushweller, Brian, on Calpine application for Infrastructure Fund, 16

Butkiewicz, James, 165, 173

CADSR. *See* University of Delaware's Center for Applied Demography &; Survey Research

Caesar Rodney Institute, 105; on Fisker Automotive, 201; on state grants, 141

Calpine, 16

Capital One, 66, 67, 75; DCRAC against, 68; Delaware workforce of, 68; Dodd-Frank Act regarding, 69; Federal Reserve in planned acquisition of ING Direct of, 68–69; hearings involving, 69; HSBC purchase of, 67; ING Direct USA purchase of, 67; renaming of, 69; state job-development incentives offered to, 67; turn-down of state grant by, 69

Capital One 360, 69, 73, 76

Carey, Kevin, 90

Carper, Tom, 22, 23, 25, 32, 68, 139, 165; on AZ's decision, 23–24; river task force transmittal letter to, 64

Carter, David, 130, 187–188

Cash Management Policy Board, 9

Castle, Mike, 63, 165

CDF. *See* Council on Development Finance

Center for Molecular Biotechnology (CMB), 141–142; Fraunhofer relationship with, 142

Cephas, Julius, 53, 55, 56, 58; on Dole, 57; on Kinder Morgan, 55, 56

Chase Bank, 10

Chase Center, 73, 76

Chevrolet Volt, caveats of, 87

Chouhan, Naresh, on AZ, 30

Christiana Mall: as popular destination, 166; traffic congestion concerns about, 167

Christina River, 41, 43; costly dredging of, 48; General Assembly resolution on future of, 63; pollution and abandoned banks of, 63

Christina River Walk, 73

Chrysler Corporation, 9, 14, 79, 91, 179, 180, 186; Delaware loan to, 8–9

Citigroup, 150

Citizens for Responsible Growth (CRG), 167; compromise agreement between Stoltz and, 167–168

City of Wilmington, 71; dilemma facing, 45; finances of, 41; locating money for Hercules, 148; state purchase of port from, 46

Clark, Paul, 168, 169

claw-backs, 16, 74, 92, 93, 100, 106

CMB. *See* Center for Molecular Biotechnology

Coastal Zone Act (CZA), 51, 58, 109, 117, 123, 126, 133; O'Mara ruling of, 130

Coastal Zone Industrial Control Board, 109, 132

Committee on Foreign Investment, 90

Condliffe, Simon, 64–65; executive summary of Motiva by, 119–120

Constitutional Convention of 1897, 2; delegate on granting corporate charters, 1–2

Consumer Reports, 84

Coons, Chris, 68, 167, 168

Council on Development Finance (CDF), 14, 81, 207; advisory role of, 13; executive sessions of, 13; in subsidy process, 13

Court of Chancery, 3

Cragg, Jeff, 84; on Markell, 110

Craig, Eleanor, 202

Credit CARD Act of 2009, 10

Crestor, 28, 29, 31

CRG. *See* Citizens for Responsible Growth

Cullis, Fred, on objections to locating businesses in Delaware, 202–203

CZA. *See* Coastal Zone Act

The Data Centers (TDC), 188, 190, 194–195; aim of, 188; excessive noise pollution concerns regarding, 189–190; hurdles faced by, 193–194; Kowalko on, 189; lease of UD land of, 188; Levin on, 188–189; opposition and support of, 191–192; political tempest over, 190–191; turbine generating power system of, 188

DCM. *See* DuPont Capital Management Corporation

DCRAC. *See* Delaware Community Reinvestment Action Council

DEDA. *See* Delaware Economic Development Authority

DEDO. *See* Delaware Economic Development Office

DEFAC. *See* Delaware Economic and Financial Advisory Council

DeFoe, Neal P., 145

Delaware, 2, 41, 145, 157–158, 170–171, 171, 182; AZ key reasons for choosing, 23; banking industry growth in, 10; Bank of America as second largest employer in, 150; Bullock on incorporation services in, 3; call for better pro-business climate in, 201–202; Capital One workforce of, 68; challenges in, of attracting and retaining businesses, 180–181; Chrysler Corporation loan from, 8–9; closing of auto assembly plants in, 180; closing of more companies in, 182–183; confronting traffic congestion regarding AZ, 25–27; courting of AstraZeneca by, 21–22; Dole Fresh Fruit Company lease extension in, 47; GM sixty years in, 79; Great Recession job loss and recovery in, 79, 174, 179; hotel industry struggle in, 75; incentive package for AstraZeneca, 22, 23, 139; incentives for

AAA Mid-Atlantic, 70, 71; incorporation in, 2–4; Kinder Morgan pollution-creating enterprise concern of, 51–52; largest state funded businesses in, 140; as leader in corporate charter market, 3; mantra of, 36; Minott on future economy of, 24; nation's financial crisis affecting jobs in, 14–15; no business tax break or funding guidelines information from, 72; other job cuts by AZ affecting, 33–35; property tax and bank franchise tax in, 174–175, 177n59; revenue from incorporations in, 3; sizable investment in AZ, 35–36; struggles with AZ, 27–28; as tax haven, 3; tax rates of, 174; three objections to businesses locating in, 202–203; unemployment rates in, 173, 181, 195n6, 205–206; use of tax credits to attract businesses to, 16

Delaware Audubon Society, 120, 127, 130, 130–131, 133–134, 187

Delaware Biotechnology Institute, 23, 24, 141, 142

Delaware City Environmental Coalition, study of PBF, 126

Delaware City Refinery, 13, 117, 189, 201; federal-state civil lawsuit of Motiva, 119; Getty Oil affecting health of residents, 117; from Getty to Star Enterprises of, 117–118; Motiva as most controversial owner of, 118–120; PBF Energy as owner of, 122–133; Premcor Inc. purchase of, 120–121; Valero Energy Corporation tenure at, 121–122. *See also* Motiva; PBF Energy; Star Enterprises

Delaware Clean Energy Jobs Act, 80

Delaware Community Reinvestment Action Council (DCRAC), 75; against Capital One, 68

Delaware Department of Labor, 14, 162, 172, 205–206

Delaware Department of Transportation (DelDOT), 25, 74, 168, 169; plan for improvements by, 26; regulatory power of, 174

Delaware Economic and Financial Advisory Council (DEFAC),

projections of, 15, 182

Delaware Economic Development Authority (DEDA), 12–13, 13, 121; financing process of, 12–13; other incentives of, 13; Strategic Fund administration responsibility of, 12; time frame for bond issuance of, 14

Delaware Economic Development Office (DEDO), 9, 10, 13, 79, 81; Allen Family Foods grants of, 145; Citigroup grant from, 150; on closing of Valero, 121; Fraunhofer relationship with, 142–143; Hayward on evolvement of, 9; Hercules grants of, 149; importance of, 10; lack of transparency in funding of businesses by, 157; Markell appointment of Levin as director of, 15, 149; mission of, 10; multiple roles of director of, 14; Nagengast on, 10; Playtex Products, Inc. two grants from, 144–145; regulations amended by, 162; Strategic Fund as principal funding mechanism for, 12; subsidies increase during Great Recession, 15; on training activities for new and existing employers, 172

Delaware Hotel & Lodging Association, 73

Delaware New Jobs Infrastructure Fund, 15–16, 73, 108

Delaware Public Employees Council 81, 92

Delaware River, 41, 43, 48, 58; dredging of, for accommodation of Panama Canal, 48, 49

Delaware River and Bay Authority, 46

Delaware Strategic Fund, 15, 16, 27, 67, 71, 73; Allen Family Foods grants from, 145; criteria on types of assistance of, 12; DCM grants from, 143; DEDA responsible for administration of, 12; findings and purpose of, 11; Invista grant from, 140; *New York Times* database information on, 157; as principal funding mechanism for DEDO, 12; Sallie Mae and Discover Bank incentives from, 150; use of, 11

Delaware Technology Park, 34, 142

Delaware Theatre Company, 73, 76
DelDOT. *See* Delaware Department of
Transportation
Delmarva Power, 100, 102, 103, 104, 109,
188, 203; "Bloom Boxes" and
surcharge of, 111–112; Bloom Energy
controversial aspect of arrangement
with, 103–104; class action lawsuit
against, 113; *News Journal* on,
104–105, 106; unpredictability of
surcharge by, 103–104
Department of Energy, U. S. (DOE), 83,
88, 93; Fisker conditional loan from, 80
Department of Justice, U. S., 119
Department of Natural Resources and
Environmental Control (DNREC), 100,
109, 113, 118, 121, 125, 147;
environmentalists call to, regarding air
pollution monitor at PBF, 130;
environmental penalties against PBF
by, 132–133; regulatory power of, 174;
report on emissions from PBF, 129
Department of Transportation, U. S., 57,
162
Diamond State Port Corporation (DSPC),
46–48, 52, 204; Dole deal with, 56–58;
infrastructure renovation costs of, 55;
Kinder Morgan assurances to, 52;
Kinder Morgan selection of, 51; losing
money and berth conditions of, 48;
proposal to federal government for
assistance, 48; reviewing investor
proposals, 50
Dimon, Jamie, 144
Discover Bank, 150
Division of Revenue, 158–159, 159–161;
report on impact of tax preferences, 158
DNREC. *See* Department of Natural
Resources and Environmental Control
Dodd-Frank Act, 69
DOE. *See* Department of Energy, U. S.
Dohnert, Edmund, 143–144
Dole Fresh Fruit Company: Cephas on, 57;
DSPC deal with, 56–58; lease extension
in Delaware of, 47; Levin on possible
move of, 57; Markell deal with, 57;
News Journal on deal with, 57; possible
move to New Jersey of, 56; as tenant of
Wilmington Marine Terminal, 57

Dormant Commerce Clause, 110
Dravo Corporation, 73; production of,
during WWII, 63
DSPC. *See* Diamond State Port
Corporation
"due diligence", 36, 199–200, 201, 207
du Pont, Pierre (Pete), 4, 9, 10, 15, 148,
149; budget bill veto problem of, 6;
creation of DEDO by, 9; cut tax rate,
7–8; economic development successes
of, 9; internal task force of, regarding
Hercules, 8
DuPont Capital Management Corporation
(DCM), 143
DuPont Company, 140, 143, 143–144
DuPont Corporation, 2, 7, 14, 79;
reincorporated in Delaware, 2–3
DuPont Environmental Education Center,
76
DuPont Experimental Station, 22, 25, 32,
143
DuPont Merck Pharmaceutical Company,
32
DuPont Pharmaceuticals, 22, 23, 24, 32

economic development, Delaware, 9;
background of, 1–2; booming economy
induced by war effort in, 42; casino
jobs in, 164–166; Christiana Mall and
Barley Mill Plaza in, 166–170;
corporate income tax return
requirement of, 158; court system
contribution to, 3–4; "due diligence" in,
36, 199–200, 201, 207; early
incorporation process in, 1; *The
Economist* on, 206; Federal Reserve
Bank of Philadelphia report on,
183–184; generate positive returns in,
112; government investments conflict
with other goals in, 203–204; as high
performer in, 26; incorporating and
subsidizing businesses as core of, 4;
incorporation in, 2–4; international
trade in, 164; Internet gambling in, 166;
markets matter in, 205; mixing of
politics with, 204–205; negative reports
regarding, 181–182; *New York Times*
database information on, 157–158;
politics always prevalent in, 194–195;

portfolio strategy in, 94; proactive management approach to, 4–5, 9; regulatory hurdles removal in, 161–162; state-funded trips abroad in, 163–164; strategies of, 4–5, 17, 199; successful investments in, 204; tax preferences in, 158–161; transparency in, 205; winners and losers in, 75; workforce development as aid to, 170–173

Economic Development Accountability Project of New Jersey Policy Perspective (NJPP), AAA Mid-Atlantic study of, 70, 71

The Economist, 206

E. I. du Pont company, 1
Energy Advisory Council, energy plan of, 101
Environmental Protection Agency, 87
Executive Order 36, 162
Executive Order 109, 63

Farmers Bank of the State of Delaware, 9; Biondi on, 5; crisis of, 5–6; FDIC intervention in, 6; state as majority stockholder in, 5
FCDA. *See* Financial Center Development Act
FDA. *See* Food and Drug Administration
FDIC. *See* Federal Deposit Insurance Corporation
Federal Department of Housing and Urban Affairs (HUD), 148
Federal Deposit Insurance Corporation (FDIC), 6
Federal Reserve, in Capital One's planned acquisition of ING Direct, 68–69
Federal Trade Commission, 29
Fehrenbacher, Katie, 110
Financial Center Development Act (FCDA), 149–150, 179, 199–200; Hayward as major player in, 10; as job growth investment, 21; tax rate adjustment of, 10
Fisker, Henrik, 79, 80, 86, 89, 91, 99
Fisker Atlantic, 89

Fisker Automotive, 15, 79, 84, 100, 180, 185, 200; A123 Systems demise affecting, 89–90; attracting of, 79–82; bankruptcy of, 91–93; blame game regarding, 92; Caesar Rodney Institute on, 201; "cash crunch" of, 82, 91; competitors of, 87–89; detailed description of project by, 80–81; DOE conditional loan to, 80; floundering of, 90–91; former GM plant purchase by, 80; Karma's embarrassing performance, 84–86; Levin on DEDO financing of, 81; management shakeup at, 86–87; *News Journal* article on, 82–83; no due diligence regarding, 201; ongoing problems with Karma, 82–84; politics during crisis of, 83–84; Project NINA of, 80; red flags in decision to invest in, 93; search for strategic partner, 91; Superstorm Sandy regarding, 91; Wanxiang America purchase of, 93
Fisker Karma (all-electric, plug-in, hybrid vehicle), 82, 82–84, 84; *Consumer Reports* negative response to, 84; cost of, 79–80; incident of fires caused by, 85; other issues of, 85–86; recall of, 82, 84, 85
Food and Drug Administration, U. S. (FDA): AstraZeneca suit against, 31; AZ elimination of 500 jobs due to, 28, 32
Fortune magazine, on Bloom financials, 110
"fracking", 103, 124, 205
Frantz, David G., 83
Fraunhofer, 140; CMB as subsidiary of, 141–142; financial support of, 142; UD, CMB and DEDO relationship between, 142–143
Frawley baseball stadium, 73, 76
Freedom of Information Act, 74, 153n2, 205
Freel, Edward J., 46
FuelCell Energy Inc., 109, 110
Funk, Vance A., III, 192

General Assembly, 1, 2, 5, 6, 7–8, 9, 53; attracting and keeping jobs during Great Recession importance to, 15; AZ waiver of traffic and deed restrictions approval by, 25–26; Fiscal Year 1996 Bond Bill of, 46; Fiscal Year 1999 Bond Bill of, 46; Fiscal Year 2011 Bond Bill of, 82, 94n8; Fiscal Year 2012 Bond Bill of, 15; on leasing to private firms, 52; legislation on RDC, 64; port construction approval by, 43; Purzycki on Westin Hotel project hearing of, 73; resolution on future of Brandywine and Christina rivers, 63; Senate Bill 3 of, 52–53

General Assembly Joint Finance Committee, 5

General Motors (GM), 2, 14, 80, 86, 179; Chevrolet Volt caveats of, 87; in Delaware sixty years, 79; reincorporated in Delaware, 2–3

Giacco, Alexander, 7–8, 147, 149; attack on state government as anti-business, 6–7; on personal income tax rate, 7; threatened to move Hercules, 7

Gingrich, Newt, 83

Girard Trust of Philadelphia, 6, 9

Glen, Robert, 68, 69

GM. *See* General Motors

Gordon, Thomas, 25, 58, 168–169

grants: to Bank of America, 151; Caesar Rodney Institute on state, 141; Capital One turn-down of state, 69; from DEDO, 144–145, 145, 149, 150; from Delaware Strategic Fund, 140, 143, 145; federal, for public education in Delaware, 171; Invista purpose of, 140–141; to JPMorgan Chase, 151; potpourri of state, to diverse recipients, 152–153; Strategic Fund to Allen Family Foods, 145

Grassley, Charles, 83

Great Recession, 10, 15, 33, 65, 67, 69, 149; casinos affected by, 165; Delaware job loss and recovery in, 79, 174, 179; financial services sector in, 179, 200; GM closed during, 79; job creation priority in, 199

Green Delaware, 51–52

Greensboro, North Carolina, 27

Harker, Patrick, 99, 107, 108, 194; on vision of STAR campus, 190

Hayward, Nathan, 7, 8; on clover-leaf traffic interchange, 26; on DEDO evolvement, 9; as major player in FCDA, 10

Hercules Corporation, 6, 8, 9, 14, 24, 140; DEDO grants to, 149; McGonegal essay on, 148–149; new building for, 148; state reduced tax rate of, 148. *See also* Giacco, Alexander

Hodas, David, 101

Hong Kong and Shanghai Banking Corporation (HSBC) Capital One purchase of, 67

hotel occupancy rate, 14

HUD. *See* Federal Department of Housing and Urban Affairs

Iacocca, Lee, 8–9

incentives, 13, 147; for AAA Mid-Atlantic, 70–71; for AZ, 21–22, 23, 139; for Bank One Delaware, 144; for Bloom Energy, 100; for Capital One, 67; to PBF Energy, 121–122; for Sallie Mae and Discover Bank, 150

"indoor inspection or resting facility," federal regulation on dairy cows regarding, 47

Industrial Relations Committee, 52

ING Direct USA, 66, 68–69, 75; Capital One purchase of, 67; Great Recession trouble of, 67; major businesses of, 66–67; overseas direct banking online only of, 67; Wilmington Riverfront corporate headquarters of, 67

"intangible investments", 3

International Longshoremen's Local 1694-1, 53, 55

Investment Company Act of 1940, 158

Invista, 140; Delaware Strategic Fund grant to, 140; lay off of 400 workers at, 141; *News Journal* on, 141; purpose of grant to, 140–141

Jensen, Arthur, 130

jobs, 67, 132, 199; attracting and keeping, 15; Bank of America cuts in, 150; at Bloom Energy, 109; Delaware casinos problem with, 164–166; elimination of 500, at AZ due to FDA, 28, 32; Great Recession loss and recovery of, 79, 174, 179; nation's financial crisis affecting, 14–15; *News Journal* on loss of, 14; other cuts by AZ, 32, 33–35; PBF increase in, 122–123; tax credits for creation of, 160; Wilmington Marine Terminal expansion impact on, 43–44

Johnson Controls Inc., 90

JPMorgan Chase, 68, 144, 151–152; funding to UD for PhD Financial Analytics program, 171–172; grants to, 151

Karlovich, Michael, 130, 131

Kenton, Glenn, 8, 10

Kern, Gene, 188, 193–194; on political tempest over data center, 190–191

Kerry, John, 124

Keystone XL oil pipeline, 124–125

Kim, Hong Kuk, 146

Kinder, Rich, 53

Kinder Morgan, 58, 59; assurances to DSPC, 52; Cephas on, 55, 56; DSPC selection of, 51; envisioned plan of, 54–56; on General Assembly's intervention, 53; Levin on deal with, 52, 53, 55; Marshall on deal with, 52; *News Journal* meeting with, 54; as pollution-creating enterprise concern of Delaware, 51–52; on projected expenditures, 54; "suspended" negotiations of, 55

Koch, Charles, 140

Koch, David, 140

Koch Industries, Inc, 140

Koehler, Bernhard, 79, 80, 86

Kott, Jonathan, 84

Kowalko, John, 74, 111–112, 186–187, 189, 192

LaSorda, Tom, 86, 89; announcement of Fisker Atlantic by, 89

Laswell, Harold, 185

Lavelle, Greg, 25, 74, 109, 112, 164, 187

Levin, Alan, 52, 55, 58, 59, 68, 69; on Calpine, 16; on DEDO financing of Fisker Automotive, 81; on Dole, 57; on financial services workforce, 151; Fisker debacle of, 201; on Fraunhofer, 142; on Kinder Morgan deal, 52, 53, 55; on leasing of AZ buildings, 34; Markell appointment of , as director of DEDO, 15, 149; on modernization of port, 49; on TDC, 188–189; on transparency, 205; on Westin Hotel, 73, 74

Lindland, Rebecca, on Fisker "cash crunch", 91

liquefied natural gas (LNG), 51

Lobdell Car Wheel Company, 43

locating a business: company and CEO personal tax bills consideration in, 7; key business factors in, 153

Lowth, Simon, 34

Malik, Navid, on AZ, 30

Markell, Jack, 15, 17, 33–34, 47, 52, 53, 58; appointment of Levin as director of DEDO, 15, 149; attracting Fisker Automotive by, 79, 80; Begatto blamed, for Fisker's demise, 92; on Bloom Energy, 99, 100, 103, 105, 109; challenged by Fisker deal, 84; clinched deal with Dole, 57; Cragg on, 110; Delaware Clean Energy Jobs Act of, 80; Delaware New Jobs Infrastructure Fund of, 15–16; Executive Order 36 of, 162; Fisker debacle of, 201; on Harim Group (Allen Family Foods), 146–147; on hot seat, 183–185; on job increase at PBF, 122–123; negotiating and incentives to PBF Energy, 121–122; on private investors for port, 49; on renewed subsidies, 17; state-funded trips abroad of, 163–164; on TDC, 190; on Westin Hotel, 74–75; on workforce training, 170

Marshall, Robert, on Kinder Morgan deal, 52, 53

Martin, Roger, on FDIC bailout of Farmers Bank, 6

Maryland Port Administration, 49

Mayor of Newark: candidates posture on power plant, 192; resignation of current, 192; special election candidates for, 192; two significant developments during race for, 192–193

McBride, David, 110

McGonegal, Kevin, 148–149

McKinney-Cherry, Judy, 33, 144

MedImmune, 30, 35

Merck & Company, 14, 22, 32

Minner, Ruth Ann, 17, 70, 139, 141, 142; Bank One Delaware pitch of, 144; on Motiva, 119

Minott, Darrell J., on Delaware's future economy, 24

Mitchell, Mike, on M & A, 30

Montgomery, Jeff, 50

Moody's Analytics, 181–182

Motiva: catastrophic explosion of acid tank by, 118–119; Condliffe's executive summary of, 119–120; federal-state civil lawsuit of, 119; Minner on, 119; as most controversial owner of Delaware City refinery, 118–120

Munroe, John, 117

Nagengast, Larry, on DEDO, 10

Nathans, Aaron, 49–50, 54

National Community Reinvestment Coalition (NCRC), merger claim of, 68–69

National Council for Public-Private Partnerships, 50

Natural Resources Defense Council, 120

NCRC. *See* National Community Reinvestment Coalition

New Castle County, 46, 71, 93, 141, 148, 164, 188; AstraZeneca regarding, 25–26; Bloom Energy involving, 103, 104, 109; Delaware City Refinery in, 117, 120; Fisker abatement of property taxes by, 80, 201; retail hub of, 167, 169, 174

New Jersey, 2, 56; economy dominated by nation's largest industrial enterprises, 2; raising revenue success in, 2; use of tax credits to attract businesses to, 17

News Journal, Wilmington, 21, 49, 50, 53, 55, 59, 84, 205; on AstraZeneca location choice, 23; on AZ cutting of jobs and tearing down buildings, 34; on Barley Mill Plaza, 168; on Bloom-

Delmarva plan and new financial pledges, 104–105, 106; citizens use of, 187–188; on DelDOT, 169; Dohnert letter to editor about Dupont company, 143–144; on Dole deal, 57; Fisker Automotive article in, 82–83; on housing in Delaware, 182; on hydrogen fuel cell powered cars, 88; on increasing cost of Bloom surcharge, 111–112; on Invista, 141; on job loss in Delaware, 14; Kinder Morgan meeting with, 54; on MedImmune payoff for AZ, 35; on PBF victory, 132; on political complexities of growing business and job creation, 186; politicians use of, 186–187; on potpourri of state grants to diverse recipients, 152–153; "special investigation" of Westin deal, 74; on traffic issue, 25

New York, use of tax credits to attract businesses to, 16–17

New York Times, 17, 29; on Capital One hearings, 69; database information on Delaware created by, 157–158

Nexium, 29

Nichols, John, as citizen activist against Bloom, 104, 109–110

NJPP. *See* Economic Development Accountability Project of New Jersey Policy Perspective

Norment, Richard, 50

Novartis, forming new crop protection business with AZ, 27

Obama, Barack, 83, 84, 91, 124, 125

oil, 117, 124–125, 129, 134

O'Malley, Thomas D., 121, 125

O'Mara, Collin, 100, 103–104, 125, 132–133; on Bloom clean energy future, 102; Coastal Zone Law ruling of, 130

O'Neill, Theodore, 85

Ormisher, Roger, 82

Panama Canal, 48, 49, 50

patent cliff, 29, 33

PBF Energy, 15, 130, 184, 205; caveat of, 123; Coastal Zone Permit and air emission control permit required of, 125–126; Delaware City Environmental Coalition study of, 126; Delaware City Refinery purchase by, 122; DNREC environmental penalties toward, 132–133; DNREC report on emissions from, 129; environmental concerns about, 125–128; environmentalists complaints about train movements regarding, 127–128; expansion planned of, 122–123; "jobs-versus-environment" conflict regarding, 132; Keystone XL oil pipeline regarding, 124–125; Markell negotiations and incentives to, 121–122; Markell on job increase at, 122–123; moves against unloading operations of, 130–131; *News Journal* on victory of, 132; outsiders join dispute about, 131–132; profitable year of, 125; public hearing regarding, 130; raise intake of crude oil by rail of, 129, 134; rally at, 130; shifting to crude-by-rail, 123–125; Sierra Club concerns with, 123–127; threat to survival of, 128–133

Penn Cinema Riverfront IMAX, 76

Pennsylvania, courting and package of incentives for AstraZeneca, 21–22, 23

Peterson, Russell, 7, 63–64, 117, 131–132

Pfizer, Inc, 32, 35

Playtex Products, Inc, 140; DeFoe on Delaware partnership with, 145; purpose of two grants from DEDO, 144–145

Politics: Who Gets What, When, How (Laswell), 185

pollution: of Christina River, 63; -creating enterprise concern of Kinder Morgan, 51–52; environmentalists call to DNREC regarding PBF air monitor, 130; Star Enterprises as subject of complaints about, 118; TDC excessive noise concerns regarding, 189–190

Port of Baltimore, 43, 44; Ports America running of, 49–50

Port of Philadelphia, 43, 44, 49

Port of Wilmington, 58; brief history of, 41–42; Delaware's state government purchase of, 41; from silted harbor to modern port, 41–43

Port of Wilmington Maritime Society, 52

Ports America, 49–50

Posawatz, Tony, 86–87, 90, 91

Powers, Rebecca, 192–193

Public Service Commission (PSC), 100, 101, 104, 188; commissioners approval and apprehension of Bloom deal, 106–107, 106–108; ratepayer opposition in hearings regarding Bloom-Delmarva, 104

Purzycki, Michael, on Westin Hotel project, 73, 74

Rangan, Rashmi, 68

RDC. *See* Riverfront Development Corporation

real estate development, 166, 170

recession. *See* Great Recession

Reichman, Mark, 53

Renewable Energy Portfolio Standards Act (REPSA), 109

Renewable Portfolio Standards (RPS), 80, 101, 203

REPSA. *See* Renewable Energy Portfolio Standards Act

Richardson, H. H., 42–43

Richman, Joshua, 99, 100

Ridge, Tom, 23

"right-to-work" law, 94, 206, 208n14

Riverfront Development Corporation (RDC), 139, 140, 204; Brown's second study report on Riverfront, 65–66; Condliffe report regarding Riverfront to, 64–65; DelDOT land purchase and resale of, 74; eminent domain use loss of, 74; General Assembly legislation on, 64; Great Recession regarding, 65; package of financial guarantees and land concessions to BPG for bank loan, 74; sought funding for Westin Hotel, 73

Riverfront Market, 73

river task force: recommendations of, 64; transmittal letter to Carper, 64

Rodrigue, Jean-Paul, 50

Roe, Amy, 126, 128, 130, 132, 189, 192–193

Romney, Mitt, 90–91

Roy, Roger, 168

RPS. *See* Renewable Portfolio Standards

Ruth, Eric: on Bank of America, 150–151; on Fisker Atlantic, 89

Sallie Mae, 150

Saulsbury, William, on bringing corporations to Delaware, 2

Save Our County (SOC), on rezoning of Barley Mill Plaza, 168, 169

Schlosser, John, 53, 55

Scott, Pam, 168

SEC. *See* U.S. Securities Exchange Commission

Seedorf, Herman, 127, 128

Seroquel, 28, 29, 31

Sharpley, George, 14–15

Shell U.S. Gas & Power, 51

Short, Danny, 184

Sierer, Polly, 192–193

Sierra Club, 127, 128, 130, 132, 133–134, 189

Sigler, John, 163

Simpson, Gary, 74, 187

SOC. *See* Save Our County

Soriot, Pascal, 34, 35

Sridhar, K. R., 108

Star Enterprises: Delaware City refinery from Getty to, 117–118; Saudi Aramco half interest in, 117–118; as subject of pollution complaints, 118

Starkey, Jonathan, 34

State Energy Coordinator, 101

Stecker, Sarah: on competition and secrecy in AAA Mid-Atlantic deal, 71; on Delaware incentives for AAA Mid-Atlantic, 71; NJPP study by, 70, 71; study conclusions of, 72

Suez Canal, 50

Supreme Court, Delaware, 3

Supreme Court, U. S., ruling on pharmaceutical companies, 29

Swayze, David, 9

Sweeney, John, 186

Syngenta, 27

tax preferences: companies managing intangibles in, 158–159; deduction of interest in, 159–160; Division of Revenue report on impact of, 158; tax credits for creation of jobs and qualified investments as, 160; tax credits for research and development as, 160–161

Taylor, John H., 73

TDC. *See* The Data Centers

Tesla Motors Inc.: Model S sedans of, 88; Tesla Roadster of, 88

Themal, Harry, on legal actions of Sierra and Audubon groups, 133–134

Thune, John, 83

TIS. *See* traffic impact study

Toprol-XL, 28, 32

Trabant, Arthur, 63–64

traffic impact study (TIS), 168–169

Tribbitt, Sherman, xi, 4, 5–6, 6, 7

UD. *See* University of Delaware

UDAG. *See* Urban Development Action Grant

University of Delaware (UD), 24, 45, 142, 188; Fraunhofer relationship with, 142–143; JPMorgan Chase funding for PhD Financial Analytics program at, 171–172; "no-cost ground lease" to Bloom by, 107; research and technology campus of, 99, 107; STEM education at, 173

University of Delaware Graduate School of Marine Studies, 41–42

University of Delaware's Center for Applied Demography & Survey Research (CADSR), 64, 65, 119

Urban Development Action Grant (UDAG), 148

U.S. Chamber of Commerce, 4

U.S. Circuit Court of Appeals, Washington, D. C., 31

U. S. District Court, Wilmington, 27

U.S. District Court of Delaware, 109

U.S. District Court of Washington, D. C., 31

U.S. Securities Exchange Commission (SEC), 123

Veasey, Norman, 3–4; on state campaign finance practices, 169–170, 195

Volkswagen, 45, 46

Wanxiang America, 93, 201

Wanxiang Group Corporation, 89–90

Weir, David, 24

Westin Hotel, 73, 76; lawmakers voiced skepticism of, 74; Levin on, 73, 74; Markell on, 75; *News Journal* "special investigation" of deal with, 74; Purzycki on, 73, 74; RDC sought funding for, 73; state government refused support for, 74

Whitehead, Christine, 133

Wilmington: from major milling center to industrial city, 41–42; shipbuilding as dominant industry in early, 63

Wilmington Marine Terminal: Board of Harbor Commissioners development plan for, 43; capital renovations of, to benefit Dole, 57–58; cold storage warehouse of, 46; competitors of, 49–51; construction of, 43; dilemma facing, 45; expansion of, impact on jobs, 44; factors in state action to take over, 45–46; five-year study of operations and facilities at, 44; future of, 58–59; import-export imbalance of, 45; as leader in imported refrigerated fruit, 47; losing money and berth conditions of, 48; as nation's largest banana port, 48; as port of choice for importing commodities, 45; pressures to expand regarding, 43–46; principal recommendations of study of, 44; private investors for, 49; shipping of dairy cows in, 47; state purchase of, 46; total cargo handled at, 43

Wilmington Port Terminal, 42; Richardson on business potential of, 42–43. *See also* Wilmington Marine Terminal

Wilmington Riverfront, 204; AAA Mid-Atlantic in, 66, 70–72; assessing development of, 75; attraction of business entities to, 66; Brown's second study report on, 65–66; Capital One in, 66, 67–69; Condliffe report regarding, 64–65; as example of brownfield redevelopment, 76; features of, 73; ING Direct USA in, 66–67; as tourist mecca, 76; Westin Hotel controversy on, 73–75

Wilmington Rotary Club, 7

Wilson, Woodrow, 2

Wolfenden, David M., 180

workforce development, 170, 172, 175; editorial on, 172; federal grant for public education in Delaware as, 171; JPMorgan Chase funding to UD for PhD Financial Analytics program as, 171–172; New Directions as school education reform initiative in, 170; report on jobs and educational requirements in Delaware, 170–171; Rodel Foundation "Vision 2015" plan in, 170; state government agencies engaged in nonacademic, 172; STEM education as, 172–173

World War II, 43; Dravo Corporation production during, 63

Zoladex, 27, 28

About the Authors

William W. Boyer is Messick Professor Emeritus of Public Administration, visiting scholar of the Center for Applied Demography and Survey Research, and former chair of the Department of Political Science and International Relations of the University of Delaware. He has also served as administrative assistant to the governor of Wisconsin, and first head of the Department of Political Science at Kansas State University.

He earned his Ph.D. in political science at the University of Wisconsin (Madison) and has lectured in many universities throughout the world. Among his other books are *Bureaucracy on Trial: Policy Making by Government Agencies* (1964); *Governing Delaware: Policy Problems in the First State* (2000); *Politics and Government of Delaware* (2009), co-authored with Edward C. Ratledge; and *Pivotal Policies in Delaware: From Desegregation to Deregulation* (2014), also coauthored with Edward C. Ratledge.

Edward C. Ratledge is a 1972 graduate of the University of Delaware (BS, MA in economics) and currently is the director of the Center for Applied Demography and Survey Research (CADSR). As a policy fellow and associate professor in the College of Arts and Sciences, Ratledge has accumulated more than forty years of experience working with state and local government at both policy and operational levels.

Ratledge is currently working with William Boyer on a series of books dealing with public policy as practiced in Delaware over the past fifty years.

Together with his colleague Joan Jacoby and others he has conducted applied research on prosecution throughout the United States. The book, *The Power of the Prosecutor: Gatekeepers of the Criminal Justice System*, is currently in production.

While Ratledge was born in Alabama during in 1943, his family traces its roots in Delaware from the 1700s. He grew up in Delaware and returned to finish school at the University of Delaware following military service in Vietnam in 1969–1970.